A Little Child Shall Lead Them

Carter G. Woodson Institute Series

Deborah E. McDowell, Editor

A Little Child Shall Lead Them

A DOCUMENTARY ACCOUNT
OF THE STRUGGLE FOR
SCHOOL DESEGREGATION IN
PRINCE EDWARD COUNTY, VIRGINIA

Edited by
BRIAN J. DAUGHERITY
AND BRIAN GROGAN

University of Virginia Press
CHARLOTTESVILLE AND LONDON

University of Virginia Press

© 2019 by the Rector and Visitors of the University of Virginia
All rights reserved

Printed in the United States of America on acid-free paper

First published 2019

1 3 5 7 9 8 6 4 2

Library of Congress Cataloging-in-Publication Data
Names: Daugherity, Brian J., 1972– editor. | Grogan, Brian, 1951– editor.
Title: A little child shall lead them : a documentary account of the
struggle for school desegregation in Prince Edward County, Virginia /
edited by Brian J. Daugherity and Brian Grogan.
Description: Charlottesville : University of Virginia Press, 2019. | Series: Carter G. Woodson
Institute series | Includes bibliographical references and index.
Identifiers: LCCN 2018060149 | ISBN 9780813942711 (cloth : alk. paper) |
ISBN 9780813942728 (pbk. : alk. paper) | ISBN 9780813942735 (e-book)
Subjects: LCSH: School integration—Virginia—Prince Edward County—History—Sources. |
Segregation in education—Virginia—Prince Edward County—History—Sources.
Classification: LCC LC214.22.V8 L37 2019 | DDC 379.2/6309755632—dc23
LC record available at https://lccn.loc.gov/2018060149

Cover art: Phyllistine Ward, Jimmy Allen, and an unidentified third student
outside the new Robert Moton High after the closing of the public schools, 1960.
(American Friends Service Committee Archives; reproduced with permission)

CONTENTS

ACKNOWLEDGMENTS

The editors of this book extend our sincerest thanks to the individuals, archives, institutions, libraries, and publications that have granted us the permission to publish the historical documents and writings comprising this volume: Albert and Shirley Small Special Collections Library, University of Virginia; Archives of the American Friends Service Committee; Associated Press; *Christian Century* magazine; *Commentary* magazine; Dwight D. Eisenhower Presidential Library; Edward H. Peeples Jr.; Edward H. Sebesta; Faith and Politics Institute; the family of Barbara Johns; the family of Reverend L. Francis Griffin; Steven Stewart and the *Farmville Herald* newspaper; Ken Woodley; *Journal of Negro Education*; Little Brown and Company publishers; Martin Luther King Jr. Center for Nonviolent Social Change; National Education Association; Oliver Hill Jr.; *Newsday* newspaper; Timothy Phelps; *The Progressive* magazine; R. C. Smith; *Richmond Times-Dispatch* newspaper; Robert Russa Moton Museum; *U.S. News and World Report* magazine; Virginia Commonwealth University Special Collections and Archives; Virginia Education Association; Beblon Parks; the *Virginian-Pilot* newspaper; Virginia State University Special Collections and Archives; William J. vanden Heuvel; and the *Washington Post* newspaper.

For permission to reproduce the included photographs and illustrations we thank the Alabama Department of Archives and History; Archives of the American Friends Service Committee; Library of Congress; Library of Virginia; National Archives and Records Administration; McClintock & Derr Design; Brian Grogan, Photography + Preservation Associates; John A. Stokes; *Richmond Times-Dispatch*; Albert and Shirley Small Special Collections Library, University of Virginia; Virginia Commonwealth University Special Collections and Archives; and Virginia Union University Archives and Special Collections.

The Dr. Martin Luther King Jr. Memorial Commission of the Virginia General Assembly provided valuable collaboration with us on the development of this historical anthology. We offer thanks to former Virginia state senator Henry L. Marsh, past chairman of the King Commission, who also played an important role in the legal cases that helped restore the Prince Edward County public schools. And a heartfelt thank you to Brenda Edwards, senior research associate in the Virginia General Assembly Division of Legislative Services, retired, and longtime administrator for the King Commission, for her enthusiasm for this project and the warmth of her friendship.

Historian Brian Lee generously shared his extensive knowledge of and research on the Prince Edward County public schools struggle. Historians James Hershman, Georgetown University, and Peter Wallenstein, Virginia Polytechnic Institute and State University, offered their critical insights and understanding of this period of Virginia history and were generous with their critiques as this work progressed. Historian Ronald Heinemann, professor emeritus, Hampden-Sydney College, and biographer of Virginia senator Harry F. Byrd, is a longtime friend who offered valued reflection and encouragement for the project.

Lawyer Jennifer Spreng, St. Mary's University School of Law, graciously shared her voluminous research on the legal chronology and numerous court cases of the legal battles for public education in Prince Edward County. We also extend our thanks to Sarah Carr and Mark Zanchelli of the Office of the Clerk, U.S. Court of Appeals for the Fourth Circuit, for their assistance in helping to abridge for a lay readership the case ruling in *Griffin v. County School Board of Prince Edward County*.

At Virginia Commonwealth University, we received assistance from University Librarian John Ulmschneider and Senior Research Associate Ray Bonis, Special Collections and Archives. Brent Tarter, formerly of the Library of Virginia, shared his encyclopedic knowledge of the library holdings, which was especially helpful.

We also received important production assistance from students at VCU, who helped digitize source materials and create the computer files needed to prepare the book manuscript. Our thanks to Virginia Andrews, Anna Bessemer, and Luke Murray. We also extend our thanks at VCU to Kathleen Murphy, VCU Department of History, for her gracious assistance with the complicated process of licensing the copyrighted material that is included in this book. The VCU History Department's F. Robert Schilling, Jr., Fund provided much-needed funding for licensing costs.

Jean Fairfax and Dr. Edward Peeples, whose deep personal experiences with the Prince Edward public schools struggle gave them a unique perspective on this history, were invaluable sources of information. With their decades-long association with the American Friends Service Committee (AFSC), they helped establish the Prince Edward County Collection within the AFSC archives, making this important material more accessible. We extend our particular thanks to Edward Peeples, our esteemed colleague and friend, who wrote the first research paper on the Prince Edward schools crisis in 1963 and has been a leading authority and advocate for presenting this history in the decades following. We are deeply indebted to him both for access to his research and the innumerable conversations we have shared on this topic.

Many friends, colleagues, and students read portions of the manuscript, provided feedback, and otherwise offered support during the conceptualization, research, and production of this book. We extend our thanks to Kathryn Bennett, Mary Berlin, the late John Egerton, Maria Gray, Kevin Grogan, Calvin Nunnally, Burwell Robinson, R. C. Smith, Robert and Helen Williams, and, at the Virginia Foundation for the Humanities, Robert Vaughan, and David Bearinger. A most appreciative thanks to Richard McClintock, who generously shared his editing and proofreading expertise to shaping the manuscript.

The staff of the University of Virginia Press has been a valued partner from the beginning. We especially thank Richard Holway, who shepherded the manuscript and provided timely and helpful advice throughout the process. Our thanks to Bonnie Gill, Helen Chandler, Nicholas Rich, and Morgan Myers for their guidance and assistance with the editorial process, and to Margaret Hogan for her deft editorial touch.

Finally, and most importantly, we wish to acknowledge the extraordinary courage and fortitude of the African American community of Prince Edward County.

We dedicate this book to the 1951 Moton High School student strikers, to the plaintiffs of the 1951 court case *Davis v. County School Board of Prince Edward County*, and to all the students who were denied their right to public education by the closing of the public schools in Prince Edward County, Virginia.

EDITORS' NOTES

A Little Child Shall Lead Them is a collection of primary documents addressing the civil rights–era struggle for public education in Prince Edward County, Virginia. The book is organized chronologically into a prologue, seven sections, and an epilogue, with the principal focus on the years 1951–66. Each section begins with an introduction by the editors to provide historical context for the documents. Each reading is accompanied by an introductory note and questions to bring out their meanings. The section titles have been chosen from the titles of readings, or language therein, and are meant to reflect the events or themes of the section.

Many of the documents presented here have been abridged to maintain a focus on events related to public school desegregation in Prince Edward County. We have indicated so with ellipses where text has been deleted. We corrected obvious misspellings, typographical errors, or inaccurate dates in the original documents. For readability and clarity, these changes are not noted in the text. When necessary to clarify an idea or phrase, we did so by adding a word or two in brackets. We standardized the usage of numbers. Otherwise, archaic spelling, nonstandard capitalization, parenthetical information, and outdated phrases or language are as they appear in the original documents. We have sought to keep the spirit of the original documents and the authors' voices intact.

Prince Edward County is located in an area of Virginia traditionally called "Southside" for its location south of the James River, east of the Blue Ridge Mountains, and west of the coastal areas of the state. The word "Southside" appears frequently throughout the documents as a name and description of the region in which this history is centered.

A Little Child Shall Lead Them includes perspectives on the struggle for public school desegregation in Prince Edward County from civil rights and segregationist leaders, students, activists, politicians, scholars, lawyers, judges, and clergy, as well as newspaper and magazine journalists. We have sought to present a diverse selection of voices from this history.

The documents come from court cases, government documents, newspaper and magazine articles, personal writings, scholarly publications, and the records of important organizations involved in the public schools crisis. Texts of speeches present the voices of important figures. Several confidential letters and reports are included, for which the writers did not envision a larger audience. Presented here they help to further illuminate the complexity and passion of this struggle.

The words "Negro," "colored," and "Afro-American" appear in the readings as the accepted, vernacular language of the particular time in which they were written. In our text, the editors have used the terms "African American" and "black" to describe the same community.

The words "desegregation" and "integration" are used to specific purpose in the editors' text. "Desegregation" is defined in the Civil Rights Act of 1964 as "the assignment of students to public schools and within such schools without regard to their race, color, religion, sex, or national origin." "Integration" describes a situation when significant numbers of whites and blacks attend school together, though not necessarily reflecting the racial makeup of the community. In Prince Edward County, the public schools were *desegregated* for many years after the 1964 Supreme Court ruling that reopened the schools, but they were not yet *integrated* as almost all white children attended the segregated, private Prince Edward Academy.[1]

In 1959, Prince Edward County officials defunded and closed the entire public school system to prevent desegregation. Historically, the number of children forced out of school has been cited as 1,700, as is noted in many of the documents in this collection. This number, however, only represents the African American student population in 1959 when the schools first closed. A study by Dr. Edward H. Peeples conducted in 2002 for the Virginia General Assembly estimated the actual number of black students affected by the five years of closed public schools at nearly 2,700.[2] This is the figure used by the editors in our commentary. Estimates from field surveys conducted by the American Friends Service Committee (AFSC) in 1964 (see p. 212) indicate that several hundred poor white children were also affected by the crisis.

It is our hope that this variety of documents will help readers understand the struggle for public education in Prince Edward County through the words of the people who experienced and observed this vitally important, though not well known, chapter in the civil rights movement.

NOTES

1. Jennifer Spreng, "Scenes from the Southside: A Desegregation Drama in Five Acts," *University of Arkansas at Little Rock Law Journal* 19, no. 3 (Spring 1997): 327–412.

2. "Estimates of the Number of Youth Denied an Education in Prince Edward County, Virginia, 1959–1964," Edward H. Peeples Prince Edward County (Va.) Public Schools Collection.

TIMELINE

	VIRGINIA AND THE NATION	PRINCE EDWARD COUNTY
1865	April 9: Robert E. Lee surrenders to Ulysses S. Grant at Appomattox Court House.	April 6: Sailor's Creek, last battle of Virginia campaign of Civil War. April 7: Lee, then Grant, passes through Farmville. July 20: Freedmen's Bureau opens first school for blacks, run by members of Philadelphia Quaker Meeting.
1870	New Virginia Constitution stipulates that "white and colored persons shall not be taught in the same school, but in separate schools, under the same general regulations."	First public schools in county open on segregated basis.
1896	*Plessy v. Ferguson* U.S. Supreme Court Case approves legal segregation, affirming the concept of "separate but equal."	W. E. B. Du Bois visits Prince Edward County.
1902	Virginia Constitutional Convention disenfranchises most black voters in Virginia.	Approximately 90 percent of black voters in county are disenfranchised by Virginia Constitutional Convention
1920s		Black parents petition for better school facilities and high school grades.
1924	Virginia Racial Integrity Act passed into law by the General Assembly.	
1930s		One additional year after elementary school added for black students.
1930s– 1940s	National Association for the Advancement of Colored People (NAACP) conducts legal campaign for equalization in all aspects of public education, including teacher pay and school facilities.	

VIRGINIA AND THE NATION	PRINCE EDWARD COUNTY
1947	State Board of Education determines Moton High School building to be inadequate.
1948	July 26: President Harry S. Truman issues executive order desegregating U.S. military.	Tar paper buildings constructed at Moton High School to alleviate overcrowding.
1950	*Sweatt v. Painter* U.S. Supreme Court case changes NAACP legal strategy from equalization to desegregation.	Enrollment at Moton High School reaches 477 students in school built for 180 students.
1951	August: Loan for new Moton High School approved by state. Advanced on priority list after *Davis* case lawsuit is filed.	April 23: Student strike at Moton High School.
		April 25: *Farmville Herald* newspaper editorial declares "student inspired" strike as "mass hookie."
		April 26: NAACP lawyers Oliver Hill and Spottswood Robinson meet with students and parents.
		May 21: First Prince Edward school lawsuit filed, *Davis v. County School Board of Prince Edward County.*
1952		March 7: Three-judge federal panel rules against plaintiffs in *Davis* case. Ruling appealed by NAACP to U.S. Supreme Court.
1953		September: New Moton High School opens. Built by county in effort to thwart lawsuit for public school desegregation.
1954	May 17: *Brown v. Board of Education* ruling by U.S. Supreme Court declares that "separate but equal" is unconstitutional.	July 12: Prince Edward County Board of Supervisors issues resolution opposing school desegregation.
	June 25: Governor Thomas Stanley states he will use all legal means to continue segregated schools in Virginia.	July: Defenders of State Sovereignty formed to resist desegregation in public schools of Virginia.
1955	*Brown II* Supreme Court ruling orders school desegregation "with all deliberate speed."	June: Prince Edward School Foundation formed to develop private school education program.

VIRGINIA AND THE NATION	PRINCE EDWARD COUNTY

1955 December 1: Rosa Parks refuses to give up her seat on a bus in Montgomery, Alabama.

1956 February 25: Senator Harry F. Byrd calls for "massive resistance" to desegregation.

March 12: Southern Manifesto issued and signed by 101 members of Congress.

August 27: Virginia governor Thomas Stanley announces package of massive resistance legislation to maintain segregation in Virginia public schools.

September 21: Virginia General Assembly passes law requiring closing of any public school that is required by court order to desegregate.

More than four thousand white citizens petition county asking not to be taxed to support integrated schools.

May 3: Board of Supervisors states that it will not appropriate money for desegregated schools.

1957 September: Central High School desegregated, Little Rock, Arkansas.

1958 September: Massive resistance laws invoked; nearly thirteen thousand white children are shut out of school in Norfolk, Charlottesville, and Warren County, Virginia.

1959 January: Courts strike down Virginia's school closing laws.

February: Public schools reopen and begin to desegregate in Arlington and Norfolk, Virginia.

September: Desegregated schools open without incident in Charlottesville, Virginia.

May 9: U.S. Court of Appeals orders Prince Edward to desegregate public schools by September 1.

June 26: Board of Supervisors refuses to appropriate funds for public schools, effectively closing public schools after eight years of court cases and delays.

September 10: Public schools are closed and Prince Edward Academy is opened for white students.

1960 February 1: Student lunch counter sit-in in Greensboro, North Carolina.

American Friends Service Committee begins efforts to send students out of county for education.

VIRGINIA AND THE NATION	PRINCE EDWARD COUNTY
1960 Virginia General Assembly passes tuition grant legislation for private education.	Prince Edward County passes local tuition grant ordinance. April 26: Prince Edward County School Board resigns.
1961 May: Freedom Rider buses travel to South.	Virginia Teachers Association organizes summer remedial education program in Prince Edward County.
1962 University of Mississippi desegregated.	March 28: Dr. Martin Luther King Jr. visits Prince Edward County. December: U.S. Department of Justice joins NAACP as friend of court in appeal of Prince Edward case.
1963 January 1: Centennial of Emancipation Proclamation. April–May: Demonstrations in Birmingham, Alabama. Summer: Protests in Danville, Virginia. June 11: George Wallace makes stand in school door at University of Alabama. June 12: Medgar Evers is assassinated in Jackson, Mississippi. August 28: March on Washington for Jobs and Freedom. September 15: Sixteenth Street Baptist Church is bombed in Birmingham, Alabama. November 22: President John Kennedy assassinated in Dallas, Texas.	February 28: President John Kennedy addresses Prince Edward public schools crisis in message to Congress. March 18: Robert Kennedy speech in Louisville, Kentucky. Continuing legal battles in school desegregation and tuition grant court cases. Summer: Street demonstrations in Farmville for desegregated public facilities and reopening of public schools. American Federation of Teachers and students from Hampton Institute, Queens College, and Yale University organize summer education programs in Prince Edward County. August: Kennedy administration organizes Free Schools Association for Prince Edward County. September 16: Free Schools Association begins classes; first formal schooling for black students since 1959.

VIRGINIA AND THE NATION	PRINCE EDWARD COUNTY
1964 January 23: 24th Amendment to the Constitution ends poll tax in federal elections. June: Freedom Summer voter registration drive begins in Mississippi. June 21: James Cheney, Andrew Goodman, and Michael Schwerner are murdered in Philadelphia, Mississippi. July 2: President Lyndon Johnson signs Civil Rights Act. August 18: NAACP files suit challenging Virginia state tuition vouchers. December: Federal court declares Virginia tuition grants unlawful.	May 11: Robert Kennedy visits Free Schools Association. May 25: *Griffin v. County School Board of Prince Edward County* Supreme Court case orders reopening of public schools. August: Free Schools Association ends eleven-month program. September 8: Public schools reopen in Prince Edward after five years of being closed.
1967–1972	Continued black protest for adequate public school funding, black teachers, and black representation on the county school board.
1968 April 4: Dr. Martin Luther King Jr. assassinated in Memphis, Tennessee.	
1971 April 20: *Swann v. Charlotte-Mecklenburg Board of Education* Supreme Court case orders strong measures to accomplish full school desegregation.	
1972	Overcrowding at one county elementary school is the same as at Moton High School at time of 1951 strike. County forced to increase public education budget by 48 percent to meet new minimum state standards.
1970s–1980s	White students gradually come back to public schools as school superintendent James M. Anderson works to establish sound public school system.

	VIRGINIA AND THE NATION	PRINCE EDWARD COUNTY
1995		Campaign to preserve former Moton High School begins when it is threatened with demolition.
1998		August 5: Robert R. Moton High School is designated a National Historic Landmark by U.S. secretary of the interior.
2001		Robert R. Moton Museum opens in former high school building, site of 1951 school strike.
2003	Virginia General Assembly passes a resolution of "profound regret" for the closing of public schools in Prince Edward County.	June 15: Prince Edward County School Board awards honorary diplomas to students who were put out of school by the closing of public schools.
2004	April 23: Virginia General Assembly establishes *Brown* Scholarship Fund to assist education of Virginia citizens impacted by school closings. May 17: Fiftieth anniversary of *Brown v. Board of Education of Topeka, Kansas.*	May 16: Honorary diplomas awarded to Prince Edward students who were put out of school by the closing of public schools at fiftieth anniversary commemoration of *Brown v. Board of Education.*
2008	July 21: Dedication of Virginia Civil Rights Memorial on the state capitol grounds in Richmond. The memorial honors the struggle for school desegregation in Prince Edward County.	July 21: Dedication of a plaque honoring Barbara Johns and 1951 school strike on lawn of Prince Edward County Court House. Illumination of a permanent Light of Reconciliation in courthouse bell tower.
2017	February 23: Commonwealth of Virginia office building housing offices of the attorney general is renamed the Barbara Johns Building to honor her pioneering stand for civil rights in education.	

A Little Child Shall Lead Them

Introduction

Twice in less than one hundred years rural Prince Edward County, Virginia, found itself as a crossroads of history.

On April 6 and 7, 1865, the last battles of the Virginia campaign of the Civil War were fought near Farmville, the main town in the county, as the Confederate and Union Armies marched through the county just days before the surrender of General Robert E. Lee to General Ulysses S. Grant at Appomattox Court House, a short distance to the west.

On April 23, 1951, in an event that foreshadowed the emergence of the modern civil rights movement, Barbara Johns, a sixteen-year-old African American student at Robert R. Moton High School, led her classmates in a two-week boycott of the overcrowded and inadequate facilities of their segregated school in Farmville. From the outset, the quest for equality of public education in Prince Edward County is remarkable for the important role of students in instigating the events.

The strike began as a demand for equality in separate educational facilities. At the urging of lawyers Oliver Hill and Spottswood Robinson of the National Association for the Advanced of Colored People (NAACP), the insistence on a better school soon became a lawsuit for school desegregation in the county and a vital part of the growing national movement for equality in all public education.

The original Prince Edward school desegregation lawsuit, *Davis v. County School Board of Prince Edward County*, was filed in May 1951, and the U.S. Supreme Court later consolidated it with four other cases under the name *Brown v. Board of Education of Topeka, Kansas*. In the Court's unanimous decision on May 17, 1954, it ruled that public school segregation was unconstitutional and must cease.

The Virginia political establishment, led by U.S. senator Harry F. Byrd, chose to fight the *Brown* decision, using the political tactics of "massive resistance," a

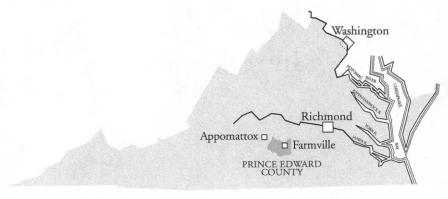

VIRGINIA

Map of Virginia and Prince Edward County. (Copyright McClintock & Derr Design; reproduced with permission)

movement dedicated to the complete nullification of the landmark Supreme
Court ruling. While massive resistance against public school desegregation
took root all over the South, it was Prince Edward County that provided the
nation with the extreme case in point.

On June 2, 1959, the Board of Supervisors of Prince Edward County, facing
a court order to desegregate the local schools the following September, voted
to eliminate all funding for its public school system, thereby closing the schools
in defiance of the Court. A private academy was immediately established for
the white children of Prince Edward and was later supported by state and local
tuition grants. For a period of five years, 1959–64, the county denied public
education to nearly 2,700 African American children and untold numbers of
poor white children, who, with only a few exceptions, remained unschooled.
Prince Edward County became the only place in the nation to close its entire
public school system to avoid desegregation.

After five years of litigation, the public schools were reopened by the U.S.
Supreme Court in *Griffin v. County School Board of Prince Edward County.*
The decision, handed down on May 25, 1964, came almost ten years to the day
after the original desegregation ruling in *Brown v. Board of Education.* Another
decade would pass as the public schools struggled in the face of official indiffer-
ence, severe financial limitations, and the challenges of teaching children who
had suffered such educational deprivation, before the gradual acceptance of
integrated public education in the county.

The historic 1954 Supreme Court decision outlawing school segregation
had its roots in the centuries-long struggle by African Americans for freedom

and education. The colonial South established laws restricting education for blacks, whether slave or free, which remained in effect until after the Civil War. The first formal education for black children came to Prince Edward County in 1865 with the Freedmen's Bureau and was supported by members of the Philadelphia Quaker Meeting. Public education was established in Virginia by the Reconstruction constitution of 1870, a condition required for readmittance to the Union following the Civil War. From its inception, however, the General Assembly stipulated that "white and colored persons shall not be taught in the same school, but in separate schools, under the same general regulations."[1]

The advent of widespread public education in the United States in the late nineteenth century reflected, in large measure, an emerging industrial society and the accompanying need for an educated work force. Public education provided access to full participation in American society, culture, and commerce. The right to education in America became symbolic of the rights of citizenship, a manifestation of the belief that the public school was the one institution that could make good on the promise of equality put forth in the Constitution. The legal and institutionalized social contract of segregation and the mores of Jim Crow culture denied that right to African American citizens for nearly one hundred years, and the consequences still trouble our society today.

The story of Prince Edward County has been generally overlooked in the historiography of the civil rights movement until recent years, as few books examined the events in detail. Excerpts from two books that were published in 1965 are included in this volume: *They Closed Their Schools*, a historical narrative by journalist Bob (R. C.) Smith, and *Bound for Freedom*, a memoir by educator Neil V. Sullivan.[2] The first scholarly books on these events were not published until 2011 and 2012, nearly fifty years later. *Brown's Battleground* by historian Jill Ogline Titus and *Southern Stalemate* by sociologist Christopher Bonastia offer modern historical perspectives including research in sources previously unavailable.[3] A number of scholarly papers and several personal memoirs have also been published since the 1960s.[4]

The history of the century-long struggle for education in Prince Edward County is representative of the need for a scholarly approach to civil rights history that calls for a broader chronology of the era. Historian Jacquelyn Dowd Hall's essay "The Long Civil Rights Movement" argues that an extended period of historical study is necessary to understanding the movement's roots and legacies.[5]

The struggle for public education in Prince Edward County lasted longer than the commonly defined chronology of the modern civil rights era. The

1951 Moton School strike was rooted in a decades-long striving by the African American community for educational opportunities against the limitations imposed by recalcitrant white control. The strike took place more than four years before Rosa Parks refused to move to the back of the bus in Montgomery, Alabama, and nine years before the lunch-counter sit-ins by black college students in Greensboro, North Carolina. The lengthy legal and moral battles for educational equality and reconciliation in the county would be ongoing for years after the death of Dr. Martin Luther King Jr. in 1968.

Much of the historiography of the civil rights movement has tended to focus on urban areas such as Montgomery, Birmingham, or Selma, Alabama; Albany, Georgia; and Memphis, Tennessee; major protests, such as the Freedom Rides and the March on Washington; or violent events, as in the murder of three civil rights workers in Philadelphia, Mississippi. Recent historical studies have presented lesser-known stories of the civil rights era, many of them local community studies, as important contributions to a nuanced and complex history that is deeply interconnected. Like these works, the intent of this volume is to contribute to the historiography of the civil rights era by presenting this story of the struggle for public education in a rural, agricultural community as a window into the history of America's racial divide.[6]

The Prince Edward County story also speaks to the role of women in the civil rights movement. Often portrayed as an "invisible" force in the movement for racial change, women helped shape and guide the struggle in countless ways. Prior histories of this era, however, frequently overlooked their contributions. In Prince Edward, student Barbara Johns (see pp. 42 and 47) led the 1951 school strike, which took the local civil rights struggle from rural Virginia to the U.S. Supreme Court. She later noted that she had been inspired, in part, by one of her schoolteachers, Inez Davenport. The American Friends Service Committee (AFSC), a Quaker peace organization founded following World War I, brought significant assistance to the black community during the years of the closed public schools. Jean Fairfax, director of southern programs for the AFSC, tirelessly campaigned the federal government to reopen the public schools. Helen Baker (see p. 136), then later Nancy Adams (see p. 212), ran the AFSC field office in Prince Edward, providing educational and moral support to the black community. As historian Laurie B. Green has written, "The shift over the last two decades from national to local civil rights studies, from stories about political leaders to those centered on the grass roots, has revealed the scope of women's activism."[7]

Prince Edward's local struggle and Virginia's massive resistance unfolded amid the Cold War era. Arguments on both sides of the bitter racial divide reflected Cold War concerns. Appealing to anticommunist sentiment, segregationists sought to discredit the civil rights drive by claiming it was a "communist influenced" movement led by radicals with subversive ideas.[8] Civil rights advocates countered with claims that removing racial barriers would actually strengthen the United States in its international contest with the Soviet Union. In 1957, Virginia NAACP state conference president Edwin B. Henderson stated, "By eliminating these laws that insult people of color in America we will win friends among the non-white races of mankind around the world and add them in the struggle against Godless communism" (see p. 102). Civil rights leaders and organizations highlighted the gap between American rhetoric and reality in an effort to convince American policymakers to support progress in racial affairs.[9]

Contemporary scholars have highlighted the connection between the segregationist fight against *Brown v. Board of Education* and the rise of modern conservatism and the growth of the private school movement. In Prince Edward County, segregationist leaders identified themselves as patriots defending the U.S. Constitution against federal interference, conspicuously naming the locally formed segregationist organization the Defenders of State Sovereignty and Individual Liberties. Their argument for constitutionality and patriotism was a means to obscure the segregationist ideology underlying their efforts. Using language in such a manner would later become a hallmark of modern conservative rhetoric, as noted by sociologist Christopher Bonastia, who writes in *Southern Stalemate*, "Many convictions of modern conservatism—such as enthusiasm for school choice, a 'fee-for-service' mentality about taxation (whereby the highest taxpayers receive the most services), and reduction of public services—have their roots in places like Prince Edward County."[10] Dr. Robert Green, who conducted educational research in Prince Edward County in 1963, stated decades later that the origins of school vouchers and charter schools can be found in the fight over public education in Prince Edward County.[11]

The concept of truth and reconciliation is also an emerging field of study in the historiography of the era, as scholars examine the process of healing in communities that were traumatized by the racism of Jim Crow society and the fight for civil rights and justice. In *Shattered Voices: Language, Violence, and the Work of Truth Commissions*, professor of law Teresa Godwin Phelps argues that traumatized societies must take proactive steps to address the needs of victims by investigating and reporting on the past. Historian Timothy B. Tyson explains in *Blood Done Sign My Name*, "Genuine healing requires a candid confrontation with our past. In any case, if there is to be reconciliation, first there must be truth."[12] Efforts toward truth and reconciliation have come to Prince

Edward County in a number of ways and events that are recounted in the epilogue to this volume.

The educational tragedy of Prince Edward County challenges an often-
presented triumphalist narrative of the civil rights movement and American
history. While in the end the legal battles were won and the schools were
reopened, it was, in many respects, a Pyrrhic victory, as the loss to the African
American community was profound. The damage wrought by this educational
deprivation is generations-deep and long-lasting.[13] "You know, what they done,
they crippled us. They crippled me," John Hurt said forty years later. "If I could
take that board that said, 'Shut these schools down'—if I could take them and
put 'em in my position where I was and let them walk around for forty-some
years that I been walking around like that . . . then that would be the answer to
my prayer. . . . Let them see some of the hell that they put me through because
they didn't want people to go to school together."[14]

It can be said then, of this community in Southside Virginia, that the Civil
War ended here and an important opening event of the modern civil rights
movement took place here. In the shadow of Appomattox, this struggle for
public education helps further illuminate the decades-long struggle for freedom of America's civil rights years. The human legacy of these tragic events
was a generation of uneducated and undereducated children who were denied
their right to education and thus their right to full participation in American
society. "The Prince Edward case posed the moral question," wrote journalist
Bob Smith, "of whether it is right and just in twentieth-century America for
a county to close its public schools, for whatever reason."[15] In no other community in the country did the far-reaching legal decision of *Brown v. Board of
Education* have a more profound effect than in the closing of the public schools
of Prince Edward County, Virginia.

NOTES

1. Virginia State Constitution of 1870 (Underwood Constitution), http://vagovernment
matters.org/primary-sources/516.

2. Smith, *They Closed Their Schools*; Sullivan, Maynard, and Yellin, *Bound for Freedom*.

3. Titus, *Brown's Battleground*; Bonastia, *Southern Stalemate*.

4. See, for example, Kara Miles Turner, "'Liberating Lifescripts': Prince Edward County,
Virginia, and the Roots of *Brown v. Board of Education*," in *From the Grassroots to the Supreme
Court: Brown v. Board of Education and American Democracy*, ed. Peter Lau (Durham, N.C.:
Duke University Press, 2004), 88–104; Amy Murrell, "The Impossible Prince Edward Case: The
Endurance of Resistance in a Southside County, 1959–64," in Lassiter and Lewis, eds., *Moderates'
Dilemma*, 134–67; and Lee and Daugherity, "Program of Action." Examples of memoirs include
Foster and Foster, *Silent Trumpets of Justice*; Green, *Something Must Be Done*; and Stokes, *Stu-
dents on Strike*. Additional examples can be found in the Selected Bibliography.

5. Jacquelyn Dowd Hall, "The Long Civil Rights Movement and the Political Uses of the Past," *Journal of American History* 91, no. 4 (March 2005): 1233–63; William A. Link, *A Hard Country and a Lonely Place: Schooling, Society, and Reform in Rural Virginia, 1870–1920* (Chapel Hill: University of North Carolina Press, 1986).

6. A growing number of studies focus on the struggle for public education at the local level. Jeffrey L. Littlejohn and Charles H. Ford, *Elusive Equality: Desegregation and Resegregation in Norfolk's Public Schools* (Charlottesville: University of Virginia Press, 2012); David Cecelski, *Along Freedom Road: Hyde County North Carolina and the Fate of Black Schools in the South* (Chapel Hill: University of North Carolina Press, 1994); and Charles McKinney, *Greater Freedom: The Evolution of the Civil Rights Struggle in Wilson, North Carolina* (Lanham, Md.: University Press of America, 2010), are pertinent examples of this scholarship.

7. Laurie B. Green, "Challenging the Civil Rights Narrative: Women, Gender, and the 'Politics of Protection,'" in *Civil Rights History from the Ground Up: Local Struggles, A National Movement,* ed. Emilye Crosby (Athens: University of Georgia Press, 2011), 53; Danielle L. McGuire, *At the Dark End of the Street: Black Women, Rape, and Resistance—A New History of the Civil Rights Movement from Rosa Parks to the Rise of Black Power* (New York: Knopf, 2010).

8. George Lewis, *The White South and the Red Menace: Segregationists, Anticommunism, and Massive Resistance, 1945–1965* (Gainesville: University Press of Florida, 2004).

9. Legal scholar Mary L. Dudziak argues that racial discrimination in the United States hindered American efforts in its ideological struggle with communist ideology. Dudziak, *Cold War Civil Rights: Race and the Image of American Democracy* (Princeton, N.J.: Princeton University Press, 2000). See also Thomas Borstelmann, *The Cold War and the Color Line: American Race Relations in the Global Arena* (Cambridge, Mass.: Harvard University Press, 2001).

10. Bonastia, *Southern Stalemate,* 8. See also Joseph Crespino, *In Search of Another Country: Mississippi and the Conservative Counterrevolution* (Princeton, N.J.: Princeton University Press, 2007).

11. Dr. Robert Green, interview by Brian Grogan, San Francisco, California, May 22, 1998.

12. Teresa Godwin Phelps, *Shattered Voices: Language, Violence, and the Work of Truth Commissions* (Philadelphia: University of Pennsylvania Press, 2004), 5–10; Timothy B. Tyson, *Blood Done Sign My Name: A True Story* (New York: Three Rivers Press, 2004), 10.

13. Titus, *Brown's Battleground,* 220–21.

14. John Hurt, interview by Brian Grogan, Farmville, Virginia, May 22, 2004.

15. Smith, *They Closed Their Schools,* 265.

Prologue

"THE NEGROES OF FARMVILLE, VIRGINIA"

Following the Civil War, the federal government oversaw the dissolution of the Confederacy and supervised the end of slavery during the era of Reconstruction. Criteria for readmission to the Union for the former Confederate states included the writing of a new state constitution and the establishment of public education. In 1865, the U.S. Congress established the Bureau of Refugees, Freedmen, and Abandoned Lands, known as the Freedmen's Bureau, in the War Department to assist former slaves and protect them from whites hostile to emancipation and civil rights for African Americans.

Congress granted African American men the right to vote in 1867 and later embodied this right in the U.S. Constitution by adoption of the Fifteenth Amendment. The ratification of the Fourteenth Amendment in 1868 granted citizenship to former slaves. These changes allowed African Americans to participate in constitutional conventions and gain election to state legislatures throughout the South.

African Americans represented Prince Edward County in the Virginia General Assembly in the 1860s, 1870s, and 1880s. In 1869, one of the first acts of the reestablished legislature, which included James W. Bland of Prince Edward County, was to ratify the Fifteenth Amendment to the U.S. Constitution. This amendment prohibited states from denying any man the right to vote because of his "race, color, or previous condition of servitude."

From the late 1860s through the 1890s, African American men in Virginia participated in local, state, and national politics. In 1867–68, black Virginians served as delegates to the state constitutional convention that was required by the federal government as a condition for readmission to the United States. Twenty-five black delegates, including Bland, participated in the constitutional process. The new constitution, known as the Underwood Constitution after convention president John C. Underwood, legalized the right of black men to vote. It also established Virginia's first public school system and required that black and white children be taught separately. The constitution initially contained provisions to disenfranchise former Confederates, but these sections were rejected by Virginia's electorate. The Underwood Constitution was ratified by public vote in 1869, went into effect in 1870, and served as the constitution of Virginia until 1902.

During the same election, however, conservative white Virginians regained control of the General Assembly and helped elect a moderate Republican as governor. The conditions required by the federal government for readmission to the Union had angered many white Virginians. Opposition to education and voting rights for African Americans was virulent and widespread. In virtually every session of the General Assembly from 1870 onward, legislative efforts were made to overturn the Underwood Constitution.[1]

In the late 1870s, the Readjusters, a coalition of African Americans and liberal whites in Virginia, temporarily assumed political control by focusing on issues supported by working-class Virginians of all races. This shaky political coalition, however, could not survive an appeal to the racial fears of white Virginians launched by conservative white southern Democrats. By focusing on opposition to, and fear of, black political participation, conservatives regained control of Virginia's state government in the early 1880s and resumed the process of disenfranchising black voters.

In 1896, the U.S. Supreme Court legalized the practice of racial segregation. In *Plessy v. Ferguson* (see p. 12), the Court endorsed the doctrine of "separate but equal," which stated that segregation was acceptable so long as the facilities provided for the two races were equal. Subsequently, Virginia and state legislatures throughout the South passed laws requiring the separation of the races in most public spaces, including businesses, parks, courtrooms, and accommodations. In most instances, facilities for black southerners were inferior and rarely equal to those provided for whites.

In May 1900, Virginians voted to call a state constitutional convention, and in 1901–2 the all-white convention produced a new state constitution that disenfranchised approximately 90 percent of eligible black voters and almost half of working-class white voters. "The Democratic party is pledged in its platform to eliminate the ignorant and worthless negro as a factor from the politics of this State," declared John Goode, president of the convention.[2] The constitution of 1902 also reinforced segregation in education with the statement, in section 140, "White and colored children shall not be taught in the same school."[3]

The Jim Crow era had arrived. White politicians expanded segregation laws in Virginia in the early 1900s and further constrained the rights of African Americans by adopting the Racial Integrity Act of 1924 (see p. 30). For the next five decades, the status of African Americans in Virginia would revert to second-class citizenship.

Black Virginians fought to maintain their legal and political rights in this changing milieu. They sued to overturn the new state constitution but were rebuffed by the courts. In 1904, the U.S. Supreme Court dismissed two lawsuits, *Jones v. Montague* and *Selden v. Montague*, challenging the legality of the 1902 constitution. Organized boycotts in several Virginia cities also resisted newly established segregation statutes for streetcars. John Mitchell, editor of the *Richmond Planet* newspaper (see p. 23), chaired the Richmond boycott committee. African Americans were now struggling against the implementation of new segregation statutes that restricted all aspects of their public lives.[4]

African Americans, who had celebrated the freedoms obtained during Reconstruction, grieved as their newfound rights were circumscribed. They would continue to demand their rights of citizenship in the decades-long struggle against segregation that followed. Yet this community never lost the "peculiar hopefulness" noted by W. E. B. Du Bois, "that one day black people will have all the rights they are now striving for" (see p. 18).

NOTES

1. Raymond H. Pulley, *Old Virginia Restored: An Interpretation of the Progressive Impulse, 1870–1930* (Charlottesville: University Press of Virginia, 1968), 5–12.

2. "No White Man to Lose His Vote in Virginia," political broadside, Library of Virginia (1901.N.68), Richmond.

3. Virginia Constitution of 1902, sec. 140, http://vagovernmentmatters.org/archive/files /vaconstitution1902_6885e65b9d.pdf.

4. Andrew Buni, *The Negro in Virginia Politics, 1902–1965* (Charlottesville: University of Virginia Press, 1967), 34–49; Blair L. M. Kelley, *Right to Ride: Streetcar Boycotts and African American Citizenship in the Era of* Plessy v. Ferguson (Chapel Hill: University of North Carolina Press, 2010), 139–63.

Plessy v. Ferguson

U.S. Supreme Court

May 18, 1896

In 1890, the state of Louisiana enacted a statute requiring racial segregation on railroad cars. Two years later, Homer Plessy, a shoemaker of mixed racial heritage, intentionally challenged the law by riding in a railroad car for white passengers in order to be arrested. Convicted by a local judge, Plessy lost his appeal to the Supreme Court of Louisiana. His attorneys took the case to the U.S. Supreme Court.

In *Plessy v. Ferguson*, the Court ruled seven to one that segregation was not discriminatory if facilities for blacks and whites were equal, thus affirming the legal precedent of "separate but equal," which would dominate race relations in the nation for the next sixty years. The decision was based in part on earlier legal precedents accepting segregation in education, including *Roberts v. City of Boston* (1850).

Justice John Marshall Harlan penned an eloquent, lonely dissent stating, "In respect of civil rights, all citizens are equal before the law. The humblest is the peer of the most powerful."

This case turns upon the constitutionality of an act of the general assembly of the state of Louisiana, passed in 1890, providing for separate railway carriages for the white and colored races. . . .

The constitutionality of this act is attacked upon the ground that it conflicts both with the Thirteenth Amendment of the Constitution, abolishing slavery, and the Fourteenth Amendment, which prohibits certain restrictive legislation on the part of the States.

That it does not conflict with the Thirteenth Amendment, which abolished slavery and involuntary servitude, except as a punishment for crime, is too clear for argument. Slavery implies involuntary servitude—a state of bondage; the ownership of mankind as a chattel, or, at least, the control of the labor and services of one man for the benefit of another, and the absence of a legal right to the disposal of his own person, property and services. . . .

A statute which implies merely a legal distinction between the white and colored races—a distinction which is founded in the color of the two races, and which must always exist so long as white men are distinguished from the other race by color—has no tendency to destroy the legal equality of the two races, or re-establish a state of involuntary servitude. Indeed, we do not understand that the Thirteenth Amendment is strenuously relied upon by the plaintiff in error in this connection.

By the Fourteenth Amendment, all persons born or naturalized in the United States, and subject to the jurisdiction thereof, are made citizens of the United States and of the state wherein they reside; and the states are forbidden from making or enforcing any law which shall abridge the privileges or immunities of citizens of the United States, or shall deprive any person of life, liberty, or property without due process of law, or deny to any person within their jurisdiction the equal protection of the laws. . . .

The object of the amendment was undoubtedly to enforce the absolute equality of the two races before the law, but, in the nature of things, it could not have been intended to abolish distinctions based upon color, or to enforce social, as distinguished from political, equality, or a commingling of the two races upon terms unsatisfactory to either. Laws permitting, and even requiring, their separation, in places where they are liable to be brought into contact do not necessarily imply the inferiority of either race to the other, and have been generally, if not universally, recognized as within the competency of the state legislatures in the exercise of their police power. The most common instance of this is connected with the establishment of separate schools for white and colored children, which has been held to be a valid exercise of the legislative power even by courts of states where the political rights of the colored race have been longest and most earnestly enforced.

One of the earliest of these cases is that of *Roberts v. City of Boston*, 5 Cush. 198, in which the Supreme Judicial Court of Massachusetts held that the general school committee of Boston had power to make provision for the instruction of colored children in separate schools established exclusively for them, and to prohibit their attendance upon the other schools. . . .

The distinction between laws interfering with the political equality of the negro and those requiring the separation of the two races in schools, theaters, and railway carriages has been frequently drawn by this court. . . .

So far, then, as a conflict with the Fourteenth Amendment is concerned, the case reduces itself to the question whether the statute of Louisiana is a reasonable regulation, and with respect to this there must necessarily be a large discretion on the part of the legislature. In determining the question of reasonableness, it is at liberty to act with reference to the established usages, customs, and traditions of the people, and with a view to the promotion of their comfort, and the preservation of the public peace and good order. Gauged by this standard, we cannot say that a law which authorizes or even requires the separation of the two races in public conveyances is unreasonable, or more obnoxious to the Fourteenth Amendment than the acts of Congress requiring separate schools for colored children in the District of Columbia, the constitutionality of which does not seem to have been questioned, or the corresponding acts of state legislatures.

We consider the underlying fallacy of the plaintiff's argument to consist in the assumption that the enforced separation of the two races stamps the colored race with a badge of inferiority. If this be so, it is not by reason of anything found in the act, but solely because the colored race chooses to put that construction upon it. The argument necessarily assumes that if, as has been more than once the case and is not unlikely to be so again, the colored race should become the dominant power in the state legislature, and should enact a law in precisely similar terms, it would thereby relegate the white race to an inferior position. We imagine that the white race, at least, would not acquiesce in this assumption. The argument also assumes that social prejudices may be overcome by legislation, and that equal rights cannot be secured to the negro except by an enforced commingling of the two races. We cannot accept this proposition. If the two races are to meet upon terms of social equality, it must be the result of natural affinities, a mutual appreciation of each other's merits, and a voluntary consent of individuals. . . . Legislation is powerless to eradicate racial instincts or to abolish distinctions based upon physical differences, and the attempt to do so can only result in accentuating the difficulties of the present situation. If the civil and political rights of both races be equal, one cannot be inferior to the other civilly or politically. If one race be inferior to the other socially, the Constitution of the United States cannot put them upon the same plane.

It is true that the question of the proportion of colored blood necessary to constitute a colored person, as distinguished from a white person, is one upon which there is a difference of opinion in the different states; some holding that any visible admixture of black blood stamps the person as belonging to the colored race . . . ; others, that it depends upon the preponderance of blood . . . ; and still others, that the predominance of white blood must only be in the proportion of three-fourths. . . . But these are questions to be determined under the laws of each state, and are not properly put in issue in this case. Under the allegations of his petition, it may undoubtedly become a question of importance whether, under the laws of Louisiana, the petitioner belongs to the white or colored race.

The judgment of the court below is therefore affirmed.

Mr. Justice Harlan, dissenting. . . .

In respect of civil rights common to all citizens, the Constitution of the United States does not, I think, permit any public authority to know the race of those entitled to be protected in the enjoyment of such rights. Every true man has pride of race, and under appropriate circumstances, when the rights of others, his equals before the law, are not to be affected, it is his privilege to express such pride and to take such action based upon it as to him seems proper. But I deny that any legislative body or judicial tribunal may have regard to the race of citizens when the civil rights of those citizens are involved. Indeed, such legislation as that here in question is inconsistent not only with that equality of rights which pertains to citizenship, national and state, but with the personal liberty enjoyed by everyone within the United States.

The Thirteenth Amendment does not permit the withholding or the deprivation of any right necessarily inhering in freedom. It not only struck down the institution of slavery as previously existing in the United States, but it prevents the imposition of any burdens or disabilities that constitute badges of slavery or servitude. It decreed universal civil freedom in this country. This court has so adjudged. But, that amendment having been found inadequate to the protection of the rights of those who had been in slavery, it was followed by the Fourteenth Amendment, which added greatly to the dignity and glory of American citizenship, and to the security of personal liberty by declaring that,

> all persons born or naturalized in the United States, and subject to the jurisdiction thereof, are citizens of the United States and of the State wherein they reside,

and that

> no state shall make or enforce any law which shall abridge the privileges or immunities of citizens of the United States; nor shall any state deprive any person of life, liberty or property without due process of law, nor deny to any person within its jurisdiction the equal protection of the laws.

These two amendments, if enforced according to their true intent and meaning, will protect all the civil rights that pertain to freedom and citizenship. Finally, and to the end that no citizen should be denied, on account of his race, the privilege of participating in the political control of his country, it was declared by the Fifteenth Amendment that "the right of citizens of the United States to vote shall not be denied or abridged by the United States or by any state on account of race, color or previous condition of servitude."

These notable additions to the fundamental law were welcomed by the friends of liberty throughout the world. They removed the race line from our governmental systems. . . .

Everyone knows that the statute in question had its origin in the purpose, not so much to exclude white persons from railroad cars occupied by blacks, as to exclude colored people from coaches occupied by or assigned to white persons. Railroad corporations of Louisiana did not make discrimination among whites in the matter of accommodation for travelers. The thing to accomplish was, under the guise of giving equal accommodation for whites and blacks, to compel the latter to keep to themselves while traveling in railroad passenger coaches. No one would be so wanting in candor as to assert the contrary. The fundamental objection, therefore, to the statute, is that it interferes with the personal freedom of citizens. . . . If a white man and a black man choose to occupy the same public conveyance on a public highway, it is their right to do so; and no government, proceeding alone on grounds of race, can prevent it without infringing the personal liberty of each. . . .

But in view of the Constitution, in the eye of the law, there is in this country no superior, dominant, ruling class of citizens. There is no caste here. Our Constitution is color-blind, and neither knows nor tolerates classes among citizens. In respect of civil rights, all citizens are equal before the law. The humblest is the peer of the most powerful. The law regards man as man, and takes no account of his surroundings or of his color when his civil rights as guaranteed by the supreme law of the land are involved. It is therefore to be regretted that this high tribunal, the final expositor of the fundamental law of the land, has reached the conclusion that it is competent for a state to regulate the enjoyment by citizens of their civil rights solely upon the basis of race. . . .

The present decision, it may well be apprehended, will not only stimulate aggressions, more or less brutal and irritating, upon the admitted rights of colored citizens, but will encourage the belief that it is possible, by means of state enactments, to defeat the beneficent purposes which the people of the United States had in view when they adopted the recent amendments of the Constitution, by one of which the blacks of this country were made citizens of the United States and of the states in which they respectively reside, and whose privileges and immunities, as citizens, the states are forbidden to abridge. Sixty millions of whites are in no danger from the presence here of eight millions of blacks. The destinies of the two races, in this country, are indissolubly linked together, and the interests of both require that the common government of all shall not permit the seeds of race hate to be planted under the sanction of law. What can more certainly arouse race hate, what more certainly create and perpetuate a feeling of distrust between these races, than state enactments which, in fact, proceed on the ground that colored citizens are so inferior and degraded that they cannot be allowed to sit in public coaches occupied by white citizens?

That, as all will admit, is the real meaning of such legislation as was enacted in Louisiana.

The sure guarantee of the peace and security of each race is the clear, distinct, unconditional recognition by our governments, national and state, of every right that inheres in civil freedom, and of the equality before the law of all citizens of the United States, without regard to race. . . .

We boast of the freedom enjoyed by our people above all other peoples. But it is difficult to reconcile that boast with a state of the law which, practically, puts the brand of servitude and degradation upon a large class of our fellow citizens—our equals before the law. The thin disguise of "equal" accommodations for passengers in railroad coaches will not mislead any one, nor atone for the wrong this day done. . . .

I am of opinion that the state of Louisiana is inconsistent with the personal liberty of citizens, white and black, in that state, and hostile to both the spirit and letter of the Constitution of the United States. If laws of like character should be enacted in the several states of the Union, the effect would be in the highest degree mischievous. Slavery, as an institution tolerated by law, would, it is true, have disappeared from our country; but there would remain a power in the states, by sinister legislation, to interfere with the full enjoyment of the blessings of freedom, to regulate civil rights, common to all citizens, upon the basis of race, and to place in a condition of legal inferiority a large body of American citizens, now constituting a part of the political community, called the "People of the United States," for whom, and by whom, through representatives, our government is administered. Such a system is inconsistent with the guarantee given by the Constitution to each state of a republican form of government, and may be stricken down by congressional action, or by the courts in the discharge of their solemn duty to maintain the supreme law of the land, anything in the constitution or laws of any state to the contrary notwithstanding.

For the reason stated, I am constrained to withhold my assent from the opinion and judgment of the majority.

163 U.S. 537 (1896).

QUESTIONS

1. Describe how the *Plessy v. Ferguson* decision circumscribed the rights of African American citizens. What justifications did the justices offer for their acceptance of segregation?

2. Justice Harlan wrote in his dissent that "the thin disguise of 'equal' accommodations for passengers in railroad coaches will not mislead anyone." Describe your understanding of this statement.

The Negroes of Farmville, Virginia: A Social Study

W. E. B. Du Bois

January 1898

William Edward Burghardt Du Bois was born in Massachusetts in 1868. Educated in public schools, Du Bois attended college at Fisk University and, in 1895, became the first African American to receive a Ph.D. from Harvard University. He became a renowned historian and sociologist, and was one of the founding members of the NAACP in 1909.

Shortly after obtaining his doctorate, Du Bois began historical and sociological research on African American communities in the United States. In 1897, he conducted a study for the U.S. Department of Labor of the black community in Farmville, now the county seat of Prince Edward County. Based on empirical research and statistical analysis, Du Bois's report sought to convey the condition of African Americans in the town thirty years after the end of the Civil War.

Prince Edward County is a small irregular quadrangle of about 300 square miles, situated in the middle country of Virginia, between the Piedmont region and tide water, about 57 miles southwest of Richmond, and midway between Petersburg and Lynchburg. This county is thus near the geographical center of the State, and is also in the center of a district that produces seven-eighths of the tobacco crop of Virginia. The county seat is Farmville, a market town of 2,500 inhabitants, situated on the upper waters of the Appomattox.

This county has had an interesting history as regards its population. A century ago it had a population of 8,000, evenly divided between whites and blacks; today it has a population of over 14,000, but the increase is almost entirely among the blacks, the number of whites still remaining under 5,000. . . .

Of the total population of the county, less than one-third live in towns of 25 or more inhabitants, leaving the great mass of the people thoroughly rural and agricultural. Before the late war more than 75 per cent of the farms were of 100 acres or over, and were worked by gangs of from 10 to 50 slaves. By 1870 these farms had become so broken up that nearly 40 per cent of them were less than 50 acres in size. . . .

Agriculture is the chief occupation of the inhabitants of the county, tobacco being the leading product. Corn, wheat, oats, and potatoes are also raised, together with dairy products and poultry. . . .

In addition to this agricultural exhibit there is a little manufacturing, and there are three lines of railway crossing the county and bringing it into touch with the markets. . . .

Turning to the Negroes of the county, we find that in 1895 the 9,924 Negroes therein owned 17,555 acres of land, which, together with buildings, was assessed at $132,189. The whites of the county, in the same year, owned 202,962 acres, and the assessed value of their lands and buildings was $1,064,180. . . .

Situated in the geographic center of an historic slave State, near the economic center of its greatest industry, tobacco culture, and also in the black belt of the State, i.e., in the region where a decided majority of the inhabitants are of Negro blood, Prince Edward County is peculiarly suited to an investigation into Negro development. The few available statistics serve to indicate how vast a revolution this region has passed through during the last century. They show the rise and fall of the plantation-slave system; the physical upheaval of war in a region where the last acts of the great civil war took place, and the moral and economic revolution of emancipation in a county where the slave property was worth at least $2,500,000. . . .

The present study does not, however, concern itself with the whole county, but merely with the condition of the Negroes in its metropolis and county seat, Farmville, where its social, political, and industrial life centers, where its agricultural products are marketed, and where its development is best epitomized and expressed.

Farmville is in the extreme northern part of Prince Edward County. It is thoroughly Virginian in character—easy-going, gossipy, and conservative, with respect for family traditions and landed property. It would hardly be called bustling, and yet it is a busy market town, with a long, low main street full of general stores, and branching streets with tobacco warehouses and tobacco factories, churches, and substantial dwellings. Of public buildings there is an opera house, a normal school for white girls, an armory, a courthouse and jail, a bank, and a depot. . . .

Farmville is the trading center of six counties. Here a large proportion of the tobacco of these counties is marketed, . . . here are a half dozen or more commission houses which deal in all sorts of agricultural products; and here, too, is the center for distributing agricultural implements, clothing, groceries, and household wares. On Saturday, the regular market day, the town population swells to nearly twice its normal size from the influx of country people—mostly Negroes—some in carriages, wagons, and ox carts, and some on foot, and a large amount of trading is done. . . .

The population of Farmville has grown steadily since 1850. Since 1890, however, the Negro population appears to have fallen off—a fact due doubtless to the large emigration to Northern cities. . . .

In 1880 the population of Farmville district, including Farmville town, was 3,310, of whom 1,120 were whites and 2,190 blacks; and in 1890 the population of the district was 3,684, of whom 1,246 were whites and 2,438 blacks.

The town of Farmville has no school for colored children, but sends them to the district school just outside the corporation limits. The schoolhouse is a large, pleasantly situated frame building with five rooms. It has one male principal, and one male and three female assistants. It is not at present, if the general testimony of the townspeople is to be taken, a very successful school. It is practically ungraded, the teachers are not particularly well equipped, except in one, possibly two, cases, and the school term is six months—September 15 to April 1. The teachers' salaries do not average over $30 a month, which confines the competition for the school to residents of the town. . . .

Of the 367 children between 5 and 15 years of age, 205, or 55.9 per cent, were in school. . . .

Between the ages of 5 and 15 years the boys and girls attend school in about the same proportion; after that the boys largely drop out and go to work. As compared with the boys, a larger proportion of the girls receive some training above that of the common grades. The effect of child labor and housework and in the tobacco factories is easily traced in the figures as to the length of school attendance during the year. Of the 205 children from 5 to 15 years of age who attended school during the year 1896–97, only 52 per cent attended the full term of six months, 33 per cent attended half the term, and 11 per cent less than three months. . . .

Even so indifferent a school system has had its effect on the illiteracy of the town. Of the 908 people reporting, 42.5 per cent could read and write, 17.5 per cent could read but could not write, while 40 per cent were wholly illiterate. . . .

Many of the Farmville boys and girls are attending various schools and academies away from home. Those most frequented, in order of popularity, are: Virginia Seminary, Lynchburg, a colored Baptist school; Virginia Normal and Collegiate Institute, Petersburg, a State school; Hartshorn Memorial College, Richmond, a school for girls; Hampton Institute, Hampton; Ingleside Seminary, Burkeville, a Presbyterian school. . . .

The opportunities for employment in Farmville explain much as to the present condition of its Negro citizens, as, for example, the migration from country to town and from town to city, the postponement of marriage, the ownership of property, and the general relations between whites and blacks. If we divide the total colored population above 10 years of age according to the popular classification of pursuits, we have in professional occupations, 22; in domestic, 287; in commercial, 45; in agricultural, 15; in industrial, 282; not engaged in gainful occupations, 259, and not reported, 14. . . .

While the range of employment open to colored men is not large, that open to women is peculiarly restricted, so that most girls have only the choice between domestic service and housewifery. . . .

There are no colored physicians or lawyers in the town, preachers and teachers being the only representatives of the learned professions. The position of preacher is the most influential of all positions among the Negroes, and brings the largest degree of personal respect and social prestige. The two leading preachers in the town . . . are graduates of theological seminaries and represent the younger and more progressive element. They use good English and no scandal attaches to their private life, so far as the investigator could learn. Their influence is, on the whole, good, although they are not particularly spiritual guides, being rather social leaders or agents. Such men are slowly but surely crowding out the ignorant but picturesque and, in many particulars, impressive preacher of slavery days. . . .

The teacher stands next to the preacher in general esteem. An increasing number of these are now young women, and those in Farmville teach the schools of the surrounding country districts. The school terms are from four to six months, and in addition there is considerable private teaching done. . . .

The Negroes of Farmville . . . and the neighboring county districts form a closed and in many respects an independent group life. They live largely in neighborhoods with one another, they have their own churches and organizations and their own social life, they read their own books and papers, and their group life touches that of the white people only in economic matters. Even here the strong influence of group attraction is being felt, and Negroes are beginning to patronize either business enterprises conducted by themselves or those conducted in a manner to attract their trade. Thus, instead of the complete economic dependence of blacks upon whites, we see growing a nicely adjusted economic interdependence of the two races, which promises much in the way of mutual forbearance and understanding.

The most highly developed and characteristic expression of Negro group life in this town, as throughout the Union, is the Negro church. The church is, among American Negroes, the primitive social group of the slaves on American soil, replacing the tribal life roughly disorganized by the slave ship, and in many respects antedating the establishment of the Negro monogamic home. The church is much more than a religious organization; it is the chief organ of social and intellectual intercourse. As such it naturally finds the free democratic organizations of the Baptists and Methodists better suited to its purpose than the stricter bonds of the Presbyterians or the more aristocratic and ceremonious Episcopalians. Of the 262 families of Farmville, only 1 is Episcopalian and 3 are Presbyterian; of the rest, 26 are Methodist and 218 Baptist. In the town of Farmville there are 3 colored church edifices, and in the surrounding country there are 3 or 4 others.

The chief and overshadowing organization is the First Baptist Church of Farmville. It owns a large brick edifice on Main street. The auditorium, which seats about 500 people, is tastefully finished in light wood with carpet, small organ, and stained glass windows. Beneath this is a large assembly room with benches. This building is really the central clubhouse of the community, and in greater degree than is true of the country church in New England or the West. Various organizations meet here, entertainments and lectures take place here, the church collects and distributes considerable sums of money, and the whole social life of the town centers here. The unifying and directing force is, however, religious exercises of some sort. The result of this is not so much that recreation and social life have become stiff and austere, but rather that religious exercises have acquired a free and easy expression and in some respects serve as amusement-giving agencies. For instance, the camp meeting is simply a picnic, with incidental sermon and singing; the rally of country churches, called the "big meeting," is the occasion of the pleasantest social intercourse, with a free barbecue; the Sunday-school convention and the various preachers' conventions are occasions of reunions and festivities. Even the weekly Sunday service serves as a pleasant meeting and greeting place for working people who find little time for visiting during the week. . . .

Finally, it remains to be noted that the whole group life of Farmville Negroes is pervaded by a peculiar hopefulness on the part of the people themselves. No one of them doubts in the least but that one day black people will have all rights they are now striving for, and that the Negro will be recognized among the earth's great peoples. Perhaps this simple faith is, of all products of emancipation, the one of the greatest social and economic value. . . .

Bulletin of the Department of Labor, no. 14 (Washington, D.C.: Department of Labor, January 1898), 1–38.

QUESTIONS

1. Du Bois noted that a significant number of local African Americans owned their own land. How might the independence offered by landownership have affected race relations in the county during this period?

2. By the 1890s, segregation was part of society in Prince Edward County. In what ways did blacks and whites interact on a regular basis, and what aspects of their lives were lived separately?

3. What was "the most highly developed and characteristic expression of Negro group life in this town"? In what ways was this institution important?

The History of the Revolutionary Body

Richmond Planet
July 13, 1901

The *Richmond Planet* was an African American newspaper founded in 1882 by former slaves. John Mitchell Jr. was appointed editor in 1884, at only twenty-one years old, beginning a long journalism career of fighting segregation and racial injustice. Although W. E. B. Du Bois wrote a positive account of a thriving black community in Prince Edward County in the years following Reconstruction (see p. 18), reactionary forces opposed to African American economic, social, and political advancement were rapidly growing across Virginia. The movement culminated in calls for a new constitution to rescind the civil rights granted to blacks in the Reconstruction constitution of 1870. In this editorial, Mitchell attacked the constitutional convention then in progress for denying black participation, for failing to follow the governing procedures of the 1870 constitution then in force, and for its stated purpose of disenfranchising black voters.

The Constitutional Convention which is now in session in this city is indeed a remarkable body. It was convened as a result of a deception by which a voter who did not vote for or against the calling of the constitutional convention involuntarily voted for it.

The avowed purpose of this body was to disfranchise all of the colored citizens without taking from any white man his right to vote.

In the meantime, the mandate went forth that the people most interested—the colored people—should be denied representation. They were not permitted to come as delegates from any county in the state, and thus in the forum, where their rights are to be sacrificed, the citizen of color is as silent as the grave.

That this was unjust, that it was unprecedented in this state, that it was the crowning act of injustice of all these years, no fair-minded man will deny.

But the most surprising part of the whole business was the action of the Constitutional Convention itself. Having been called under the old constitution, it threw off all restraints by declining to require the members to take the oath of office. The effect of taking this oath would have been primarily to cause all of the judges, senators and other officials to either retire from the convention or yield the offices which they held.

The feature of the whole affair is the disposition to nullify and over-ride the 14th and 15th Amendments to the Constitution of the United States and the disregard of the compact entered into with the national government, by which Virginia was readmitted into the union.

It is safe to say that no constitution will be lasting which has race prejudice for its foundation stone and class legislation for its temporary support. To build for the present only is to make trouble for future generations.

History has its lessons and students of it should be guided thereby. It is impossible to permanently check the progress of the colored people by vicious legislation even though it is engrafted in the constitution of the commonwealth.

No representative upon the floor of the Constitutional Convention has called for the statistics bearing upon the progress of the citizens of color as a producer. They dare not call for it.

Still, it is an undeniable fact that in eleven southern states the colored people produce ($600,000,000) six hundred million dollars worth of wealth per annum which is an average of over ($54,000,000) fifty-four million dollars in each one of the states.

Yet, this wealth producing people is ridiculed as paying no taxes, when they really furnish the money with which the white brother in the south pays his taxes.

It is a sad condition of affairs now prevailing, but the end of this long night of oppression and misrepresentation must be just beyond. He who tramples upon the helpless in the zenith of his power will live to rue the day and suffer for his heartlessness. This is as true of races as it is of individuals.

QUESTIONS

1. What was the avowed purpose of the constitutional convention described in the editorial? Why were African Americans denied representation in the convention?

2. The editorial states that the convention was invalidating its responsibility to the U.S. Constitution and the conditions under which Virginia was readmitted to the Union after the Civil War. Describe these actions.

Dedication of the Lincoln Memorial

Robert Russa Moton

May 30, 1922

Robert Russa Moton delivered the keynote address at the dedication of the Abraham Lincoln Memorial in Washington, D.C., in May 1922. Born in 1867, the son of freed slaves, Moton was raised on a plantation in Prince Edward County, graduated from Hampton Institute, and served as the principal of Tuskegee Institute from 1915 to 1935. When the first high school was built for African Americans in Prince Edward County in 1939, it was named Robert Russa Moton High School.

Moton's stature among white political and social leaders was founded, in part, on his advocacy of accommodation in race relations. He supported the premise that black Americans should advance the cause of their rights in society by earning through their behavior and achievements the goodwill of white Americans.

Moton prepared a speech, however, that strongly criticized the state of American race relations and the diminishing rights of African American citizens. The memorial commission, led by chief justice of the Supreme Court and former U.S. president William Howard Taft, required Moton to temper his remarks prior to the dedication ceremony. Although Moton had a seat of honor on the dais as the keynote speaker, all African Americans in the audience were required to sit in a segregated area. The following text is the original address written by Robert Russa Moton.[1]

When the Pilgrim Fathers set foot upon the shores of America in 1620, they laid the foundations of our national existence upon the bed-rock of liberty. From that day to this, liberty has been the watchword, liberty has been the rallying call, liberty has been the battle-cry of our united people. In 1776, the altars of a new nation were set up in the name of liberty and the flag of freedom unfurled before the nations of the earth. In 1812, in the name of liberty, we bared our youthful might, and struck for the freedom of the seas. Again, in '61, when the charter of the nation's birth was assailed, the sons of liberty declared anew the principles of their fathers and liberty became co-extensive with the union. In '98, the call once more was heard and freedom became co-extensive with the hemisphere. And as we stand in solemn silence here today before this newly consecrated shrine of liberty, there still comes rumbling out of the East the slowly dying echoes of the last great struggle to make freedom co-extensive with the seven seas. Freedom is the life-blood of the nation. Freedom is the heritage bequeathed to all her sons. For sage and scholar, for poet and prophet, for soldier and statesman, freedom is the underlying philosophy of our national existence.

But at the same time, another influence was working within the nation. While the Mayflower was riding at anchor preparing for her epoch-making voyage, another ship had already arrived at Jamestown, Virginia. The first was to bear the pioneers of freedom, freedom of thought and freedom of conscience; the latter had already borne the pioneers of bondage, a bondage degrading alike to body, mind and spirit. Here then, upon American soil, within a year, met the two great forces that were to shape the destiny of the nation. They developed side by side. Freedom was the great compelling force that dominated all and, like a great and shining light, beckoned the oppressed of every nation to the hospitality of these shores. But slavery like a brittle thread in a beautiful garment was woven year by year into the fabric of the nation's life. They who for themselves sought liberty and paid the price thereof in precious blood and priceless treasure, somehow still found it possible while defending its eternal principles for themselves, to deny that same precious boon to others.

And how shall we account for it, except it be that in the Providence of God the black race in America was thrust across the path of the onward-marching white race to demonstrate not only for America, but for the world whether the principles of freedom were of universal application. From the ends of the earth were brought together the extremes of humanity to prove whether the right to life, liberty and the pursuit of happiness should apply with equal force to all mankind.

In the process of time, these two great forces met, as was inevitable, in open conflict upon the field of battle. And how strange it is that by the same over-ruling Providence, the children of those who bought and sold their fellows into bondage should be the very ones to cast aside ties of language, of race, of religion and even of kinship, in order that a people not of their own race, nor primarily of their own creed or color, but brethren withal, should have the same measure of liberty and freedom which they enjoyed.

What a costly sacrifice upon the altar of freedom! How costly the world can never know nor estimate! The flower of the nation's manhood and the accumulated treasure of two hundred and fifty years of unremitting toil: and at length, when the bitter strife was over, when the marshalled hosts had turned again to broken, desolated firesides, a cruel fate, unsatisfied with the awful toll of four long years of carnage, struck at the nation's head and brought to the dust the already wearied frame of him, whose patient fortitude, whose unembittered charity, whose never failing trust in the guiding hand of God had brought the nation, weltering through a sea of blood, yet one and indivisible, to the placid plains of peace. On that day, Abraham Lincoln laid down his life for America, the last and costliest sacrifice upon the altar of freedom.

We do well to raise here this symbol of our gratitude. Here today assemble all those who are blessed by that sacrifice. The united nation stands about this memorial mingling its reverent praise with tokens of eternal gratitude: and not America only, but every nation where liberty is loved and freedom flourishes, joins the chorus of universal praise for him, who with his death, sealed forever the pledge of liberty for all mankind.

But in all this vast assemblage, there are none more grateful, none more reverent, than those who, representing twelve millions of black Americans, gather with their fellow-citizens of every race and creed to pay devout homage to him who was for them, more truly than for any other group, the author of their freedom. There is no question that this man died to save the union. It is equally true that to the last extremity he defended the rights of states. But, when the last veteran has stacked his arms on fame's eternal camping ground; when only the memory of high courage and deep devotion remains to inspire the noble sons of valiant fathers; at such a time, the united voice of grateful posterity will say: the claim of greatness for Abraham Lincoln lies in this, that amid doubt and distrust, against the counsel of his chosen advisors, in the hour of the nation's utter peril, he put his trust in God and spoke the word that gave freedom to a race, and vindicated the honor of a nation conceived in liberty and dedicated to the proposition that all men are created equal.

But someone will ask: Has such a sacrifice been justified? Has such a martyrdom produced its worthy fruits? I speak for the Negro race. Upon us, more perhaps than upon any other group of the nation, rests the immediate obligation to justify so dear a price for our emancipation. In answer let me review the Negro's past upon American soil. No group has been more loyal. Whether bond or free, he has served alike his country's need. Let it never be omitted from the nation's annals that the blood of a black man—Crispus Attucks—was the first to be shed for the nation's freedom; and first his name appears in the long list of the nation's martyred dead. So again, when a world was threatened with disaster and the deciding hand of America was lifted to stay the peril, her black soldiers were among the first to cross the treacherous sea; and when the cause was won, and the record made of those who shared the cruel hardship, these same black soldiers had been longest in the trenches, nearest to the enemy and first to cross their border. All too well does the black man know his wrongs. No one is more sensible than he of his incongruous position in the great American republic. But be it recorded to his everlasting credit, that no failure on the part of the nation to deal fairly with him as a citizen has, in the least degree, ever qualified his loyalty.

In like manner has he served his country in the pursuits of peace. From the first blows that won the virgin soil from the woods and wilderness to the sudden, marvelous expansion of our industry that went so far to win the war, the Negro has been the nation's greatest single asset in the development of its vast resources. Especially is this true in the South where his unrequited toil sustained the splendors of that life which gave to the nation a Washington and a Jefferson, a Jackson and a Lee. And afterwards, when devastating war had leveled this fair structure with the ground, the labor of the freedman restored it to its present proportions, more substantial than before.

While all this was going on, in spite of limitations within and restrictions without, he still found the way to buy land, to build homes, to erect churches, to establish schools and to lay the foundations of future development in industry, integrity and thrift. It is no mere accident that Negroes in America after less than sixty years of freedom own 22,000,000 acres of land, 600,000 homes and 45,000 churches. It is no mere accident that after so short a time Negroes should operate 78 banks, 100 insurance companies, and 50,000 business enterprises representing a combined capital value of more than $150,000,000. Neither is it an accident that there are within the race 60,000 professional men, 44,000 school teachers and 400 newspapers and magazines; that general illiteracy has been reduced to twenty per cent. Still the Negro race is only in the infancy of its development, so that, if anything in its history could justify the sacrifice that has been made, it is this: that a race that has exhibited such wonderful capacities for advancement should have the restrictions of bondage removed and be given the opportunity in freedom to develop its powers to the utmost, not only for itself, but for the nation and for humanity. Any race that could produce a Frederick Douglass in the midst of slavery, and a Booker Washington in the aftermath of Reconstruction has a just claim to the fullest opportunity for developments.

But Lincoln died, not for the Negro alone, but to vindicate the honor of a nation pledged to the sacred cause of human freedom. Upon the field of Gettysburg he dedicated the nation to the great unfinished work of making sure that "government of the people, for the people and by the people should not perish from the earth." And this means all the people. So long as any group within our nation is denied the full protection of the law; that task is still unfinished.

So long as any group within the nation is denied an equal opportunity for life, liberty and the pursuit of happiness, that task is still unfinished. So long as any group is denied the fullest privilege of a citizen to share both the making and the execution of the law which shapes its destiny—so long as any group does not enjoy every right and every privilege that belongs to every American citizen without regard to race, creed or color, that task for which the immortal Lincoln gave the last full measure of devotion—that task is still unfinished. What nobler thing can the nation do as it dedicates this shrine for him whose deed has made his name immortal—what nobler thing can the nation do than here about this shrine to dedicate itself by its own determined will to fulfill to the last letter the lofty task imposed upon it by the sacred dead?

More than sixty years ago he said in prophetic warning: "This nation cannot endure half slave and half free: it will become all one thing or all the other." With equal truth, it can be said today: no more can the nation endure half privileged and half repressed; half educated and half uneducated; half protected and half unprotected; half prosperous and half in poverty; half in health and half in sickness; half content and half in discontent; yes, half free and half yet in bondage.

My fellow citizens, in the great name which we honor here today, I say unto you that this memorial which we erect in token of our veneration is but a hollow mockery, a symbol of hypocrisy, unless we together can make real in our national life, in every state and in every section, the things for which he died. This is a fair and goodly land. Much right have we, both black and white, to be proud of our achievements at home and our increasing service in all the world. In like manner, there is abundant cause for rejoicing that sectional rancours and racial antagonisms are softening more and more into mutual understanding and increasing sectional and inter-racial cooperation. But unless here at home we are willing to grant to the least and humblest citizen the full enjoyment of every constitutional privilege, our boast is but a mockery and our professions as sounding brass and a tinkling cymbal before the nations of the earth. This is the only way to peace and security at home, to honor and respect abroad.

Sometimes I think the national government itself has not always set the best example for the states in this regard. A government which can venture abroad to put an end to injustice and mob-violence in another country can surely find a way to put an end to these same evils within our own borders. The Negro race is not insensible of the difficulties that such a task presents; but unless we can together, North and South, East and West, black and white, find the way out of these difficulties and square ourselves with the enlightened conscience and public opinion of all mankind, we must stand convicted not only of inconsistency and hypocrisy, but of the deepest ingratitude that could stain the nation's honor. Twelve million black men and women in this country are proud of their American citizenship, but they are determined that it shall mean for them no less than for any other group, the largest enjoyment of opportunity and the fullest blessings of freedom. We ask no special privileges; we claim no superior title; but we do expect in loyal cooperation with all true lovers of our common country to do our full share in lifting our country above reproach and saving her flag from stain or humiliation. Let us, therefore, with malice toward none, with charity for all, with firmness in the right as God gives us to see the right—let us strive on to finish the work which he so nobly began, to make America the symbol for equal justice and equal opportunity for all.

Robert Russa Moton Papers, box 11, Library of Congress, Washington, D.C.

NOTE

1. See Adam Fairclough, "Civil Rights and the Lincoln Memorial: The Censored Speeches of Robert R. Moton (1922) and John Lewis (1963)," *Journal of Negro History* 82, no. 4 (Autumn 1997): 408–16.

QUESTIONS

1. In what ways were black Americans justifying the "dear price of Emancipation," as described by Robert Moton?
2. Which passages of Moton's speech may have so displeased the organizers of the Lincoln Memorial dedication committee that they asked him to revise his remarks?
3. How did Moton state that the nation could best fulfill the unfinished legacy of Abraham Lincoln?

Race Measure Becomes Law

Farmville Herald
March 21, 1924

Southern states had established and enforced laws classifying citizens by race since colonial times. In Virginia, individuals with one-quarter or more "Negro blood" were classified as black. Legislation enacted in 1910 required that Virginians with one-sixteenth or more black blood be classified as black. In 1924, the General Assembly passed the Racial Integrity Act, establishing the "one-drop rule," which mandated that citizens with any black blood be classified as nonwhite.[1] Enactment of this law, only two years after the dedication of the Lincoln Memorial, confirmed the concerns expressed by Robert Moton regarding the diminishing rights of African American citizens. The new legislation was strictly enforced by Virginia's Bureau of Vital Statistics, created in 1912 and headed by Walter A. Plecker, an ardent white supremacist, and proved another step by the state government to institutionalize the strictures of racial segregation.

The *Farmville Herald* printed this report on the Racial Integrity Act provided by the Bureau of Vital Statistics. Established in 1890 and published weekly, the newspaper was the primary source of news in Prince Edward County. Owned since 1921 by publisher and editor J. Barrye Wall, the *Herald* presented a conservative, segregationist perspective on local and state affairs.

Designed to Correct Great Out-Standing Evil of State and Nation

Senate Bill 219 to preserve racial integrity, passed the House March 8, 1924, and is now a law of this state.

This bill aims at correcting a condition which only the more thoughtful people of Virginia know the existence of.

It is estimated that there are in the State from 10,000 to 20,000, possibly more, near white people, who are known to possess an intermixture of colored blood, in some cases to a slight extent it is true, but still enough to prevent them from being white.

In the past, it has been possible for these people to declare themselves as white or even to have the Court so declare them. Then they have demanded the admittance of their children into the white schools, and in not a few cases have intermarried with white people.

In many countries they exist as distinct colonies holding themselves aloof from negroes, but not being admitted by the white people as of their race.

In any large gathering or school of colored people, especially in the cities, many will be observed who are scarcely distinguishable as colored.

These persons however are not white in reality, nor by the new definition of this law, that a white person is one with no trace of the blood of another race, except that a person with one-sixteenth of the American Indian, if there is no other race mixture, may be classed as white.

Their children are likely to revert to the distinctly negro type even if all apparent evidence of mixture has disappeared.

The Virginia Bureau of Vital Statistics has been called upon for evidence by two lawyers within the last month who were employed to assist people of this type to force their children into the white public schools, and by another employed by the school trustees of a district to prevent this action.

In each case evidence was found to show that either the people themselves or their connections were reported to our office to be of mixed blood.

Our Bureau has kept a watchful eye upon the situation, and has guarded the welfare of the State as far as possible with inadequate law and power. The condition has gone on however, and is rapidly increasing in importance.

Unless radical measures are used to prevent it, Virginia and other parts of the Nation must surely in time go the way of all other countries in which people of two or more races have lived in close contact. With the exception of the Hebrew race, complete intermixture or amalgamation has been the inevitable result.

To succeed, the intermarriage of the white race with mixed stock must be made impossible. But that is not sufficient, public sentiment must be so aroused that intermixture out of wedlock will cease.

The public must be led to look with scorn and contempt upon the man who will degrade himself, and do harm to society, by such abhorrent deeds.

The Bureau of Vital Statistics, clerks who issue marriage licenses, and the school authorities are the barriers placed by this law between the danger and the safety of the Commonwealth.

NOTE

1. There was an exception granted for a small number of white Virginians who claimed historical lineage to Native American members of the Powhatan Confederation, which lived in Virginia when Jamestown was established.

QUESTIONS

1. What were the goals of the 1924 Racial Integrity Act? How might this legislation have affected race relations in Prince Edward County?
2. In what ways did the Racial Integrity Act reflect the diminishing rights of African Americans as described by Robert Moton in his original speech for the dedication of the Lincoln Memorial?

I

"A Little Child Shall Lead Them"

Segregation affected every aspect of southern life by the early twentieth century. Laws required the separation of the races in transportation, assemblies, accommodations, neighborhoods, and public schools. In practice, however, segregation violated the key tenet of the 1896 *Plessy v. Ferguson* Supreme Court decision (see p. 12), which justified segregation with the legal concept of "separate but equal." During the Jim Crow era, separate was rarely, if ever, equal.

"An obsessive preoccupation with race and class was the central cause of the South's tragic neglect of public education," explained journalist John Egerton. "All too many of the white men who dominated political and cultural life in the region for decades after Reconstruction viewed education as a privilege reserved primarily for their sons and others of the same station; they had little concern for the schooling of women and almost no interest at all in the education of blacks or poor whites."[1] In the first decades of the twentieth century, major funding for public education in the South came from northern businessmen and philanthropists. As late as 1935, only three of the eleven former Confederate states provided free textbooks to children.

Virginia's public schools had been segregated since their inception in 1870, and funding disparities plagued the system from the beginning. In 1925, the Commonwealth of Virginia spent an average of $40.27 per year on each white public school student but only $10.47 on each black student. Facilities for black students, black teacher salaries, course offerings, and educational resources suffered as a result.[2]

In Prince Edward County, extreme educational disparities existed throughout the Jim Crow era. Following many years of persistent requests from the black community, the first high school for African Americans was built in 1939 under the Public Works Administration of the Franklin Roosevelt presidency. The school was named for Robert Russa Moton (see p. 25), a native of the region who had risen to national prominence as an educator and black leader.

At the time of construction, the Moton School was one of only twelve high schools for African Americans in rural Virginia. Limited in size by traditional reluctance to fund black education, the building soon became hopelessly over-crowded. Three classes were held simultaneously in the school auditorium and one classroom was located in a school bus. In 1948, three temporary classrooms were built to ease overcrowding and quickly dubbed "tar paper shacks" (see p. 35) due to their appearance and cheap construction. Built in 1939 for 180 students, enrollment at the school was 477 in 1950.

As the Moton High School was being constructed, state and federal money was also used to renovate Farmville High School for white students. A compar-ison of the facilities highlighted the inequities of black and white education in the county. Farmville High was a far superior facility that included science labs, a gymnasium, and a cafeteria—none of which existed at the Moton School.

The first branches of the NAACP in Virginia were established in the 1910s, and were among the first in the South. In the 1930s and 1940s, the NAACP pursued a policy of legal challenges to the inequities that permeated segregated education. The long legal battles produced a modicum of progress. In Virginia, court challenges led by lawyer Oliver Hill prodded the state toward educational equality within segregation, leading to improvements in black teacher salaries, school facilities, curricula, and transportation. Even with favorable court rul-ings, however, implementation of equality was difficult to achieve. In one case, a county school board in Virginia dropped classes in chemistry, physics, biology, and geometry from the white high school curriculum rather than expend more funds on black education.[3]

In Prince Edward County, the extreme educational disparities continued. Members of the Moton Parent Teacher Association (PTA) made numerous, unsuccessful appeals to the school board for a new building, but their requests were ignored. In early 1951, the all-white board instructed the black PTA mem-bers to stop attending board meetings and to submit no further requests.

As the NAACP battled in the courts for school equality, a new approach emerged from students. During and after World War II, students participated in boycotts, protests, and marches protesting the inequities of Jim Crow educa-tion in more than two dozen cities in both the North and South between 1943 and 1953.[4] In the spring of 1951, this movement found voice in Prince Edward County under the leadership of Barbara Rose Johns (see p. 42), a sixteen-year-old student at Robert R. Moton High School. The push for better educational opportunities for the black children of Prince Edward was now on the shoulders of a younger generation, whose actions would bring about the NAACP lawsuit for school desegregation in the county, *Davis v. County School Board of Prince Edward County* (see p. 55).

NOTES

1. Egerton, *Speak Now against the Day*, 127–28.
2. J. Douglas Smith, *Managing White Supremacy: Race, Politics, and Citizenship in Jim Crow Virginia* (Chapel Hill: University of North Carolina Press, 2002), 135; see also 234–35.
3. Peter Wallenstein, *Cradle of America: Four Centuries of Virginia History* (Lawrence: University Press of Kansas, 2007), 334–35.
4. August Meier and Elliott Rudwick, *Along the Color Line* (Champaign: University of Illinois Press, 1976), 359–60; Thomas J. Sugrue, *Sweet Land of Liberty: The Forgotten Struggle for Civil Rights in the North* (New York: Random House, 2008), 169–71.

A Little Child Shall Lead Them

Bob Smith

1965

Journalist Bob Smith wrote the first book-length account of the school desegregation crisis in the county, *They Closed Their Schools: Prince Edward County, Virginia, 1951–1964*. Published in 1965, the account was based on dozens of visits to the county and numerous interviews as the school closing crisis took place. The book served as the principal work on this subject for nearly fifty years. In this selection, from chapter 2 of the book, Smith discusses the life of Moton High School student Barbara Johns in the late 1940s and early 1950s.

Barbara Rose Johns had roots deep in Prince Edward County. Her grandparents and parents all had been born there. Her father, a solid, silent man, owned land in the Darlington Heights section. Her uncle, the Reverend Vernon Johns, preached there when he was not off preaching somewhere else, denouncing the country Negroes who filled the churches where he spoke for their impenetrable docility, for not caring enough.

Barbara was born in New York City. Her mother and father had hoped to get away from the farm and the slow, rural existence with its drab promise for the future. . . . When Barbara was fourteen months old, the family moved back to the county and then, in 1942, to Washington, where her mother, Violet

Johns, had found work with the government. Robert Johns entered the army that year, and the next year Barbara was moved back to the county to live with her grandparents. She was enrolled in Public School 14, a one-room school set in a patch of pine.

Barbara feels that she was protected from the realities of life during this time. She remembers no personal experience of color in her early years, but at night she and occasionally one of the more venturesome of her three younger brothers and one younger sister would slip out of bed to the door of the room where the family was gathered around talking: "You could hear stories about slavery and about the way Negroes were living in the old days. I don't know about whether any of this was real experience for them or what, and I know none of them actually had been slaves of course. . . . But I remember stories. . . . There was one story about a young white woman with this particular horse that she wanted groomed just right. She would come out and wipe a clean white cloth across the horse's body to see if it got any dirt. If it did the slave got whipped. . . . I remember that the story ended, and I know it sounds mean, but I always felt glad somehow. . . . Anyway the way it ended the horse threw her and she died. . . ."

In 1945 Barbara's father got out of the army and her mother left her job in Washington to return to the county. Violet Johns had an opportunity to see more of her ten-year-old daughter. She remembers that "Barbara was sort of strange, sort of—deep. I don't know. Anyway she would play for a while and then she would stop just as abruptly. I guess you could say that she was selfish. . . . She liked to be by herself quite a bit and she thought that a lot of the things other kids were interested in were silly. . . ."

Before he had gone into the army, Robert Johns had operated a general store owned by Vernon Johns in a section of Darlington Heights, in which Negro farmers predominated. When he came out, Robert took over the store entirely. Despite the nature of the immediate neighborhood, the clientele was thoroughly mixed. White farmers were regular customers, white salesmen were regular visitors. Mrs. Johns remembers having difficulty adjusting back from the manners of Washington to rural Virginia: "People used to come in and I used to get so angry that they would . . . call you by your first name. 'Violet, how about this'—and that kind of thing. I would tell them I thought only my personal friends called me by my first name. We used to have a verbal fight almost every day with some salesman or another."

She remembers when Barbara was quite small that a white boy came into the store and asked for "Uncle Robert" and that she had to explain to her daughter that her father was not really the little boy's uncle.

When Barbara was twelve and thirteen she worked in the store, waiting on customers, when school was out. Of the job, she recalls, "I used to feel proud that I was able to give this service rather than go to them for service. . . . My father was on good terms with all the whites around. . . . They would come, some of them, and sit around and play cards. . . . Well they were all poor dirt farmers, you know, and it didn't matter much to them . . . one white farmer's wife used to come over and talk and sit. . . . I remember she had a daughter and I used to think she was such a beautiful girl. She went to Farmville and got a job in the five and ten and I came in one day and she just turned away. . . . All the times we had talked and just this little thing turned her head. . . ."

Barbara seethed, but smothered her flame. If she erupted at all, it was privately, in something she wrote down, or in brief, savage outbursts of anger. Mostly, she internalized her revenge. Years later, she wrote: "I remember as a youngster getting a special surge of pride out of discovering that the superior white man wasn't too superior after all. This came from visiting the Rose's and Newberry's five- and ten-cent stores in Farmville and finding out that the salesgirls couldn't count worth a darn. Example: I remember getting several (say five) 10-cent items and one 19-cent item. Instead of figuring 69 cents right off the bat, she got pencil and pad and wrote a list of five 10- and one 19-cent items and then added it up to be 79 cents. I asked her to recheck and she came up with 59 cents. Instead of taking advantage of her ignorance I got a greater kick from taking each item and counting them correctly out for her and seeing her face turn a crimson red and muttering 'Oh, yes, that's right.'" . . .

Barbara read incessantly. Her mother remembers occasions when she searched the grounds and the house proper for her daughter only to find her, at last, perched in the attic with a book. She read Booker T. Washington's *Up From Slavery* and remembered Washington's gentleness and the way in which he refused to picture the white man as cruel but instead showed how white and Negro depended upon each other. She read *Little Women* and *Little Men* and, not much later, Richard Wright's *Native Son*. She even tackled H. G. Wells's *Outline of History* from her Uncle Vernon's library. Barbara read, and her grandmother Croner was impressed: "She was quiet, serious, Barbara was . . . didn't seem to want to get out much . . . seemed she had to do a lot of thinking and studying. She read good books, didn't fool with any of these funny books. . . . Then, too, there were people who influenced her. Vernon Johns was often in the home and you know she didn't get nothing but encouragement from him to do better. . . ."

Her mother, too, saw Barbara's frankness as another link between her daughter and the Johns side of the family. She could not get Barbara to attend church regularly. . . . Her daughter "had a temper and she was sort of . . . stubborn, and anything she believed in she was determined to continue to believe in and if you wanted to change her mind you had to give a lot of reasons. . . . She was very outspoken, a little like her Uncle Vernon in that respect."

Barbara considers that her life began to change when she entered R. R. Moton High School. Her classmates remember her during her freshman and sophomore years as a quiet girl, intelligent, and active in school affairs. Barbara joined the drama guild, the New Homemakers of America, the high school chorus, and she was elected to the student council. She traveled a good deal as a result of this office. She began to think that Moton High School was a blight on the county, on all the Negroes in the county, on her.

She saw Huntington High School in Newport News, Solomon Russell High School in Lawrenceville, the Ralph E. Bunche High School in King George. She saw the Farmville High School closer to home, and in the forbidden distance from which she saw it glamour was attached. It was like the banana split she had seen in the window of the Southside Drug Store and had wanted to sit at a counter and eat. . . .

The worst thing about Moton was the palliative the school board had found for the overcrowding, the tar paper shacks. Each of the shacks had a single wood stove for heat, and the students who sat close to the stove stripped off their sweaters while those who sat farther away wrapped up in overcoats. The teachers had to pause in their lessons to stoke the fire. The shacks leaked in some places, and colds were the usual thing in the winter.

These circumstances bothered Barbara perhaps more than any of her classmates. She was troubled by the reports of the boys who worked after school around the Farmville High School and who spoke of the excellent equipment in the shops. She was troubled by the fact that the students at Moton had to leave for school an hour early in order to be there on time because the buses used to haul the Negro students were so few and so dilapidated. They were largely hand-me-down buses, abandoned by the white school system when new ones were obtained there; this troubled Barbara most of all, that the school and all about it seemed makeshift, hand-me-down, second-rate.

The students talked about these conditions over lunch. They talked but they did nothing, for most of them could conceive of nothing to do. Barbara realized that they would never act. She and they heard reports from their parents or other sources that the negotiations with the school board were not proving fruitful. Time hung heavily.

Barbara liked the school principal, M. Boyd Jones. She found him straight-forward, not the kind of principal who would tell the students that all was well in the world. Jones taught fair play, she remembers, and she considers that he had a considerable influence over the course that events took, if only because his teaching made it all seem inevitable.

But it was not easy to talk to one's principal about the things that made anger well up. Jones was seeing a good deal of one of his teachers, a Miss Inez Davenport, whom he married shortly afterwards. Barbara went to Miss Davenport: "I told her how sick and tired I was of the inadequate buildings and facilities and how I wished to hell (I know I wasn't this profane in speaking to her but that's how I felt) something could be done about it. After hearing me out she asked simply, 'Why don't you do something about it?' I recall smiling at her, dropping the subject, and going about my other activities. But I didn't forget that statement, for it stuck with me for several days and out of it was conceived the idea of the strike."

One of the first students Barbara Johns thought of was John Stokes. Any planning would have to include him, and he and his sister, Carrie, would have to be in favor of the plan.

The Stokes family in Prince Edward County was unusual. One measure of this fact was that *The Farmville Herald* had carried a full-length feature on John when he was elected state president of the New Farmers of America (the Negro 4-H). It was rare that the *Herald* carried stories about Negro achievements of longer than brief "colored news" length. In the story John was described as the son of Luther Stokes, a farmer, and head of an "outstanding" county family. One older sister, Lieutenant Martha Stokes, a graduate of St. Philip's Hospital in Richmond, was with the United States Marine Corps at Fort Dix, New Jersey. Three older brothers had served as noncommissioned officers in the army during World War II. . . . John's younger sister, Carrie, was president of the student council at Moton.

John Stokes, himself, had a record any high school student might have envied. He was vice-president of the student council, business manager of the "Motonian," a top student, a track star, and orator for the New Farmers of America. Like Barbara Johns, he used his opportunities as a student leader to travel. Twice he went to Atlanta and made frequent shorter trips around Virginia. He thinks that getting out of the county and listening to his older brothers and sisters talk about life in the north and in other countries contributed to his dissatisfaction with conditions at Moton: "I believe my brothers and sisters had influenced me more than anyone else. They had taught me the importance of being a good student so that I would not be hampered by my color, and the importance of not believing that I was inferior. . . ."

The Stokes family was "outstanding" in ways that the *Herald* did not know. The home was one in which could be found the latest books, magazines, and newspapers that ranged far beyond the confines of Virginia. The Stokeses were thoughtful people to whom many of the farmers in their section of the country came for advice. They were genuine opinion leaders for the county's Negro population.

The feature story about John Stokes appeared in the *Herald* of September 15, 1950. Dates of student meetings that ensued were never recorded, but it was not more than two months later that John Stokes was taking part in a student conspiracy directed at the authority of school officials of the county.

John Stokes remembers that Barbara Johns privately collared about five of Moton's student leaders—among them John and his sister, Carrie—and asked them to meet her in the bleachers around the athletic field one afternoon late in the fall. The students knew what the meeting would be about, although Barbara's plan was a mystery to them. The meeting was sure to be about conditions at the high school. John Stokes was prepared to agree that something had to be done: "The buildings, the shacks themselves, well to tell you frankly I used to catch colds in them. They were drafty and they were cold. If you sat around the stove you were too warm and if you sat away from it you were too cold. It was no way to be taught, and we considered that we were not getting the best education that way. . . . And we used to be embarrassed. People would stop by the highway and ask what those buildings were. We would say they were part of the school. They would say: 'School! Looks like a poultry farm!'"

John knew from his travels that the situation of Negro high school students elsewhere in Virginia was superior to that of the Moton students. He was not hard for Barbara to persuade. He found that "she opened our eyes to a lot of things. I guess it was her environment that made her such a person. You know she was quiet, very slow spoken. She talked to us just that way that day. But I guess maybe her uncle had quite an influence on her."

Barbara spoke to the students about the efforts their parents were making through the Moton PTA to get improvements in the school, and she contrasted Moton with other, more modern, Negro high schools in the state. She asked them why they thought their parents could make no progress with the school board in looking toward a new school. She asked the student leaders to watch the results of the next PTA—school-board meeting to see what progress was made. John Stokes recalls: "Then she said our parents ask us to follow them but in some instances—and I remember her saying this very vividly—a little child shall lead them. She said we could make a move that would broadcast Prince Edward County all over the world."

The meeting ended with Barbara asking the student leaders each to bring one more reliable student to a meeting that would follow soon. This second meeting, John Stokes recalls, was held indoors at the school during the winter of 1950. About ten student leaders were on hand. Barbara told the students that their parents were not taking a stand. She talked about action. She suggested that the students assembled there make plans to take the entire school out on strike in the spring. They would make and carry placards just like any other strikers. They would not come back until the school board promised a new school. Stokes recalls that those in attendance agreed wholeheartedly to the plan.

On Barbara's advice the students present agreed to keep the plan to themselves. The atmosphere of conspiracy was thought to be necessary as much for the protection of Moton authorities as for the plan itself. Barbara emphasizes that the students did not want Principal Jones, who was generally admired, to be hurt by what they did.

A third meeting of the student leaders—now grown to between fifteen and twenty in number—was held after Barbara and John had attended a Moton PTA meeting, possibly the one in April, 1951. Reasonably complete machinery was organized to set the rebellion in motion. It was not decided what the students would do once the entire school was out on strike. Stokes remembers that one plan was for the students to carry placards to advertise their plight and, if this did not bring action, to walk over to the white school, take seats, and stay until removed. Stokes later labeled this idea as "crazy" and it is one that never was tried. The placards, however, were made.

There was doubt about method but none about goals. The students wanted a new school. Barbara, John, and other student leaders were agreed on this point. The NAACP had by this time filed its first desegregation suit, in Clarendon County, South Carolina, but it is doubtful if the Moton students were even conscious of this. On Sunday, April 22, delegates of the Fourth District NAACP conference met in Sussex County, to hear the respected Virginia NAACP lawyer Spottswood Robinson speak. Robinson talked about Clarendon County: "Before the end of 1951 we hope to see a judicial declaration of the invalidity of racial segregation in at least one Southern school system . . . this nullification may come from the Supreme Court of the United States. . . . The NAACP has undertaken its non-segregation policy after realizing that previous experiences had proven that there can exist no equality in a segregated school system."

The Moton students did not know about Robinson's speech, but on the other hand, he did not know about them. While Farmville High School seniors were being given a guided tour of Washington, D. C., a small group of Moton conspirators were spreading the word of the plan for Monday to a picked group of juniors and seniors who were considered reliable enough to be told in advance. There would be enough of them, of the right sort, to carry the entire student body out of the school.

From *They Closed Their Schools: Prince Edward County, Virginia, 1951–1964* (Chapel Hill: University of North Carolina Press, 1965), 27–35.

QUESTIONS

1. In what ways did Barbara Johns's family shape her upbringing and her attitudes about race and racial equality?
2. Johns's father was a World War II veteran. How might this have affected her feelings about racial equality?
3. How did Johns's experiences at Moton High School influence her view of race relations in Prince Edward County? How did the administrators and teachers at the school influence her?

Recollections

Barbara Johns
Undated

Despite the challenges of southern race relations, Barbara Johns experienced a typical rural life during her years in Prince Edward County. In this undated reflection written years later, she shared memories of family life and farm work.

Johns also reflected on the county's African American schools and her frustration with their shortcomings, which led her to organize the student strike to protest the unsafe and unequal conditions at Moton High School. Following the strike, Johns's parents, fearing for her safety, sent her to Alabama to live with her uncle, Reverend Vernon Johns, and complete high school. Barbara Johns later expressed a sense of guilt that the school strike led to the public school closings and the difficulties inflicted on the children, who suffered the loss of their education.[1] Johns attended Spelman College, then Antioch College, completed a master's degree from Drexel University, and had a career as a librarian in the Philadelphia public school system.

My first recollection of Cullen, Virginia was in the year of 1942. I arrived by train from Washington, D. C. to Richmond, VA. In Richmond, we were picked up by my uncle and transported to my grandmother's home in Cullen, Va.

The ride on the train had been exciting—mainly because it was my 1st train ride, but mostly, because it was crowded with soldiers. I was fascinated by all of them in my imagination, they were big, tall, not-so tall men who looked so handsome and polished in their uniforms. I was particularly impressed by them because my own Daddy had been called into the army and though I had not seen him in his uniform—I imagined he must look as handsome as these men. In fact, the very reason my Mother, brother, sister and I left Washington to live in Va. was because my Daddy was in the service, and he felt we would fare better in the country.

My Grandmother owned 175 acres of land, and farming, raising pigs, cows, tobacco, corn and other crops was as important to her and my Grandfather's existence as they became to our own when my Dad returned from the war.

My Mother left us in our Grandmother's care and returned to Washington to live with her sister and work for the government at the Pentagon. I was enrolled in school at the Mary E. Branch Elementary School in Farmville, VA, where I remained through the 8th grade....

Finally, my Dad returned from the war and we settled down to family life in a simple white building belonging to my uncle which served as a store and a residence. Attached to it was a living room with fireplace, 3 bedrooms and a kitchen.

Here our chief occupation, Daddy and ours was to run the store, and pump gasoline....

These were happy days. We greeted the customers, fulfilled their needs, ate Big Towns and Johnny candies, and peanuts when our Dad wasn't looking—and generally lived an uncomplicated life. The fireplace in the living room was flanked by two ceiling to floor book shelves full of books left by my uncle who had moved to Montgomery, Ala. We spent many nights reading by the warmth of the fireplace. Here I read "The Postman Always Rings Twice," H. G. Wells' "War of the Worlds," and many other good books.

In between his trips from Montgomery to VA, my uncle would make sure we spent some of our time devouring the books he kept in the big house—particularly the encyclopedias. We were required to start with Volume A—and work up to Volume Z. Needless to say, I didn't relish this type of imposed and restricted reading—so I managed to circumvent this by inserting a few Archie and Veronica comic books, or some other material between the pages.

Of course, one of my brilliant, obedient cousins never took this shortcut, and that's why she graduated Phi Beta Kappa and I didn't.

My mother continued working in Washington, while we remained at the store. Soon plans were under way to build our own house on the 127 acres of land my father purchased from his brother.

Finally, the big day arrived. There stood our beautiful white house with a wrap-around porch perched upon a hill. It was a beautiful sight. We were excited and eager to move in. Mom soon arrived and we were assigned to our rooms. My brothers were given a first floor bedroom—across from my parents room—my sister and I were assigned to the second floor attic room as our house was a story and a half. There was also a living, dining room, kitchen and plenty of outdoor space. . . .

We planted tobacco (a vicious crop), corn, soybeans, watermelons, and a regular garden for family consumption. We planted apple trees, pear trees, black walnut trees, shade trees, and sunflowers. Our summertime days were spent "working" the tobacco, hoeing the corn, "slopping" the pigs, feeding the chickens, gathering the eggs, weeding the vegetable garden, milking the cows, killing chickens for dinner. In the winter—hog killing time was horrible. I always managed to disappear because I could not stand the slaughtering of the hogs. They were shot, their throat slit and then cut up for the meat. . . .

From Sept. to May—we went to school daily. I arose early in the morning to fix breakfast and lunch for my sister and brothers and to see that they were properly dressed for school. My mother had returned to her job in Washington to help supplement the income produced by the farm. . . .

I was "mother" to my siblings and therefore arrived home each day from school not with frivolous considerations of what I wanted to do—but already I had begun formulating in my mind as I rode the bus home which foods I would prepare for supper that evening. . . .

My Daddy was very strict about homework and each night you had to devote one hour to homework even if you had none. My Grandmother would often suggest that we write about the day's events and then she would grade the papers—and you would receive hilarious comments on the paper—plus we always got an "A."

At school, I enjoyed my French classes, music classes, English classes and History. Math, Science and Gym were not among my favored courses. Still, I got good grades. I belonged to the debating team, the Student Council and other activities. . . .

We were fond of our teachers. My favorite and the one who had the greatest impact upon my young life was Miss Davenport—my music teacher who later became Mrs. Jones, wife of the Principal of the school. Besides introducing us to the beauty of classical music, she permitted full expression in her classes, something quite foreign to most of the classes because most teachers taught and you listened and responded when requested. But Miss Davenport felt that everything in life lent itself to a variety of opinions, thoughts, moods, moments—much the same as music—and she encouraged you to respond that way. I got to know her more intimately when she became music teacher for my sister and me when we took piano lessons. I felt I could share my innermost thoughts with her and she wouldn't consider them ridiculous. This is how I happened to mention how unhappy I was with the school facility and its inadequacies to her. I told her it wasn't fair that we had such a poor facility, equipment, etc., when our white counterparts enjoyed science laboratories, a huge facility—separate gym dept., etc. I warmed to my subject and looked to her for some answer to my frustration—and she paused for a few moments and said, "Why don't you do something about it?" I was surprised at her answer but it didn't occur to me to ask what she meant—I just slowly turned away—as I felt she had dismissed me with that reply.

What one could do about such a situation, I had no idea. But I spent many days in my favorite hangout in the woods on my favorite stump contemplating it all. . . . My imagination would run rampant—and I would dream that some mighty man of great wealth through his kind generosity built us a new school building or that our parents got together and surprised us with this grand new building and we had a big celebration—and I even imagined that a great storm came through and blew down the main building and splattered the shacks to splinters—and out of this wreckage rose this magnificent building and all the students were joyous and even the teachers cried.

But then reality would set in and I would be forced to acknowledge that nothing magical was going to produce a new school.

And then there were times—I just prayed—"God please grant us a new school. Please let us have a warm place to stay where we won't have to keep our coats on all day to stay warm. God, please help us. We are your children, too."

This type of thinking went on for months, sometimes as I chopped the wood, sometimes as I fed the pigs—as I did my work, as I sat quietly, it would crop up in my mind—because I felt we were not treated like any other students. Their classes were not held in the auditorium, they were not cold. They didn't have to leave one building and transfer to another, their buses weren't overcrowded. Their teacher/bus driver didn't have to make the fire before he could start classes.

One morning—I was so busy rushing my brothers and sister down the hill to school, that I forgot my own lunch and had to rush back up the hill to retrieve it. In the meantime, the bus arrived, picked them up and left me standing there by the roadside waiting to thumb a ride with whomever came by.

About an hour later, I was still waiting, when the "white school bus" drives by—half empty on its way to Farmville High School. It would have to pass by my school to get to that school and I couldn't ride with them.

Right then and there, I decided indeed something had to be done about this inequality—but I still didn't know what. All day my mind and thoughts were whirling and as I lay in my bed that night—I prayed for help. That night, whether in a dream or whether I was awake, but I felt I was awake, a plan began to formulate in my mind. A plan I felt was divinely inspired, because I hadn't been able to think of anything until then. That plan was to assemble together the student council members whom I considered the "creme de la creme" of the school—because they were smart and thinkers. I knew them and trusted them and I was a part of them. From this we would formulate plans to go on a strike. We would make signs and I would give a speech stating our dissatisfaction and we would march out the school and people would hear us and see us and understand our difficulty and would sympathize with our plight and would grant us our new school building and our teachers would be proud and the students would learn more, and it would be grand. And we would live happily ever after. Fully confident that all of this would transpire, I rose early the next morning, rushed to get everyone out, could hardly wait to get to school to call this meeting.

I was self-sufficient and independent because my Mother was not around to rely upon or to consult. My Father was too busy plowing and planting and harvesting to have time for any fantasy of mine—and he would have considered it foolish—never agreed with it—but he wouldn't have stopped me. I was permitted free rein in my thinking and actions—as he put it I was too stubborn, too determined to have my way, anyway—so why hassle ourselves.

I didn't consult my Uncle because he wasn't around. And really, I didn't feel a need to consult anyone, anyway. It had been given to me. All I had to do—was do it.

From a copy in possession of the editors, provided by the Johns family.

NOTE

1. Joan Johns Cobbs recounted conversations with her sister Barbara Johns. Interview by Brian Grogan, Richmond, September 12, 2017.

QUESTIONS

1. How did Barbara Johns's family encourage her education?
2. What things about the public schools in Prince Edward County disturbed Johns?
3. Near the end of her writing, Johns explained that the idea she had conceived to address the unequal conditions in the black schools was her idea alone. Why do you think she felt it was important to make this point?

Letter from the Moton High School Strike Leaders

Barbara Johns and Carrie Stokes
April 23, 1951

Following months of planning, Barbara Johns and fellow student leaders initiated the student strike on April 23, 1951. The principal was lured away from the school with a ruse telephone call from a student. Johns then led approximately 450 classmates in the walkout. The student strike at Moton High School distinguishes this story from other locales involved in the battle for school desegregation. In Prince Edward, the students were leaders in the movement for change.

Student leaders reached out to adults for help, seeking the guidance of Farmville minister Reverend L. Francis Griffin, who would become the community leader in the long struggle for educational rights. They also contacted Oliver W. Hill and Spottswood Robinson, lawyers for the NAACP, who would become central figures in the struggle for racial and educational equality in Prince Edward County.

Gentlemen:

We hate to impose as we are doing, but under the circumstances that we are facing, we have to ask for your help.

Due to the fact that the facilities and building in the name of Robert R. Moton High School, are inadequate, we understand that your help is available to us. This morning, April 23, 1951 the students refused to attend classes under any circumstances. You know that this is a very serious matter because we are out of school, there are seniors to be graduated and it can't be done by staying at home. Please we beg you to come down at the first of this week. If possible Wednesday, April 25 between 9:00 a.m. and 3:00 p.m.

We will provide a place for you to stay.

We will go into detail when you arrive.

Yours truly,
Barbara Johns
Carrie Stokes

"Desegregation Move Started with Letter," *Richmond Times-Dispatch*, April 2, 1967.

QUESTIONS

1. Why do you believe Barbara Johns felt NAACP "help is available to us"?
2. How do you think Oliver Hill and Spottswood Robinson might have reacted when they received this letter?

Negro Pupils at Farmville Go on Strike

Richmond Times-Dispatch
April 25, 1951

Soon after the Moton High School student strike began, the *Richmond Times-Dispatch* reported on the event. One of Virginia's leading newspapers, the *Times-Dispatch* presented a conservative view of local, state, and national affairs. The paper published the following report on the student strike.

The entire student body of the R. R. Moton Negro high school walked out yesterday, protesting against "inadequate" facilities at the school, and were still on "strike" today.

Four hundred and fifty-five pupils left school shortly before noon after attending an assembly they said "was so overcrowded that breathing was difficult." One of the students said the school auditorium seats only 300, and the students who must stand in the aisles create a serious fire hazard.

School officials were slightly dismayed at the action, pointing out that a new $800,000 high school is in the planning stage.

Superintendent T. J. McIlwaine said negotiations were in progress for a site. In Richmond, Dowell J. Howard, State Superintendent of Public Instruction, said the State Education Department had approved the new school as part of Prince Edward County's four-year school development program.

The program also includes plans for three new Negro elementary schools. All told, the county intends to spend $1,925,000 improving Negro school facilities, as against $675,000 for white schools.

The new Moton school, which as now planned would take care of 700 pupils, was approved by the State Education Department January 25.

However, the county school board must submit another application for monetary help before any State funds can be released for construction of the school.

McIlwaine said the strike apparently was a protest against conditions at the present school and delay in the construction of the new school. He said he didn't know how much longer it would be before work started.

The superintendent said the walkout "seemed to be student-inspired." In answer to a query he declared it had "nothing in the world" to do with a recent rail crossing accident in which five Moton students were killed when a school bus was struck by a train.

A member of the student "strike committee" complained that a new school building had been promised for five years, and "all we get is tar-paper shacks." Three temporary wooden buildings were erected to relieve overcrowding at the school. The student said that they are improperly heated, have leaky roofs and lack sanitary facilities. She said there are only two lavatories and four drinking fountains for the 455 pupils, all located in the main building.

QUESTIONS

1. The newspaper placed "inadequate" and "strike" in quotation marks in the first paragraph. What does that suggest about the editor's view of the situation?
2. The newspaper noted that county officials were in the midst of efforts to equalize the black schools in Prince Edward. Why might the newspaper have placed such emphasis on this aspect of the situation?

A Problem Becomes an Issue

Farmville Herald
May 8, 1951

The Moton High School student strike grew dramatically in importance after student leaders contacted the NAACP for help. During the previous twenty years, the NAACP had waged a legal campaign for equality in education based on the doctrine of "separate but equal." Attorneys Oliver Hill and Spottswood Robinson visited the county on April 25 and explained to the African American community that the NAACP was now seeking plaintiffs for lawsuits challenging the constitutionality of segregation itself.

In meetings attended by thousands of black county residents, the NAACP attorneys sought and obtained support for a lawsuit against segregation in education. On May 3, 1951, Hill and Robinson formally petitioned the county school board to end segregation in the public schools. The *Farmville Herald* had initially dismissed the school strike as "mass hookie." This editorial now presented the NAACP lawsuit, and the potential ramifications in Prince Edward County, as a threat to the southern way of life.

If the student strike at R. R. Moton High School was a local effort to hasten the construction of a new school building, it can no longer be so considered. If the students initiated the movement they are no longer in command of the situation. The National Association for the Advancement of Colored People has assumed control and, according to the announced purpose, an effort will be made to discontinue racial segregation in secondary schools in Virginia. Instead of a local effort to improve school conditions, the movement has become a movement to eliminate racial segregation from the Virginia Constitution.

We regret that Prince Edward was chosen for this test case on the law of segregation. One, who has seen the great progress of public education during the past twenty years, can but feel that such a movement will greatly retard the future development of education. The progress of the South, of Virginia, of any section or community where two races must live together, depends upon the principles of segregation. Early in the Reconstruction Period it was seen as a necessity by leaders of both races. Readjustments have been accomplished and progress has been made through an understanding between the white people and the colored people of the South. Until this incident, the leaders of the races in Prince Edward County have worked together for the benefit of each. Local problems have been discussed and resolved by co-operation and understanding.

It is particularly unfortunate that the NAACP has chosen this time in the history of the United States to seek a change in the age old principles by which the South has made such marked progress. Facing a World War in which every person will be called upon to do a share in its prosecution, any program which threatens to divide the communities is to be regretted. If ever a united front, a happy people, a determined effort to preserve our way of life was needed, it is today.

We can not believe that the majority of either the Prince Edward white or Negro citizens advocate non-segregation, or would be happier thereby. Our community has been precipitated into a State controversy. It will be to our advantage to use the best judgment of which we are capable to the end that the future development of our community will not be retarded. Calm considerations, temperate words and a charitable understanding must be used to meet a situation, which we believe is not of the making of the majority of our citizens nor has the support of the majority of either race.

The problem becomes an issue. The movement which purportedly was begun locally to focus attention on the need for a new school building for Prince Edward Negroes, has become a state issue on segregation. The challenge must be accepted by the School Board and by the elected officials of the State of Virginia, who are sworn to preserve the State Constitution.

It may be well that this question of segregation be settled before further plans are made to build a new high school for Negroes. It would be folly to proceed to burden the county with a huge debt for a high school, which might be unsuitable for use in a future system. At any rate, the Constitution of the State of Virginia has been challenged. This must be resolved before any further plans for new school buildings can be made intelligently in Virginia.

QUESTIONS

1. The *Farmville Herald* stated that the NAACP had taken control of the situation in Prince Edward County and that local black leaders did not support its challenge of segregation. What was the basis for this claim?

2. The editorial said that in the past, "Local problems have been discussed and resolved by co-operation and understanding." Based on what you know, how might the local black community have responded to this point?

The Prophecy of Equalization

L. Francis Griffin

July 28, 1951

Reverend L. Francis Griffin became a trusted advisor to the student strike leaders. Raised in Farmville, Griffin fought in World War II in the famed 758th Negro tank battalion, the first such unit in the U.S. Army. Following the war, he studied theology at Shaw College before returning to Farmville in 1949 to assume his father's pastorate at

First Baptist Church. Strongly influenced by the theological views of Reinhold Niebuhr and the Social Gospel movement, Griffin pressed members of the black community to demand social justice. In the late 1940s and early 1950s, as a father and a leader of the local PTA, Griffin also led efforts to improve the county's black schools.

By 1951, Griffin, like the NAACP, supported a direct assault on segregation itself and called for change in this sermon, which he delivered in his church. He gave it in response to attempts to remove him from the pastorate of First Baptist Church amid criticism of his support for the school integration lawsuit.

"Every valley shall be exalted, and every mountain and hill shall be made low; and the crooked shall be made straight and the rough places plain; and the Glory of the Lord shall be revealed, and all flesh shall see it together; for the mouth of the Lord hath spoken it."—Isaiah 40:4–5.

One of the greatest evidences of our ignorance is our attempt to separate human races according to pigmentation of skin, shape of skull and the subsequent theory of the superiority of one people over another.

Despite the findings of science and the self-evident facts concerning man's biological, physiological, and psychological background, we tenaciously hold that races are unequal. No greater misstatement of fact has appeared in history. It is in conflict with all universal law and against the will of God. Yet we fail to realize that individual freedom is inextricably bound up with the freedom of all other human beings. Nonetheless, God is displeased over our actions.

The great leveling process of which the prophet Isaiah writes in our morning text is evidence enough that Christianity could never support any "separate but equal" doctrine and be true to the light that has been revealed.

There can be no compromise with corrupt inclinations which tend to contradict righteousness. There can only be exalted valleys, leveled hills and straight places. When the Great Arbiter shall come, life must be on a level, races must dissolve; justice, liberty and human dignity must prevail. . . .

We are all familiar with the findings of science on the race theory. Therefore we shall not go into a lengthy argument to prove the fallacy of race, but we all may rest assured whatever else might be said, God does not believe in segregation. . . .

Let us look at our little community for example. It differs from some southern communities in that while it is vicious, the viciousness is not obvious, therefore no resistance has been shown. Reinhold Niebuhr is manifestly right, "Good men do not easily realize how selfish they are if someone does not resist their selfishness; and they are not inclined to abridge their power if someone does not challenge their right to hold it."

Recently, a mild atomic explosion took place among the other race; our own children resisted the silent oppression that has existed here since slavery. In doing this they acted in a manner more spiritual than most Christians of long record, for the best definition of Spirituality is "the subordination of practical and material considerations to ideal ends." They weighed out their problems and faced them fearlessly.

The majority of us Christians believe in a safe Christianity that does not attack our status quo. No man can be a Christian who does not resist injustice regardless of the hazardous and dangerous risks involved. "For this cause," Jesus said, "came I into the world." Realizing the hazards involved in taking a stand against His contemporaries, Jesus nevertheless moved forward with faith because faith for Him was the courage that acts by understanding. . . .

When is it that every Southern church and clergymen will proclaim the "accepted year of the Lord?" When shall men clamor for brotherhood and there shall be no man bound by the chains of circumstance? When can every citizen look to his leadership with veneration and respect? How long, Lord, how long? . . .

Of course, there are those who will cry that if you do not like the South, MOVE. How silly! There is no record which says you can solve a problem by running away from it. Furthermore, it is generally conceded that people desire the clime in which they were born, and as free moral agents they desire the privilege of going where they want, when they want, without interference. Still there are those who would sell their race in order to secure themselves and families. If their families can live in comparative good circumstances all is well with the world. . . .

To carry our point further, let us examine the case of the firing of our principal, Mr. Jones. Five hundred citizens, the very best of the race, the majority of whom had children in school, signed a petition expressing their desire to have Mr. Jones direct their children's education.

This petition was ignored in a democratic world.

You can have no say over who leads your child; it is entirely out of your hands. This decision is left to those who are unwilling to sit with you, eat with you, sleep with you, to die with you.

They are persons who manifest no interest in your cause, yet will not permit you to select your children's leaders.

It is deplorable to think that we have men who would negotiate with such people.

No colored citizen is safe to live under such misused power, power that should only be in the hands of God. In order to be true to God and my fellow-man, I must speak against such a miscarriage of justice. Such wanton disregard for human dignity!

If one does not build in opposition to such, our womanhood will remain unsafe, and our children will remain victims of a cruel system of philosophy for which they are not responsible.

Because I know that God does not desire segregation and desires equaliza-tion in its true sense—Because my heart is made sad when I think of cruelty heaped upon the colored men in slavery when white men raped their women, harassed their children and brutalized the men, I must take my stand. When I think of the years of economical exploitation made on my people by the white race, and the hatred thrown against us, I must, in all sincerity, fight against such inhumanity to man with every ounce of energy given to me by God. I must resist with the ferocity of a prophet set on fire by the sights of injustice everywhere present. . . .

This is my belief, this is my conviction, this is my hope. It can be no other. Therefore the words of Martin Luther, I too must say, "Here I stand, God help me, I can do no other."

So to those who can appreciate my position, I say, "God bless you." And to those who cannot see the truth of it, "God bless you, also." . . .

If this is agreeable with the majority of the members of this church and con-gregation I will remain as your pastor. If not I will offer a resignation without any sign of livelihood, believing that God will take care of me.

For, when it is that we shall meet the Great Arbiter face to face, somewhere behind the curtains of the human race, I wish to be able to say, despite my sins, which are many, Master, despite my shortcomings and neglect, I did the best I could to bring about human justice and liberty to all by preaching Thy Holy Word as it was revealed to me.

"Here I stand, God help me, I can do no other."

(At the conclusion, the majority of the congregation expressed the desire to keep Mr. Griffin as pastor of the Church.)

Richmond Afro-American, July 28, 1951.

QUESTIONS

1. Why did Reverend L. Francis Griffin feel the concept of equalization was inadequate to address the educational disparities between blacks and whites in Prince Edward County?
2. In what ways did Griffin use religious language and references to motivate his supporters and attack those who supported segregation in Prince Edward County?
3. Griffin's solidarity with the student leaders symbolized an important development. How was the growing role of black ministers important to the civil rights movement?

Davis v. County School Board of Prince Edward County

U.S. District Court, Eastern District of Virginia
March 7, 1952

On May 23, 1951, NAACP attorneys Oliver Hill and Spottswood Robinson filed suit in federal court to end segregation in the public schools of Prince Edward County. The case was named after Dorothy E. Davis, a Moton High School student who was the first named plaintiff in the filing. Seventy-four families were listed as plaintiffs in the case.

Observers at the time called *Davis v. County School Board of Prince Edward County* the most comprehensive school desegregation lawsuit yet brought by the NAACP.[1] The case argued that segregation violated the equal protection clause of the Fourteenth Amendment to the U.S. Constitution, which guarantees equal treatment for all citizens. The suit also requested that the county's black schools be made equal to the white schools should the request to eliminate segregation be denied. The case opened in U.S. District Court on February 25, 1952.

Prince Edward is a county of 15,000 people in the southern part of Virginia. Slightly more than one-half of its inhabitants are Negroes. They compose 59% of the county school population. At the high school plane the average pupil attendance is 386 colored, 346 white. For themselves and their classmates, a large number of these Negro students, their parents, or guardians now demand that their county school board and school superintendent refrain from further observance of the mandate of section 140 of the Constitution of Virginia and its statutory counterpart, the former reading: "White and colored children shall not be taught in the same school." Defendants' adherence to this command, it is averred, creates a positive discrimination against the colored child solely because of his race or color, constituting both a deprivation of his privileges and immunities as a citizen of the United States and a denial to him of the equal protection of the laws. The prohibition is denounced as a breach of the Civil Rights Act and as inimical to section 1 of the 14th Amendment of the Federal constitution.

Demandants pray a declaration of the invalidity, and an injunction against the enforcement, of the separation provisions. In the alternative, they ask a decree noting and correcting certain specified inequalities between the white and colored schools. That the schools are maintained with public tax moneys, that the defendants are public officials, and that they separate the children according to race in obedience to the State law are concessa. The Commonwealth of Virginia intervenes to defend.

Plaintiffs urge upon us that Virginia's separation of the Negro youth from his white contemporary stigmatizes the former as an unwanted, that the impress is alike on the minds of the colored and the white, the parents as well as the children, and indeed of the public generally, and that the stamp is deeper and the more indelible because imposed by law. Its necessary and natural effect, they say, is to prejudice the colored child in the sight of his community, to implant unjustly in him a sense of inferiority as a human being to other human beings, and to seed his mind with hopeless frustration. They argue that in spirit and in truth the colored youth is, by the segregation law, barred from association with the white child, not the white from the colored, that actually it is ostracism for the Negro child, and that the exclusion deprives him of the equal opportunity with the Caucasian of receiving an education unmarked, an immunity and privilege protected by the statutes and constitution of the United States.

Eminent educators, anthropologists, psychologists and psychiatrists appeared for the plaintiffs, unanimously expressed dispraise of segregation in schools, and unequivocally testified the opinion that such separation distorted the child's natural attitude, throttled his mental development, especially the adolescent, and immeasurably abridged his educational opportunities. For the defendants, equally distinguished and qualified educationists and leaders in the other fields emphatically vouched the view that, given equivalent physical facilities, offerings and instruction, the Negro would receive in a separate school the same educational opportunity as he would obtain in the classroom and on the campus of a mixed school. Each witness offered cogent and appealing grounds for his conclusion.

On this fact issue the Court cannot say that the plaintiffs' evidence over-balances the defendants'. But on the same presentation by the plaintiffs as just recited, Federal courts have rejected the proposition, in respect to elementary and junior high schools, that the required separation of the races is in law offensive to the National statutes and constitution. They have refused to decree that segregation be abolished incontinently. We accept these decisions as apt and able precedent. Indeed we might ground our conclusion on their opinions alone. But the facts proved in our case, almost without division and perhaps peculiar here, so potently demonstrate why nullification of the cited sections of the statutes and constitution of Virginia is not warranted, that they should speak our conclusion.

Regulations by the State of the education of persons within its marches is the exercise of its police power—"the power to legislate with respect to the safety, morals, health and general welfare." The only discipline of this power by the 14th Amendment and the Civil Rights Acts of Congress is the requirement that the regulation be reasonable and uniform. We will measure the instant facts by that yardwand.

It indisputably appears from the evidence that the separation provision rests neither upon prejudice, nor caprice, nor upon any other measureless founda-tion. Rather the proof is that it declares one of the ways of life in Virginia. Separation of white and colored "children" in the public schools of Virginia has for generations been a part of the mores of her people. To have separate schools has been their use and wont.

The school laws chronicle separation as an unbroken usage in Virginia for more than eighty years. The General Assembly of Virginia in its session of 1869–70, in providing for public free schools, stipulated "that white and colored persons shall not be taught in the same school, but in separate schools, under the same general regulations as to management, usefulness and efficiency." It was repeated at the session 1871–2, and carried into the Code of 1873. As is well known, all this legislation occurred in the period of readjustment follow-ing the Civil War when the interests of the Negro in Virginia were scrupu-lously guarded. The same statute was reenacted by the Legislature of 1877 and again in 1878, still within the Reconstruction years of Virginia. In almost the same words separation in the schools was carried into the Acts of Assembly of 1881–2, and similarly embodied in the Code of 1887, in the Code of 1919, and now it is placed in the Code of 1950, in a single section, 22–221, in the same words: "White and colored persons shall not be taught in the same school, but shall be taught in separate schools, under the same general regulations as to management, usefulness and efficiency." The importance of the school separation clause to the people of the State is signalized by the fact that it is the only racial segregation direction contained in the constitution of Virginia.

Maintenance of the separated systems in Virginia has not been social despotism, the testimony points out, and suggests that whatever its demerits in theory, in practice it has begotten greater opportunities for the Negro. Virginia alone employs as many Negro teachers in her public schools, according to undenied testimony, as are employed in all of the thirty-one non-segregating States. Likewise it was shown that in 29 of the even hundred counties in Virginia, the schools and facilities for the colored are equal to the white schools, in 17 more they are now superior, and upon completion of work authorized or in progress, another 5 will be superior. Of the twenty-seven cities, 5 have Negro schools and facilities equal to the white and 8 more have better Negro schools than white.

So ingrained and wrought in the texture of their life is the principle of separate schools, that the president of the University of Virginia expressed to the Court his judgment that its involuntary elimination would severely lessen the interest of the people of the State in the public schools, lessen the financial support, and so injure both races. His testimony, corroborated by others, was especially impressive because of his candid and knowledgeable discussion of the problem. A scholar and a former Governor and legislator of the State, we believe him delicately sensible of the customs, the mind, and the temper of both races in Virginia. With the whites comprising more than three-quarters of the entire population of the Commonwealth, the point he makes is a weighty practical factor to be considered in determining whether a reasonable basis has been shown to exist for the continuation of the school segregation.

In this milieu we cannot say that Virginia's separation of white and colored children in the public schools is without substance in fact or reason. We have found no hurt or harm to either race. This ends our inquiry. It is not for us to adjudge the policy as right or wrong—that, the Commonwealth of Virginia "shall determine for itself."

On the second phase of this case, the inequality in the Negro schools when compared with the white, the defendants confess that the buildings and facilities furnished for Negro high school education are below those of the white school. We think the discrepancy extends further. We find inequality also in the curricula of the schools and in the provision for transportation of the students.

Undoubtedly frankness required admission by the defendants of their dereliction in furnishing an adequate school plant and facilities for the Negro. His high school is the Robert R. Moton. It is composed of one permanent brick building and three temporary, one-story, frame buildings. No gymnasiums are provided, no shower or dressing rooms to accompany physical education or athletics, no cafeteria, no teachers' rest room and no infirmary, to give some of the items absent in Moton but present in the white high school. Moton's science facilities and equipment are lacking and inadequate. No industrial art shop is provided, and in many other ways the structures and facilities do not meet the level of the white school.

In offerings we find physics, world history, Latin, advanced typing and stenography, wood, metal and machine shop work, and drawing, not offered at Moton, but given in the white schools. While the school authorities tender their willingness to give any course in the Negro school now obtainable in the white school, all courses in the latter should be made more readily available to the students of Moton.

In supplying school buses the Negro students have not been accorded their share of the newer vehicles. This practice must cease. In the allocation of new conveyances, as replacements or additional equipment, there must be no preference in favor of the white students.

On the issue of actual inequality our decree will declare its existence in respect to buildings, facilities, curricula and buses. We will restrain immediately its continuance in respect to the curricula and conveyances. We will order the defendant to pursue with diligence and dispatch their present program, now afoot and progressing, to replace the Moton buildings and facilities with a new building and new equipment, or otherwise remove the inequality in them.

The frame structures at Moton were erected in 1948 and 1949 as temporary expedients, upon the advice and authority of the State Board of Education. Through the activities of the school board and the division superintendent, defendants here, $840,000.00 has been obtained, the land acquired, and plans completed, for a new high school and necessary facilities for the Negroes. Both local and State authorities are moving with speed to complete the new program. An injunction could accomplish no more.

A decree will be entered in accordance with this opinion.

103 F. Supp. 337 (1952).

NOTE

1. "Public School Segregation Cases, November 26, 1952, Including Prince Edward County," part 2, box C212, Papers of the National Association for the Advancement of Colored People, Library of Congress, Washington, D.C.

QUESTIONS

1. What is the basis of the claim in the NAACP's lawsuit that segregation harmed black students?
2. What was the court's ruling and the justification for the decision? What did the ruling require of Prince Edward County officials?

2

"Separate but Equal Has No Place"

Achieving social change through legal action is a prolonged process, and *Davis v. County School Board of Prince Edward County* (see p. 55) was no exception. Originally filed in May 1951, the lawsuit was denied in federal court in 1952 and then appealed to the U.S. Supreme Court. For three years, the NAACP contended with local and state officials in the federal courts while life carried on in Prince Edward County.

Following the two-week strike, the students of Moton High returned to the classroom to complete the school year. That summer, they learned with dismay that the Prince Edward County School Board had refused to renew the contract of their principal, M. Boyd Jones. Although Jones had not been involved in the strike, county officials held him accountable.

In response to the lawsuit, local and state officials hastened the construction of a new black high school. School superintendent T. J. McIlwaine requested state funds for the endeavor, and state officials quickly complied. In July 1951, the same month Principal Jones's contract was not renewed, the school board authorized the purchase of a tract of land for the building. The county's decision to expedite construction of a new black high school was intended, in part, to undermine the local black community's commitment to desegregation. Similar steps were taken in other localities confronted with school desegregation lawsuits, in the belief that new schools with modern facilities, staffed by black teachers and administrators, might be seen as more desirable than attending local white schools. In Prince Edward, a new black high school, not desegregation, had been the original goal of the student strike.

The black community of Prince Edward County, however, had rallied behind the effort to end segregation in the county's schools. Although a small number of blacks opposed the lawsuit in 1951, the vast majority supported the legal effort. The hope of white officials that a new school building would lead to the abandonment of the *Davis* lawsuit was in vain.

The *Davis* case was one of a group of lawsuits that the NAACP hoped would end segregation in public education. NAACP attorneys had previously filed similar lawsuits in South Carolina and Kansas. Additional suits followed in Delaware and the District of Columbia. In four of these cases, including *Davis*, the NAACP argued that segregation violated the equal protection clause of the Fourteenth Amendment, which granted all Americans the right to be treated equally without regard to race. In the fifth case, based in Washington, D.C., the NAACP based its attack on segregation on the Fifth Amendment's due process clause. Unique among the five, the *Davis* lawsuit was the only case that had been inspired by student action.

Davis v. County School Board of Prince Edward County was heard in federal district court in Richmond, Virginia. In March 1952, the court ruled unanimously against the plaintiffs and found no reason to end segregation in education. The court concluded, "We have found no hurt or harm to either race."

The NAACP appealed this decision directly to the U.S. Supreme Court, which was also asked to hear the appeals of the cases from South Carolina, Kansas, Delaware, and the District of Columbia. The Supreme Court consolidated the five cases under the name of the Kansas case, *Brown v. Board of Education of Topeka*, and arguments before the Court began in December 1952. In a unanimous decision handed down on May 17, 1954, the Court declared that segregation in public education was unconstitutional.

Opposition to the *Brown* decision was immediate, emerging both from segregationist principles and from the belief of white southerners that the decision infringed on state sovereignty and their personal liberties. Paramount among these was the ability to educate their children as they pleased, without interference from the federal government. Segregationists argued that the United States was a compact among sovereign states, and the southern states had a duty to resist encroachments on their sovereign powers. As civil rights scholar Christopher Bonastia has noted, those who resisted often viewed themselves as "patriotic constitutionalists" as opposed to "diehard segregationists." As contemporary scholarship has shown, the language of individual liberties, the sovereign rights of states, and opposition to the federal government would become fundamental political doctrine of the modern conservative movement.[1]

NOTE

1. Bonastia, *Southern Stalemate*, 7–8.

Brown v. Board of Education of Topeka, Kansas

U.S. Supreme Court

May 17, 1954

On May 17, 1954, the Supreme Court issued its historic decision. The unanimous ruling, written by Chief Justice Earl Warren, stated that "in the field of public education 'separate but equal' has no place." Segregation in public education was declared
unconstitutional, overturning school segregation in seventeen southern and border
states, and ending optional segregation policies in four others.

Mr. Chief Justice Warren delivered the opinion of the Court.

These cases come to us from the States of Kansas, South Carolina, Virginia,
and Delaware. They are premised on different facts and different local conditions, but a common legal question justifies their consideration together in this
consolidated opinion. . . .

In each of the cases, minors of the Negro race, through their legal representatives, seek the aid of the courts in obtaining admission to the public schools
of their community on a nonsegregated basis. In each instance, they had been
denied admission to schools attended by white children under laws requiring
or permitting segregation according to race. This segregation was alleged to
deprive the plaintiffs of the equal protection of the laws under the Fourteenth
Amendment. . . .

The plaintiffs contend that segregated public schools are not "equal" and cannot be made "equal," and that hence they are deprived of the equal protection
of the laws. Because of the obvious importance of the question presented, the
Court took jurisdiction. Argument was heard in the 1952 Term, and reargument was heard this Term on certain questions propounded by the Court.

Reargument was largely devoted to the circumstances surrounding the
adoption of the Fourteenth Amendment in 1868. It covered exhaustively consideration of the Amendment in Congress, ratification by the states, then existing practices in racial segregation, and the views of proponents and opponents
of the Amendment. This discussion and our own investigation convince us
that, although these sources cast some light, it is not enough to resolve the
problem with which we are faced. At best, they are inconclusive. The most

avid proponents of the post-War Amendments undoubtedly intended them to remove all legal distinctions among "all persons born or naturalized in the United States." Their opponents, just as certainly, were antagonistic to both the letter and the spirit of the Amendments and wished them to have the most limited effect. What others in Congress and the state legislatures had in mind cannot be determined with any degree of certainty.

An additional reason for the inconclusive nature of the Amendment's history, with respect to segregated schools, is the status of public education at that time. In the South, the movement toward free common schools, supported by general taxation, had not yet taken hold. Education of white children was largely in the hands of private groups. Education of Negroes was almost non-existent, and practically all of the race were illiterate. In fact, any education of the Negroes was forbidden by law in some states. Today, in contrast, many Negroes have achieved outstanding success in the arts and sciences as well as in the business and professional world. It is true that public school education at the time of the Amendment had advanced further in the North, but the effect of the Amendment on Northern States was generally ignored in the congressional debates. Even in the North, the conditions of public education did not approximate those existing today. The curriculum was usually rudimentary; ungraded schools were common in rural areas; the school term was but three months a year in many states; and compulsory school attendance was virtually unknown. As a consequence, it is not surprising that there should be so little in the history of the Fourteenth Amendment relating to its intended effect on public education. . . .

In the first cases in this Court construing the Fourteenth Amendment, decided shortly after its adoption, the Court interpreted it as proscribing all state-imposed discriminations against the Negro race. The doctrine of "separate but equal" did not make its appearance in this Court until 1896 in the case of *Plessy v. Ferguson*, involving not education but transportation. American courts have since labored with the doctrine for over half a century. In this Court, there have been six cases involving the "separate but equal" doctrine in the field of public education. . . . In none of these cases was it necessary to reexamine the doctrine to grant relief to the Negro plaintiff. . . .

In the instant cases, that question is directly presented. Here . . . there are findings below that the Negro and white schools involved have been equalized, or are being equalized, with respect to buildings, curricula, qualifications and salaries of teachers, and other "tangible" factors. Our decision, therefore, cannot turn on merely a comparison of these tangible factors in the Negro and white schools involved in each of the cases. We must look instead to the effect of seg-regation itself on public education. . . .

In approaching this problem, we cannot turn the clock back to 1868 when the Amendment was adopted, or even to 1896 when *Plessy v. Ferguson* was writ-ten. We must consider public education in the light of its full development and its present place in American life throughout the Nation. Only in this way can it be determined if segregation in public schools deprives these plaintiffs of the equal protection of the laws.

Today, education is perhaps the most important function of state and local governments. Compulsory school attendance laws and the great expenditures for education both demonstrate our recognition of the importance of educa-tion to our democratic society. It is required in the performance of our most basic public responsibilities, even service in the armed forces. It is the very foundation of good citizenship. Today it is a principal instrument in awaken-ing the child to cultural values, in preparing him for later professional training, and in helping him to adjust normally to his environment. In these days, it is doubtful that any child may reasonably be expected to succeed in life if he is denied the opportunity of an education. Such an opportunity, where the state has undertaken to provide it, is a right which must be made available to all on equal terms.

We come then to the question presented: Does segregation of children in public schools solely on the basis of race, even though the physical facilities and other "tangible" factors may be equal, deprive the children of the minority group of equal educational opportunities? We believe that it does. . . .

To separate them from others of similar age and qualifications solely because of their race generates a feeling of inferiority as to their status in the commu-nity that may affect their hearts and minds in a way unlikely ever to be undone. The effect of this separation on their educational opportunities was well stated by a finding in the Kansas case by a court which nevertheless felt compelled to rule against the Negro plaintiffs:

"Segregation of white and colored children in public schools has a detri-mental effect upon the colored children. The impact is greater when it has the sanction of the law; for the policy of separating the races is usually interpreted as denoting the inferiority of the negro group. A sense of inferiority affects the motivation of a child to learn. Segregation with the sanction of law, therefore, has a tendency to (retard) the educational and mental development of Negro children and to deprive them of some of the benefits they would receive in a racial(ly) integrated school system."

Whatever may have been the extent of psychological knowledge at the time of *Plessy v. Ferguson*, this finding is amply supported by modern authority. Any language in *Plessy v. Ferguson* contrary to this finding is rejected.

We conclude that in the field of public education the doctrine of "separate but equal" has no place. Separate educational facilities are inherently unequal. Therefore, we hold that the plaintiffs and others similarly situated for whom the actions have been brought are, by reason of the segregation complained of, deprived of the equal protection of the laws guaranteed by the Fourteenth Amendment. This disposition makes unnecessary any discussion whether such segregation also violates the Due Process Clause of the Fourteenth Amendment.

Because these are class actions, because of the wide applicability of this decision, and because of the great variety of local conditions, the formulation of decrees in these cases presents problems of considerable complexity. On reargument, the consideration of appropriate relief was necessarily subordinated to the primary question—the constitutionality of segregation in public education. We have now announced that such segregation is a denial of the equal protection of the laws. In order that we may have the full assistance of the parties in formulating decrees, the cases will be restored to the docket, and the parties are requested to present further argument. . . .

It is so ordered.

347 U.S. 483 (1954).

QUESTIONS

1. What was the Supreme Court's justification for ending public school segregation in *Brown v. Board of Education*?
2. The justices stated that segregation in education had a harmful effect on African American school children. Describe their reasoning.
3. Why was this U.S. Supreme Court decision so important?

Statement of Senator Harry F. Byrd

May 17, 1954

A descendant of the powerful Byrd family of colonial Virginia, Harry F. Byrd was Virginia's most powerful political figure for more than four decades. Elected governor in 1925, Byrd reorganized Virginia's government, reducing the number of statewide

elected positions and consolidating political power, to assemble a political organization that dominated Virginia politics from the 1930s through the 1960s.

In 1933, Byrd entered the U.S. Senate, where he served until 1965. Compared to other
southern political figures of the day, Byrd was relatively restrained when it came to
racial issues. As governor in the 1920s, he had signed the South's first anti-lynching bill
and battled the influence of the Ku Klux Klan in Virginia. Byrd was a white supremacist, however, strongly committed to segregation. To Senator Byrd, the *Brown* decision
represented a threat to both public education and the sovereign rights of the states.

The unanimous decision of the Supreme Court to abolish segregation in public education is not only sweeping but will bring implications and dangers of
the greatest consequence. It is the most serious blow that has yet been struck
against the rights of the states in a matter vitally affecting their authority
and welfare.

The Supreme Court reversed its previous decision directing "separate but
equal" facilities for the education of both races. Nothing now remains for the
Supreme Court to do except to determine the effective date and the method of
the application of its decision.

One of the cruel results arising out of this "about-face" of the Supreme Court
is that the Southern States, accepting the validity of the previous decision in
recent years have expended hundreds of millions of dollars for construction of
new Negro school facilities to conform with the policy previously laid down by
the Court.

Great progress has been made at tremendous cost throughout the Southern
States to carry out that which our Southern State Governments had the right
to believe was the law of the land. This reversal by the Supreme Court from
its "separate but equal" policy to complete abolition of segregation will create
problems such as have never confronted us before.

The decision will be deplored by millions of Americans, and, instead of promoting the education of our children, it is my belief that it will have the opposite effect in many areas of the country. In Virginia we are facing now a crisis of
the first magnitude.

Those in authority, and the parents directly affected in the education of their
children, should exercise the greatest wisdom in shaping our future course.

Whatever is done should be based on our most matured judgment after
sober and exhaustive consideration.

Harry F. Byrd Papers, box 408, University of Virginia Special Collections, Charlottesville.

QUESTIONS

1. What dangers and problems did Senator Harry Byrd claim would result from the *Brown v. Board of Education* decision?
2. Byrd referred to the *Brown* decision as a reversal of the previous Supreme Court ruling on segregation. To which decision was he referring, and what might be some of the reasons he made this argument?

Supreme Court Decision

Farmville Herald

May 21, 1954

The vast majority of white residents of Prince Edward County opposed the *Brown v. Board of Education* decision. They feared the impact of integration on their children's education and the possibility of interracial relationships among students. The Court's willingness to overturn longstanding social patterns angered the white community, which immediately voiced forceful opposition. This editorial appeared in the *Farmville Herald* shortly after the decision was handed down.

The decision of the United States Supreme Court announced Monday declaring segregation in public schools to be unconstitutional in view of the Fourteenth Amendment to the Constitution shocked the people of the Southern States. Officials and private citizens are still in a state of shock, and no definite suggestion of procedure has been made. The court postponed until next October hearings on its final decree which will designate how and when the practice of non-segregation will be put into effect.

Northern states with little or no Negro population received the decision with approval, but seventeen Southern states with heavy Negro population view the decision gravely. The new opinion, contrary to the history and mores of the South for 300 years, presents a history making landmark but grave problems present themselves in the practicability of early adoption. The court's decision not to issue specific decrees apparently recognizes the social and psychological adjustments necessary to carry out such a far reaching concept, so foreign to that which has allowed the development of the races on a segregated basis for generations.

The development of public education, particularly within the past fifty years has been remarkable. Regardless of equities or inequities, from a racial, or urban-rural point of view, the fact remains that notable progress has been made. Education has been made available within the accepted manners and mores of states where there were two definite racial groups. Every effort has been made to develop the races as races in which each might take pride. The segregated races formed a citizenship, and a way of living together, which has brought phenomenal developments into the South, particularly, industrial progress, now reaching its peak.

This is now being changed. The opening wedge is public education on an integrated basis. It is a wholly new concept for the people of both the white and Negro races. To place into practice the edict of the United States Supreme Court will require a reassessment of working principles and mores ingrained in the life of the South for many generations. Physical facilities can be obtained, provided there are sufficient funds made available, but the change in racial, social and natural relationships present grave problems, incapable of solution in any definite period. Changes in such relationships are viewed with concern by members of both races, and, we believe in a majority of cases, Negroes would be as reluctant to receive whites into their schools as is the case with the whites.

The change has varying degrees within the states. In Virginia, the problem in Shenandoah county with 1½ per cent Negro population, differs in intensity with Charles City county with 78 per cent Negro population. Obviously, a state program would not be practical in all of its counties. Therefore, we believe, the solution will be found at the county level, so far as it relates to elementary and secondary education. If this be true, serious consideration must be given to conferences with the several groups to formulate basic county policy.

The impact of the decision on higher education, the desirability of teaching positions in integrated schools, the school transportation system, indicate the far-reaching effect and the adjustments required to make such an edict practical in its execution.

Until the final decrees of the Supreme Court have been written the severity of the adjustments will not be known. In the meantime, clear thinking and expression of well considered opinions will make a solution easier to formulate.

Since Prince Edward County is one of the principals in this decision, it is to be expected that more attention will be focused upon it. As we have pointed out before, some national organizations, the press, and possibly other phases of communication seeking the sensational may attempt to find "grist for the mill" in our community. The problem is ours, we must solve it! Unfortunately, our county was made a principal in this momentous suit. It came about because we failed to seek a solution of our own. Those who had but little interest in our happiness or welfare, carried far afield the original intention of the unsuspecting. A reoccurrence should be avoided.

Through the long court proceedings, the people of this community have conducted themselves admirably. Future relations and a solution to the grave problem confronting us depends upon our ability to think clearly and logically.

This newspaper continues its firm belief in the principles of segregation in public schools in Southside Virginia, and hopes that a plan can be formulated to continue development [of] the schools on a segregated basis, within the framework of the decision. We believe it is in the best interests of all our people.

QUESTIONS

1. How did this editorial describe the potential impact of the *Brown* ruling on southern society?
2. The editorial stated, "We believe in a majority of cases Negroes would be as reluctant to receive whites into their schools as is the case with the whites." Based on the previous readings, do you think this statement is accurate? Why or why not?

Atlanta Declaration

National Association for the Advancement of Colored People
May 23, 1954

Before the *Brown* decision, officials at the NAACP's national headquarters in New York City planned a meeting of southern NAACP leaders to be held immediately after the Supreme Court ruling. The conference in Atlanta, held the weekend after the decision, was attended by the leadership of the Virginia State Conference, including attorneys Oliver Hill and Spottswood Robinson. National NAACP officials recommended a program of community cooperation for the implementation of *Brown v. Board of Education* that was approved by the assembled representatives.

We, as representatives of the National Association for the Advancement of Colored People from seventeen Southern and Border States and the District of Columbia, have assembled here in Atlanta, Georgia, May 22–23, for the purpose of collectively developing a program to meet the vital and urgent issues arising out of the historic United States Supreme Court decision of May 17 banning segregation in public schools.

All Americans are now relieved to have the law of the land declare in the clearest language: ". . . in the field of public education the doctrine of 'separate but equal' has no place. Separate educational facilities are inherently unequal." Segregation in public education is now not only unlawful; it is un-American. True Americans are grateful for this decision. Now that the law is made clear, we look to the future. Having canvassed the situation in each of our States, we approach the future with the utmost confidence. This confidence is based upon many factors including the pledges of support and compliance by governors, attorneys general, mayors, and education officials; and by enlightened guidance of newspapers, radio, television and other organs of public communication and comment.

We stand ready to work with other law abiding citizens who are anxious to translate this decision into a program of action to eradicate racial segregation in public education as speedily as possible.

We are instructing all of our Branches in every affected area to petition their local school boards to abolish segregation without delay and to assist these agencies in working out ways and means of implementing the Court's ruling. The total resources of the NAACP will be made available to facilitate this great project of ending the artificial separation of America's children on the irrelevant basis of race and color.

While we recognize that school officials will have certain administrative problems in transferring from a segregated to a non-segregated system, we will resist the use of any tactics contrived for the sole purpose of delaying desegregation.

In pursuit of our objectives, we will accelerate our community action program to win public acceptance of the Court's desegregation order from all segments of the population. To this end, we are confident of the support of teachers, parents, labor, church, civic, fraternal, social, business and professional organizations.

We insist that there should be integration at all levels including the assignment of teacher-personnel on a non-discriminatory basis. The fullest resources of the Association, including the legal staff, the research staff and educational specialists on the staff, will be utilized to insure that there will be no discrimination against teachers as a result of integration.

We are aware that our region has been overburdened in its effort to provide education for all children—in part because of the dual system—and accordingly, we strongly support federal aid to assist our states in the building of new schools and the expansion of educational facilities for all our children, provided that any such legislation contains the necessary safeguards to insure the distribution of funds in accordance with the requirements of the Court's decision.

We look upon this memorable decision not as a victory for Negroes alone, but for the whole American people and as a vindication of America's leadership of the free world.

Lest there be any misunderstanding of our position, we here rededicate ourselves to the removal of all racial segregation in public education and reiterate our determination to achieve this goal without compromise of principle.

Papers of the National Association for the Advancement of Colored People, part 5, box V2595, Library of Congress, Washington, D.C.

QUESTIONS

1. What aspects of the *Brown v. Board of Education* decision did the NAACP highlight in this public statement?
2. During this period, the NAACP preferred a policy of community cooperation to bring about the implementation of *Brown*, rather than relying on litigation. Why did the NAACP choose this strategy for school integration?

Resolution of the Prince Edward County Board of Supervisors

July 12, 1954

Elected officials in Prince Edward County reacted strongly against the *Brown v. Board of Education* decision. In July 1954, the county Board of Supervisors issued the following statement. Similar resolutions opposing school desegregation were adopted by many other Virginia counties.

Whereas, the Supreme Court of the United States has in a recent decision purportedly held the provisions of the Constitution of Virginia requiring segregation in public schools to be unconstitutional, and the said court has indicated its intention to enter a decree implementing the decision some time in the future; and

Whereas it is the opinion of this board that such decision is to the detriment of public education in Virginia and an invasion of the rights of the citizens of the Commonwealth;

Now, therefore, be it resolved by the Board of Supervisors of Prince Edward County, Virginia:

First, that the said board is unalterably opposed to the operation of non-segregated public schools in the Commonwealth of Virginia;

Second, that this board is of the opinion that it is not only impracticable, but that it will be impossible to operate a non-segregated school system in the Commonwealth of Virginia;

Third, that the said board intends to use its power, authority and efforts to insure a continuation of a segregated school system in the Commonwealth of Virginia;

Fourth, that it urges all of the officials of the Commonwealth to take such action as may be necessary to insure the continuation of a segregated school system in the Commonwealth of Virginia;

Fifth, that the clerk of this board be instructed to send a copy of this resolution to the Governor, Attorney General, State Senators and Representatives in the House of Delegates.

Minutes of the Board of Supervisors, 1954, Office of the Clerk of the Court, Farmville, Virginia.

QUESTIONS

1. Why did the county Board of Supervisors feel that it would be impossible to operate non-segregated public schools in Virginia?
2. What does this statement suggest in terms of how the *Brown* decision would be implemented in Prince Edward County?

Basic Principles

Farmville Herald
November 24, 1955

In this editorial, the *Farmville Herald* challenged the role of the federal government in Virginia and presented the ideas of William Old, a Virginia lawyer who promoted the concept of the sovereign right of states, to oppose the Supreme Court. Old's writings also influenced James J. Kilpatrick, the editor of the *Richmond News Leader*. Old, Kilpatrick, and J. Barrye Wall, publisher and editor of the *Herald*, provided the intellectual argument for the defiance of the Supreme Court, and their ideas pervaded the massive resistance era.

There comes a time in the life of nations as it does in the life of individuals, when it is necessary to evaluate basic principles. The point is reached in making momentous decisions when in order to chart a future course lessons of experience must be drawn from the past. It seems to us that Virginia has reached that point, when it becomes necessary to stand upon basic principles and to be guided by past history.

Centralization of power in the Federal Government has been recognized as a growing evil for many years, more especially during the past thirty years. In declaring emergency after emergency in the 1930's, President Roosevelt assumed more and more power for the executive branch of the government. His attempt to pack the U.S. Supreme Court for the purpose of further concentration of power was met in no unmistakable terms by the reaction of the people.

In a Republic the delegation of power and the fine lines of checks and balances were principles receiving most attention by the framers of the Constitution of the United States. Let it not be forgotten that the Federal Government is a creature of the states. It derives its power through a compact of the states, which in the Constitution plainly set forth those which were delegated to the Federal Government, and all others not specifically designated were reserved to the several states of the compact. Upon this basic principle rests the freedom and liberty guaranteed by the Constitution. Needless to say, on several occasions the demarcation of these powers has been established.

William Old, an attorney and student of constitutional law, of Chesterfield, Va., has recently published a treatise on this subject. From it we will quote: . . .

"There has grown up in the minds of our people . . . an assumption that the Supreme Court is indeed supreme in every field, and that it alone of all the departments and agencies of the government, federal and local, is without checks and balances to hold it within its proper judicial orbit. No further action of any kind can be taken before the Court, either by legal action or by petition for the redress of grievances, for as far as the Court is concerned the die is cast. However, a constitutional debacle of vital proportions has been precipitated. Unless the states can maintain full sovereignty and authority on the question of segregation in the public schools and otherwise, we will be doomed to decades of turmoil, conflict and chaos. Moreover, the reasoning contained in Chief Justice Warren's opinion, if extended in the future to other governmental functions of the states, may well encompass the destruction of the states as sovereign governments." . . .

For several years the growing trends toward usurpation of powers reserved to the states by creatures of the Federal Government have been alarming. Nibbling here and there the rights of the states have been abridged little by little.

No concerted stand has been taken for the simple reason that the loss of powers and of individual liberties have affected only segments of the public. Therefore, those affected have been submissive.

It has remained for usurpation to affect the body politic in order that these losses of liberties to the individuals and sovereignty to the States be pointed up. The May 17 decision of the U.S. Supreme Court, in effect taking from the several states the power and right to manage its internal affairs, definitely a power reserved in the Constitution, finally appears in its rightful perspective. The usurpation has touched the heartstrings of the people, threatening to change the established customs and practices of a third of the nation. The time has come to stand, not only that public education may be continued efficiently in many states, but that once again the growing and dangerous practice to which both individuals and the states have supinely submitted, may be definitely curtailed; and again the delicate principle of balances and checks be taught not only to the people but to those who are entrusted with the continuation of the Republic.

Will some leader come forth in Virginia, learned in constitutional law; fired with the zeal to save those rights sacredly guaranteed; determined to place again in perspective the sovereignty of the states and the powers of the Federal Government? The answer is to be found in the people of Virginia, once they have been informed and can understand. Only the people, through their constituted legislative branches can exert such power. The Supreme Court is the last constituted judicial body; the executive branch has no power; only the people, through their state legislative branches, have the power to protect and perpetuate this basic principle of the Republic, the sovereignty of the several states and the liberties of the individual. Will Virginia lead?

QUESTIONS

1. What are the main arguments of the editorial? What perceived danger does it point out?
2. The editorial states that the *Brown v. Board of Education* decision was part of an attempt to increase the power of the federal government and reduce the power of the states. What was the justification for this claim?

Statement to the Virginia General Assembly

Oliver W. Hill

November 30, 1955

In late 1955, the Virginia legislature debated whether to call a referendum to amend the state constitution to allow the state to distribute public monies to parents to use for private school tuition in the event of court orders requiring public school desegregation. Oliver Hill, head of the state NAACP's legal team, addressed the General Assembly during its debate and renounced attempts to avoid the implementation of *Brown v. Board of Education.*

Gentlemen:

I appear before you today in a dual capacity. I represent the Virginia State Conference of NAACP Branches and, more importantly, I appear as an individual American citizen, resident of and domiciled in the Commonwealth of Virginia.

The Association which I represent, and I as an individual, fervently believe in, and have striven and will continue to strive to bring about the development of, the concept of individual liberty and human dignity exemplified and expressed in the American Declaration of Independence. The action under consideration, coupled with the proposals which are to follow, constitutes a negation of those principals of individual liberty and human dignity. It is for these reasons we add our voice to those of the other good and responsible citizens of this Commonwealth who may appear before you in opposition to the course of action under consideration.

You have been convened to consider a resolution changing a salutary provision of our State Constitution which, up until this very day, has served to bulwark, strengthen and materially aid in the development of the free public schools, the cornerstone of American Democracy.

It is common knowledge that the present proposal is simply an initial step in a series of proposals which, we believe, promulgated into law, can only serve to create a condition of strife, turmoil and confusion in the days immediately ahead until corrected by some future Legislature, the people of this Commonwealth, or by the United States Government. This course of action—designed to circumvent the ruling of the United States Supreme Court and to continue to deny citizens of the United States their constitutional rights because they are Negroes—if taken, conceived as it is in iniquity, can produce only harmful results.

Many good and responsible citizens of this Commonwealth will urge you to refrain from proposing that Section 141 of the Constitution of Virginia be repealed or in anywise tampered with on the grounds that the overall and underlying proposals are illegal, unchristian and un-American.

We believe that anyone who objectively considers the basic premise underlying the Report of the Gray Commission and the convening of this special session of the Legislature—that is, the maintenance of a system of racial segregation in the elementary, secondary and collegiate schools of this Commonwealth, fostered by law—will be compelled to conclude that this premise is wrong irrespective of whether it is considered from the viewpoint of science, religion, politics or historical facts.

The limitations of time will not permit an exhaustive presentation of any of these phases of the matter, thus I will limit myself to one small, but highly important, consideration which may not otherwise be urged.

The opponents of desegregation and of integration protest long and loudly about the Tenth Amendment to the Constitution of the United States as if no further amendments had been enacted. . . .

The adherents of racial segregation ignore entirely the virtual revolution created in the Federal-State relationship by the people of the United States, of which Virginia is still a part, when the people enacted the 14th Amendment in 1868. Prior to the enactment of the 14th Amendment, citizens of the several states derived their rights, privileges and immunities from the state in which they held legal residence. Unquestionably each citizen owed primary allegiance to his state. This condition of affairs was changed by the people of the United States. The sovereignty of the states was reduced. Section 1 of the 14th Amendment provides: "All persons born or naturalized in the United States, and subject to the jurisdiction thereof, are citizens of the United States and of the State wherein they reside."

Today, gentlemen, all loyal persons subject to the jurisdiction of the United States, irrespective of whether they reside in Oregon or Florida, Texas or Maine, California or Virginia, or even Mississippi, owe their primary allegiance to the United States. It is time that we pause and consider this fact and stop this irresponsible talking and irrational action now taking place in Virginia and elsewhere in the South.

The Supreme Court simply gave recognition to the fact that all American citizens are entitled to be treated with the individual respect and dignity set forth in the Declaration of Independence, guaranteed by the Constitution of the United States, and consistent with the principles of a sovereign democratic power.

The action presently urged upon you by persons, many of whom are racial fanatics, is predicated upon superstitious myths having no basis in reality or fact. If it is your wish to hasten the increase of federal power and further reduce the prerogatives of local government over the affairs of the people of this Commonwealth, then carry out the bidding of the racial fanatics—for which purpose you have been convened. But we do not believe that the most powerful government ever to exist on the face of the earth, which gives succor to those made destitute by the ravages of nature, will find itself impotent to protect its citizens from the ravages of a handful of officeholders who, when afforded an opportunity to rise to the role of statesmen, either from lack of vision or moral courage, degenerate into mere politicians.

It does not take any great vision to recognize the fact that if the present devices could be successfully maintained, the final outcome would result only in a continued deterioration in the structure of our free public schools with resulting chaos and damage to all persons in the lower economic strata—white as well as Negro. This would be inevitable because a large portion of the state's finances would go into the development of private schools. It is a well known fact that the per pupil cost of education of students in private schools is considerably higher than that of students in public schools. It is also a matter of common knowledge that, with the public schools receiving the entire appropriation made available for the education of school children, our public schools are woefully deficient when compared with the public schools in the more progressive sections of this country. It is significant to note that Virginia is now almost at the bottom of the list in terms of facilities and educational content offered to our children. With the draining off of a large portion of the public funds into private schools, the progress made in recent years in the public school system will cease and, actually and comparatively, our public schools will decline.

I tell you with all the earnestness at my command that, if you succumb to the hue and cry raised in certain quarters of this Commonwealth, principally by those who have no faith in democracy, public education, or anything else that makes democracy meaningful to the ordinary person, then you shall have cast the die characterizing yourselves as petty politicians.

Oliver W. Hill Sr., *The Big Bang: Brown v. Board of Education and Beyond* (Winter Park, Fla.: FOUR-G, 2000), 171–73.

QUESTIONS

1. What were the primary reasons Oliver Hill opposed the actions being considered by the Virginia General Assembly in the fall of 1955?
2. What was the importance of the Fourteenth Amendment, and how was that amendment relevant to the battle over school integration in the South, as stated by Oliver Hill?

3

"Massive Resistance"

Although the *Brown* decision is regarded as one of the most important Supreme Court decisions of the twentieth century, the ruling had little immediate impact on public education in the South. The Court's implementation decree, known as *Brown II*, was issued on May 31, 1955, and called for school desegregation "with all deliberate speed." It did not, however, establish a timeframe for the action and left the responsibility for compliance with local school boards.

Reaction against the implementation decree in Prince Edward County was immediate from segregationists, school officials, and political leaders. The Board of Supervisors voted to authorize only the legal annual minimum of $150,000 for the public school budget, henceforth operating the schools on a month-by-month basis. The move announced in effect that the county was prepared to close its public schools in defiance of the desegregation ruling. As reported by the *Richmond News Leader*, "It could be said that the courts ruled at noon that Negroes must be admitted to Prince Edward public schools, to which the county responded at 8 o'clock there will be no public schools."[1]

One week later on June 7, 1955, a mass meeting was held at Longwood College in Farmville, orchestrated by local segregationist leaders who were also prominent members of the Virginia segregationist group Defenders of State Sovereignty and Individual Liberties. The meeting resulted in the creation of the Prince Edward Educational Corporation to raise money for private education. The Defenders' plan from the group's inception looked to a future of private schools, rather than public education. Organizers presented a motion to guarantee the salaries of white teachers; it was overwhelmingly approved. The crowd vehemently opposed a proposal to also guarantee salaries for black teachers. Over the next month, the new Prince Edward Educational

Corporation would collect $180,000 in pledges for a future private school program. Only a very few white voices were raised in support of public education. James Bash, principal of the white Farmville High School, stated, "I am a public school man. I would be unable to accept a check from a private corporation of this kind." A short time later he resigned and moved away from the county (see p. 242).[2]

During the winter of 1955–56, resistance to school desegregation continued to grow among Virginia's political leaders. In a series of editorials written for the *Richmond News Leader* in late fall 1955 and early 1956, editor James J. Kilpatrick (see p. 107) promoted the political doctrine of "interposition," which held that state governments had a constitutional duty to oppose any perceived encroachment of federal power. Kilpatrick's writings helped fuel the rise of segregationist resistance in Virginia and throughout the South.

In November 1955, Virginia governor Thomas Stanley had called the legislature into special session to debate an amendment to the state constitution that would allow the state to pay tuition grants to the parents of children enrolled in schools threatened by court-ordered desegregation. Virginians voted overwhelmingly in favor of the proposal in a statewide referendum in January 1956, and the tuition grants amendment was enacted that spring. This was the first of many legislative steps aimed at preventing school desegregation in Virginia.

In December 1955, prominent southern segregationists met in Memphis, Tennessee, to establish a national organization to "fight the [Supreme] Court [and] fight the NAACP." Among those in attendance were representatives of the Citizens' Council of Mississippi, the States Rights Council of Georgia, the North Carolina Patriots, the Ku Klux Klan, and the Defenders of State Sovereignty and Individual Liberties. Members of the Defenders present included former Virginia governor William Tuck; Congressman Watkins M. Abbitt, representative for Prince Edward County; and Judge J. Segar Gravatt, the legal counsel for Prince Edward County in its ongoing court battles over school segregation.[3]

In February 1956, Senator Harry F. Byrd called for a program of "massive resistance" to the Supreme Court and desegregation in the South (see p. 83). That same month, the Virginia General Assembly adopted a "Resolution of Interposition," which pledged to oppose the implementation of *Brown v. Board of Education* in Virginia. Southern members of Congress signed a similar statement in March 1956 called the "Declaration of Constitutional Principles," which was introduced by Virginia representative Howard W. Smith. Commonly known as the "Southern Manifesto," the declaration decried the *Brown* ruling as an abuse of judicial power, calling for a complete reversal of the decision and the maintenance of segregation in the South. The signatories included nineteen senators and eighty-two members of the House of Representatives. Senator Byrd played a key role in its development, and every Virginia member of Congress signed the document. Intractable opposition to public school desegregation was now evident across the South.

The reluctance of President Dwight Eisenhower to publicly support the Supreme Court ruling encouraged segregationist opposition. While the president expressed the need to act in compliance with the law, he never endorsed the ruling itself.[4] NAACP executive secretary Roy Wilkins later commented, "President Eisenhower was a fine general and a good, decent man, but if he had fought World War II the way he fought for civil rights, we would all be speaking German today."[5]

Following the *Brown* decision, the NAACP proposed a program of cooperation with local authorities to encourage the adoption of school integration plans (see p. 70). By late 1955, however, it was clear that this policy had failed: school desegregation had occurred in only limited localities in the South, and opposition was increasing. In early 1956, NAACP leaders adopted a more aggressive strategy to achieve implementation of *Brown v. Board of Education*. The organization filed a series of school desegregation lawsuits against school boards throughout the former Confederacy.

The NAACP's legal campaign to implement *Brown v. Board of Education* exacerbated racial tensions throughout the region. The Virginia state legislature held a special session in late August 1956 and passed a package of legislation to prevent school desegregation. The most important provisions were known as the school closing laws, a group of related bills that authorized the governor to close any public school ordered by the federal courts to integrate. Additional legislation targeted the proponents of school desegregation in Virginia, including the NAACP.

Between 1956 and 1959, the battle over school desegregation in Virginia continued in the courts. NAACP attorneys filed desegregation lawsuits in Norfolk, Newport News, Arlington, and Charlottesville. They renewed their case against Prince Edward County in the spring of 1956. They argued that state-mandated segregation violated the *Brown* decision and that state laws aimed at avoiding integration were unconstitutional. Newly elected Virginia governor J. Lindsay Almond offered a battle-cry to segregationists in his inaugural speech on January 11, 1958, declaring, "Integration anywhere means destruction everywhere."[6] After numerous court rulings and appeals, federal judges ordered the commencement of school desegregation in several Virginia communities in the fall of 1958.

In September, however, Governor Almond closed white public schools in Charlottesville, Norfolk, and Warren County rather than allow desegregation. Ironically, the first school closings affected white students as nine white schools enrolling nearly thirteen thousand students were closed.[7] Both the NAACP and concerned white parents petitioned the courts to overturn Almond's decision. In January 1959, both state and federal courts ruled that the school closings violated the law, and the schools were reopened.

These court rulings reopened the schools and opened the door for public school desegregation in Virginia. On February 2, 1959, the process began when twenty-one African American students entered seven formerly all-white schools in Arlington and Norfolk. The number of localities experiencing school desegregation gradually increased over the course of the next several years. The General Assembly, however, also passed new legislation known as "freedom of choice of association," which through parental school choice and tuition grants effectively hindered widespread school desegregation for years to come. Prince Edward County, rather than comply with a court order for desegregation in June 1959, would instead close its entire public school system.

NOTES

1. Smith, *They Closed Their Schools*, 102.

2. Ibid., 116–24.

3. Anthony Lewis, "Segregation Group Confers in Secret," *New York Times*, December 30, 1955. See also Pete Daniel, *Lost Revolutions: The South in the 1950s* (Chapel Hill: University of North Carolina Press, 2000), 197.

4. Robert A. Caro, *Master of the Senate; The Years of Lyndon Johnson* (New York, Random House, 2003), 778.

5. Roy Wilkins and Tom Mathews, *Standing Fast: The Autobiography of Roy Wilkins* (Cambridge, Mass.: Da Capo Press, 1994), 222.

6. Inaugural Address of Governor J. Lindsay Almond Jr. to the General Assembly and the People of Virginia, January 11, 1958, Senate Document No. 3, J. Lindsay Almond Papers, 1850–1987 (Mss1 AL685 a FA2), Virginia Historical Society, Richmond.

7. Lassiter and Lewis, eds., *Moderate's Dilemma*, 7.

Byrd Calls on South to Challenge Court

New York Times
February 26, 1956

In February 1956, Senator Harry F. Byrd called for massive resistance to the *Brown v. Board of Education* decision, giving a formal name to the evolving opposition to school desegregation throughout the South. Byrd's comments highlighted the rise of a more extreme reaction against the Court's ruling. For the next several years, Virginia's political leaders pursued every legal strategy to preserve segregation in the public schools. Byrd's statement put Virginia at the forefront of southern resistance to *Brown*, much as Virginia had helped lead the South during the Civil War.

Senator Harry F. Byrd called today for "massive resistance" in the South to challenge the Supreme Court's order for racial integration in the public schools.

The Virginia Democrat made it clear in an interview he was not advocating or condoning violence in opposing enforcement of the order. But he said he wanted Southern States to stand together in declaring the court's opinion unconstitutional.

"If we can organize the Southern States for massive resistance to this order I think that in time the rest of the country will realize that racial integration is not going to be accepted in the South," he said.

"In interposition, the South has a perfectly legal means of appeal from the Supreme Court's order."

Interposition is a doctrine that some students of constitutional government contend enables the states to refuse to implement a Supreme Court decision they believe to be unconstitutional. Legislatures of some of the Southern States have passed resolutions of this type.

Though it has been tried several times in both the North and the South, the constitutionality of interposition has never been finally determined by the courts.

The doctrine was first used 157 years ago when Virginia and Kentucky opposed the Alien and Sedition Laws, but those measures expired before the challenge was tested.

While Mr. Byrd did not cast it in that light, his call for Southern unity on the school issue apparently was akin to the "passive resistance" urged by some proponents of racial integration.

Mr. Byrd's call for unified Southern support of interposition was in line with the study being given to the question by a group of eighteen Southern Senators who met recently under the leadership of Senator Walter F. George, Democrat of Georgia. The group named Senators Richard B. Russell, Democrat of Georgia; John C. Stennis, Democrat of Mississippi; and Samuel J. Ervin, Democrat of North Carolina, as a subcommittee to draft a manifesto the eighteen might sign setting forth their opposition to carrying out the Supreme Court order.

1. How did Senator Harry Byrd's opposition to school integration influence events in Prince Edward County, in Virginia, and across the South?
2. This article discusses the concept of interposition. What were the principal points made about interposition by the author, and by Byrd?

Declaration and Affirmation

Prince Edward County Board of Supervisors
May 3, 1956

In the spring of 1956, segregationists in Prince Edward County circulated a petition that stated, "We prefer to abandon public schools and educate our children in some other way if that be necessary to preserve separation of the races in the schools of this County." The petition collected over four thousand signatures, about one thousand more than the total number of qualified voters in the county. The "Declaration of the People of Prince Edward," issued by the Board of Supervisors, supported states' rights and segregation. It echoed the calls of Senator Harry Byrd and the Southern Manifesto for massive resistance to school desegregation.

Declaration

The power of the Federal Courts being once again invoked against the administrative officers of our public schools for the purpose of causing children of the white and negro race to be taught together therein, we the people of Prince Edward County, Virginia, deem it appropriate that we should make known to all men our convictions and our purposes.

We first affirm our deep and abiding loyalty and devotion to our country and its institutions. We acknowledge the Constitution to be the supreme law of the land and the bulwark of our liberties, ever subject to the sovereign powers reserved by it to the states and to the people. We know that the liberties of all Americans of all races rests upon the Constitution and the division of powers ordained therein. We deem it the obligation of free men to preserve the powers reserved under the Constitution to the states and to the people and to preserve the constitutional separation of the powers of government in the legislative, executive and judicial branches separately.

We believe that the best educational, social and cultural welfare and growth of both the white and negro races is best served by separation of the races in the public schools.

We believe the tranquillity, harmony, progress and advancement of the negro and white races, who must live together in Virginia and in Prince Edward County, is absolutely dependent upon the mutual good will and mutual respect of each race for the other.

We believe that a policy which undertakes to force the association of one race with the other against the will of either, by court decree, under threat of fine or imprisonment, is destructive of mutual good will and respect, breeds resentment and animosities, and is injurious to the true interests of both races.

We believe that the molding of the minds and characters of our children is the sacred duty and the priceless natural right and obligation of parents.

Freedom of decision with respect to these considerations touching as they do the most intimate relations of the people of our community and the most cherished natural rights and duties of parenthood is absolutely essential to the maintenance, operation, management and control of our public schools. We conceive this freedom to be among the sacred rights "retained by the people" under the Ninth Amendment of the Federal Constitution.

Among the reserved rights and powers of the states, guaranteed to the State of Virginia under the Tenth Amendment, is the power to maintain racially separate public schools. We do not perceive that the exercise of this power has ever been prohibited to the states by any provision of the Federal Constitution. We believe that this power can be prohibited to the states only by the states themselves. To concede the right of a Federal Court to withdraw this power from the individual states is to concede that all rights and powers of the states and of the people are enjoyed at the sufferance of the judiciary and that the guarantees of the liberties of the people are no longer fixed in the Constitution itself.

We do not intend to speak disrespectfully. The gravity of the issues requires that we speak plainly: By its decision of May 17, 1954 and subsequent decisions, the Supreme Court of the United States has flagrantly exceeded its lawful and intended authority, trespassed upon the rights of the people and dangerously encroached upon the reserved rights of the states.

Holding these convictions, it is not possible for us to submit the children of Prince Edward County to conditions which we most deeply and conscientiously believe to be pernicious. Nor can we as the heirs of liberty, purchased at so great a sacrifice by those who have gone before, submit to this judicial breaking of the constitutional chains forged to restrain tyranny for all generations of Americans. We, therefore, pledge ourselves firmly to use every honorable, legal and constitutional means at our command to oppose this assault upon the Constitution and upon the liberties of our people.

Therefore, if courts refuse to recognize these most fundamental, intimate and sacred rights and the profound necessity that they be respected, then we proclaim our resort to that first American tenet of liberty: that men should not be taxed against their will and without their consent for a purpose to which they are deeply and conscientiously opposed. We ask our Board of Supervisors as our legislative representatives to proceed at the appropriate time to enact and adopt whatever ordinances and resolutions may be required to prohibit the levying of any tax or the appropriation of any funds for the operation of racially mixed schools within Prince Edward County to the end that all public schools of the County may be closed upon the entry of a court order requiring the mixing of the races in any school of this County.

We further call upon our School Board to make known to the District Court the determination of the people of Prince Edward County here expressed. The issues are too profound and the consequences to our people too grave to leave any doubt of the impossibility of our compliance or of the resolute mind of our people. An order to mix the races in our schools can only result in the destruction of the opportunity for a public education for all children of this County.

We also call upon the Governor of Virginia and all officials of the Commonwealth in control thereof to pay state revenue to Prince Edward County for school purposes in accordance with the policy adopted by the Board of Supervisors for the payment of local funds for school purposes, thus and thereby giving effect to the "Interposition Resolution" of the General Assembly of Virginia, adopted on February 1, 1956, fixing the policy of this Commonwealth, "to take all appropriate measures honorably, legally and constitutionally available to us, to resist this illegal encroachment upon our sovereign powers."

It is with the most profound regret that we have been forced to set this course. The history of the people of Prince Edward County demonstrates their love and appreciation of the value of educational opportunity. We act with no animus toward any man or body of men. We do not act in oppression of the negro people of this County. We propose, in every way that we can, to preserve every proper constitutional right of all the people of Prince Edward County. However deeply convinced as we are of the wrongness and imprudence of intimate racial integration, we cannot and will not place merely supposed rights, newly created by judicial mandate, above the conscience of our people and above rights and powers, which for generations have been exercised honorably and constitutionally by the people of our county.

It is our earnest hope that other counties and the Commonwealth of Virginia will repudiate the spurious allurements of expediency and stratagem in order that Virginia may stand as she has always stood, dedicated to the protection of the rights of a free people against tyranny from any quarter. If we fail in this solemn obligation now our rights will be extinguished one by one.

Affirmation

We, the undersigned citizens of Prince Edward County, Virginia, hereby affirm our conviction that the separation of the races in the public schools of this County is absolutely necessary and do affirm that we prefer to abandon public schools and educate our children in some other way if that be necessary to preserve separation of the races in the schools of this County.

We pledge our support of the Board of Supervisors of Prince Edward County in their firm maintenance of this policy.

I, Horace Adams, Clerk of the Board of Supervisors of Prince Edward County, do hereby certify that the foregoing is a true and correct copy of the "Declaration" and the "Affirmation" filed with the Board of Supervisors of Prince Edward County at a meeting on Thursday, May 3, 1956, and I do further certify that said affirmation appears to have been signed by more than four thousand (4,000) persons and that statement was made to the Board that a number of additional signatures would be obtained and filed later.

At a regular meeting of the Board of Supervisors of Prince Edward County held at the Court House thereof, on the 3rd day of May, 1956, at which meeting all members of the Board were present, the following resolutions were adopted unanimously:

1. Be It Resolved, by the Board of Supervisors that we do hereby express to the people of Prince Edward County our gratitude that they have made known to this Board so clearly their views upon the grave problems with which we are confronted with respect to our schools. The support of our people makes the burden of our responsibilities lighter and the course of our future action clearer. We trust the people of the County will continue to make known to us their views as we go forward to meet our problems together.

2. Be It Resolved that the Board of Supervisors of Prince Edward County as the elected representatives of the people of Prince Edward County do hereby declare it to be the policy and intention of said Board in accordance with the will of the people of said County that no tax levy shall be made upon the said people nor public revenue derived from local taxes shall be appropriated

for the operation and maintenance of public schools in said County wherein white and colored children are taught together under any plan or arrangement whatsoever.

3. Be It Resolved by the Board of Supervisors of Prince Edward County that the Governor of Virginia, the Superintendent of Public Instruction, and the State Board of Education are hereby requested to pay any state revenue to the School Board of Prince Edward County in support of Public Schools in accordance with the policy adopted by the Board of Supervisors of said County for the payment of local revenue to said School Board.

4. Be It Further Resolved by the Board of Supervisors of Prince Edward County that the "Affirmation" signed by citizens and school patrons of the County is hereby received and directed to be filed with records of the Board and it is further resolved that the "Statement of Convictions and Purposes" adopted by the citizens of this County present at this meeting (being approximately 250 in number) be received by the Board and it is directed that the same be filed with the records of the Board.

And the Clerk of this Board is directed to prepare copies of the affirmation with a statement attached thereto showing the number of the citizens whose names are signed thereto together with copies of the "Statement of Convictions and Purposes" and that one copy of each be transmitted to the School Board of Prince Edward County, the Governor of Virginia, the Superintendent of Public Instruction, the Attorney General of Virginia, the State Board of Education, Representative J. H. Daniel and Senator J. D. Hagood, together with a copy of this resolution, and of the resolution this day adopted stating the policy and intention of this Board with respect to the levy of taxes and appropriation of local revenue for school purposes.

5. Be It Resolved by the Board of Supervisors of Prince Edward County that the Governor be and he is hereby respectfully requested not to call a special session of the Legislature of Virginia for the purpose of presenting any legislative plan which would require, permit or authorize under the laws of Virginia the teaching of white and negro children together in the public schools of Prince Edward County.

Minutes of the Board of Supervisors, 1956, Office of the Clerk of the Court, Farmville, Virginia.

QUESTIONS

1. The declaration asserts that the Supreme Court "flagrantly exceeded its lawful authority, trespassed upon the rights of the people and dangerously encroached

upon the reserved rights of the states." What evidence does the document offer to support this statement?

2. The Board of Supervisors stated, "We propose, in every way that we can, to preserve every proper constitutional right of all the people of Prince Edward County." How does this position contrast with the county's treatment of its African American citizens?

Prince Edward Stand Steady

Farmville Herald

May 8, 1956

J. Barrye Wall, publisher and editor of the *Farmville Herald*, exercised significant political influence as a leading segregationist voice in the county. In this editorial, written shortly after the NAACP renewed its school integration lawsuit in the county, Wall echoed a Civil War battle-cry—"Prince Edward stand steady"—which he and other segregationists across the South would repeat frequently in the years to come.

The people of Prince Edward County have made known to the Board of Supervisors their wishes in regard to forced racially mixed public schools. A simple statement signed by over 4,200 citizens affirms, or reaffirms, the belief of the people "that separation of the races in public schools of this county is absolutely necessary" and that they "prefer to abandon public schools and educate our children in some other way if that be necessary to preserve separation of the races in the county." This reaffirms the position taken by the Board of Supervisors and the people in mass meeting last year.

Prince Edward County rests its case. There is nothing more which can be done by the white people to make known their wishes.

State policy was set in February 1956 by the General Assembly of Virginia in Senate Joint Resolution No. 3, widely known as the "Interposition Resolution," which states:

"The General Assembly still believes the power to operate separate schools, provided only that such schools are substantially equal, is a power reserved to this State until the power be prohibited to the States by clear amendment of the (Federal) Constitution . . . Recognizing . . . the prospect of incalculable harm to the public schools of this State and the disruption of the education of her children, Virginia is duty bound to interpose against these most serious consequences, and earnestly to challenge the usurped authority that would inflict them upon her citizens . . . that, until the question here asserted by the State of Virginia be settled by clear Constitutional amendment, we pledge our firm intention to take all appropriate measures honorably, legally and constitutionally available to us, to resist this illegal encroachment upon our sovereign power."

NAACP legal counsel has filed a motion before the District Federal Court to order integration of Prince Edward County school beginning September of 1956. The case has been set for hearing by the court on July 9. In the meantime the Prince Edward School Board must plan for operation of public schools for the coming year. It is to be presumed that the same procedure will be in effect as last year, namely, that the Board of Supervisors will provide funds for the schools on a month-to-month basis, thereby remaining in a position to close the public schools when integration is ordered.

These presumptions being taken as a premise, the Prince Edward Educational Corporation can complete its plans for the operation of white schools in event the public schools system becomes inoperative. Certainly white teachers should be assured. Their loyalty, cooperation and efficiency have been tested before and certainly the people will again assure them.

Prince Edward's position is well founded. The action of the people is determined but not emotional. The strength of their position lies in the calmness, the lack of racial tension, and the resoluteness which people can maintain, believing their position to be right.

Prince Edward stands steady.

QUESTIONS

1. J. Barrye Wall explained how the school board should act "when integration is ordered" by the federal courts, implying such orders were inevitable. How is this position reflected in his other statements here?
2. What evidence did Wall cite to show that "Prince Edward stands steady"?

Desegregation:
Prince Edward County, Virginia

James Rorty
May 1956

Shortly after World War II, the American Jewish Committee launched a new monthly publication, *Commentary*. Focused on Jewish affairs and contemporary world issues, the journal supported human rights and spoke out against bigotry. James Rorty, a founding contributor, wrote for the publication for over a decade. Writing about Prince Edward County in the spring of 1956, Rorty reviewed the county's racial history and sought to convey the rationale and policies of white resistance to school integration.

A beaten and exhausted Confederacy fought its last battles in Prince Edward County in southern Virginia's Black Belt. Ninety years later Prince Edward County became the defendant in one of the five cases on which the United States Supreme Court based its already historic decision outlawing segregated education in the public schools....

It was in Farmville that General Robert E. Lee spent his last night before crossing over the county line to Appomattox Court House on April 9, 1865, to surrender to General U. S. Grant. Steeped in the history and legend of the War Between the States, the leading citizens of Prince Edward County attach a symbolic significance to the fact that at the surrender General Lee and his officers were permitted to retain their sidearms. True peace did not come, they say, until many years later when the conservative Redeemers of Virginia's traditional society triumphed at last over the "foul conspiracy" of carpetbaggers, scalawags, and Populists that had imposed Negro rule on the South.

The Supreme Court broke that peace, they insist, by its May 17, 1954, decision which suddenly outlawed the "separate but equal" covenant on which the relations of the races had been based over the preceding half century. Rather than submit to so abominable a betrayal, they will fight, say Virginia's Defenders of State Sovereignty and Individual Liberties. They will fight in the courts and in the legislatures under the banner of "interposition"; if Yankee troops were again to invade the sovereign state of Virginia to enforce the Court's decision, they would fight, they tell you more or less in William Faulkner's words, in the streets and on the farms.

The Redeemers of yesterday are the Defenders of today, and many of them bear the same names. Their president is Robert B. Crawford, owner of Farmville's Kilkare Laundry, Bible school teacher, and for fifteen years a member of Prince Edward County's school board. Mr. Crawford's gray eminence is J. B. Wall, the able, cultivated editor of the Farmville Herald, which has long been regarded as one of the best edited weeklies in the South. Farmville is one of the major manufacturing and trade centers for Virginia's tobacco-growing South Side counties, whose farmers and businessmen have a vested interest in a segregated and unorganized labor force.

In short, Prince Edward County—where again, as this is written, the National Association for the Advancement of Colored People is pressing for the implementation of the Court's desegregation order—is the heart and center of Virginia's effort to retain, in the schools as elsewhere, the separation of the races and the supremacy of the whites on which its social, economic, and political institutions are based.

Not that Prince Edward County can be considered as representative of Virginia's collective will. On the contrary. If they were permitted to do so, most of the counties and cities of the Old Dominion could and would begin desegregating their schools tomorrow, although without enthusiasm as far as most of the whites are concerned. They can't because, on the issue of the perpetuation of Virginia's anachronistic and slowly disintegrating dual society, they are temporarily the prisoners of the twenty South Side counties, whose representatives hold the balance of power in the ruling political oligarchy that reporters refer to, accurately enough, as "the Byrd machine."

The Defenders have persuaded themselves, and would like to persuade others, that Virginia's present tightly segregated dual society has back of it a hallowed, centuries old tradition, unbroken save by the horrific interlude of the Reconstruction. Actually, this is largely myth. Slavery was not like that—it entailed the opposite of racial segregation—nor was it like that in the memories of Negroes now living. As late as the turn of the century, Negroes were serving on grand and petit juries in most of the South Side counties. The present *de facto* disfranchisement of the race, which chiefly explains the overwhelming South Side vote on January 9, 1956, in favor of amending Virginia's state constitution to permit the use of tax money for the support of private schools, became effective only after the adoption of the State Constitution of 1902. After that date there came a rapid accumulation of state laws and local ordinances introducing segregation into practically every aspect of life and work. As Professor C. Vann Woodward remarks in *The Strange Career of Jim Crow*: "Few have any idea of the relative recency of the Jim Crow laws, or any clear notion of how, when, and why the system arose. There is nothing in their history books that gives them much help. And there is considerable in the books that is likely to mislead and confuse them."

One might expect to find this judgment applying with special force to books of local history. Yet in Herbert Clarence Bradshaw's excellent *History of Prince Edward County, Virginia* one finds plenty of data to support Professor Woodward's thesis about the status of Negroes both during and after slavery. . . .

The triumph of white supremacy was consolidated by the adoption of the 1902 state constitution under the virulently racist leadership of Carter Glass.

Under the new constitution illiterates were disfranchised and the Negro vote in Prince Edward County was reduced to about 10 per cent of what it had been. Before 1900, the Farmville district counted 600 to 800 votes; under the new law there remained only 277 white voters and 40 Negro.

"The possibility of Negro domination of local government," writes Bradshaw, "always a threat under the old suffrage law, was removed."

During the 70's, 80's, and 90's, Negroes had voted in large numbers in Prince Edward County, as in other South Side counties, where they constituted, as they still do, a majority of the population. Indeed, as Professor Woodward notes, qualified and acknowledged leaders of Southern white opinion went on record as saying that it was proper, inevitable, and desirable that Negroes should vote. After 1902, however, they ceased to vote. And in 1956, over fifty years later, they were still not voting, as evidenced by Prince Edward County's adoption by a vote of 2,835 to 350 of the amendment to Virginia's constitution permitting public funds to be used for private schools.

Disfranchisement was not enough, however, in Prince Edward County or elsewhere. Previously, the only Jim Crow legislation adopted by the majority of Southern states was to enforce segregation on trains, and in 1900 Virginia was the last to adopt such a law. But in that year the *Richmond Times* demanded that the principle of segregation be applied rigidly "in every relation of Southern life," on the ground that "God Almighty drew the color line and it cannot be obliterated." In the next two decades there ensued—as I have said—a spate of segregation laws and ordinances that had no precedent or warrant in the traditional folkways of the South. In Prince Edward County, and elsewhere in Virginia, Jim Crow signs blossomed over waiting rooms, water fountains, toilets, ticket windows. The poor, the sick, the insane, even prostitutes were segregated. Courts went to the length of providing Jim Crow Bibles for Negro witnesses.

Before the Civil War there was no public education in Virginia for Negroes— and none for the whites, except for indigent white children. . . .

After the war a public school system was set up under the Reconstruction Constitution of 1867–68, but did not make its appearance in Prince Edward County until 1871. A decade later there were 764 white pupils receiving instruction in twenty-seven white schools and 984 Negroes in 20 Negro schools. The actual working out of the earlier "separate but equal" rulings of the Supreme Court may be judged from the steady increase of Negro enrollment during the succeeding decades, with relatively little increase in Negro school facilities. In 1890 there were 884 whites in 32 schools and 2,217 Negroes in 33 schools. White schools in Farmville customarily operated for eight and a half months; Negro schools for six months. By 1911 there were 84 schools in Prince Edward divided equally between whites and Negroes, but the Negro enrollment was approximately twice that of the whites. As early as 1882 Negro parents vainly petitioned for the appointment of a Negro teacher in the Farmville colored school. By 1920 there were forty-eight Negro teachers in Negro elementary schools, but still no Negro high school teachers—and in fact, no Negro high schools. "The interest in high school development," writes Bradshaw, "seemed entirely confined to the white people." Farmville's first Negro high school was named for R. R. Moton, a former president of Tuskegee who had lived as a boy in Prince Edward County. . . .

From 1939 to 1946 the chairman of Prince Edward County's school board was Robert B. Crawford, now president of the Defenders of State Sovereignty and Individual Liberties. During this period the Negro parents petitioned repeatedly for the construction of a new high school, only to be told that no funds were available for that purpose. When they persisted, a delegation of the Negro Parent-Teachers' Association, led by the Reverend L. Francis Griffin, pastor of the Negro Baptist church, was told not to come again until they were invited. . . .

The Defenders of Prince Edward County regard the Reverend Griffin as one of the chief authors of the County's current troubles. He is a somewhat corpulent six-footer, now in his middle thirties, and reputedly a considerable pulpit orator. During World War II he served in North Africa and Italy. He finished his training for the ministry in 1949 and came to Farmville after the death of his father, a greatly respected clergyman to whom several of Farmville's leading citizens pay high tribute. A good Negro and a fine Christian, they say; he knew the only way to get anything for his people was to ask the white people for it. True, the record shows that his son asked the white folks too, but in a different manner. It was he, they insist, who, along with the school principal, another war veteran, instigated the strike of students in Farmville's Negro high school. This led to the suit subsequently brought by the NAACP—one of the five through which the constitutionality of segregation in schools was successfully challenged.

The NAACP lawyers tell a different story. Oliver Hill, the NAACP attorney in Richmond, says that the first he heard of the strike was when his office received a telephone call from the striking students. He, Spottswood Robinson, who is another NAACP attorney, and Thomas H. Henderson, dean of Virginia Union University in Richmond . . . agreed to stop off in Farmville . . . although, since the NAACP had planned no action in Prince Edward County, they expected that they could do nothing except advise the children to go back to their classes.

When they arrived at Farmville, however, they found that the strikers had real grievances; the Negro high school was a leaky and inadequate makeshift and had been so regarded for years, even by the white school board. The strike was well organized; while student patrols kept the younger children off the street, strike meetings were held in the basement of the Baptist church.

The Reverend Griffin insists that he had no part in instigating the strike, but acknowledges that he participated actively once it had started. The NAACP took the case only after the students had agreed to enlarge their demands for a new school to include a collateral demand for desegregation; by 1951 that had become the NAACP tactic in all such cases....

In Farmville it was only after the strike and the filing of the NAACP suit that the School Board found the money to build the new R. R. Moton High School for Negroes. It is a handsome modern structure and cost $850,000, this being over twice the total appropriations for new Negro school construction during the preceding twenty years....

The NAACP suit was instituted in May of 1951; the white leaders of Prince Edward County made at least one effort to induce the Negro complainants to drop it in exchange for a commitment by the school board to build the new Negro high school. At a meeting held in Mr. Crawford's laundry, the Reverend Griffin was urged to accept this settlement on behalf of his followers. He refused, walked out of the meeting, and has subsequently, he believes, paid a heavy price for his recalcitrancy. Tradesmen who formerly gave him credit now demanded cash. A faction of his congregation turned against him. Harassed by accumulating financial embarrassments and social pressures—the white segregationists stopped speaking to him—he became ill and his wife suffered a nervous breakdown....

"I'd have gone long ago if the kids hadn't started this thing with their strike," said the Reverend Griffin when I saw him in the bare living room of the Baptist parsonage, stripped long since of its repossessed furniture. "I've got four young children and I need more income. My service in Farmville has been sacrificial from the beginning." Then, turning to the poetry which he is said to use effectively in the pulpit, he quoted: "Chill penury hath repressed my noble rage."

Robert B. Crawford is a tall, lean countryman in his early sixties who exemplifies admirably the solid middle-class white citizenship that the Defenders of State Sovereignty and Individual Liberties claim to represent. A devout Presbyterian who for years has taught a popular interdenominational Bible class, Mr. Crawford makes it clear that he didn't lay his Bible down when he became president of the Defenders two years ago....

Mr. Crawford consented to serve as president of the Defenders, he says, when leading white citizens came to him and said: "Mr. Bob, if we are to avoid the eruption of violence by the lower strata of whites, we must keep the leadership of this movement in responsible hands." With 49 organized chapters and an estimated membership of 10,000, the Defenders feel that they are now well on their way to their announced goal of a chapter in every one of Virginia's 98 counties and cities. Careful screening of applicants, says Mr. Crawford, has kept out the Klu Kluxers and the "nigger haters."

As an organization the Defenders have publicly repudiated economic pressure as a means of penalizing NAACP activists; what individual Defenders may do is another matter. And the organization itself is not above distributing the pamphlet literature of less finicky groups such as the Citizens' Grass Roots Crusade of Carolina and the Citizens Councils of Mississippi. They also circulate some of the learned theological dissertations that cite the Scriptural account of the drunkenness of Noah and the curse pronounced on the sons of Ham as proof that the segregation of the races was part of God's plan and purpose as revealed in the Bible.

Many leading Defenders are members of the county school boards that followed the lead of Prince Edward County in voting to close the schools rather than integrate them; over fifty of these boards have petitioned the state Board of Education to forbid integration of the schools anywhere, at any level. Their resistance does not permit compromise in terms of the Supreme Court's implementing requirements of "deliberate speed." ... Mr. William S. Maxey Jr. executive director of the Defenders, was even more explicit on this point. To permit county or local autonomy in integration, would mean that in the twenty South Side counties, where Negroes constitute a majority of the population but rarely vote, they might eventually exercise their suffrage in sufficient numbers to bring about the implementation of the Supreme Court's order. ...

A year ago, Prince Edward County's response to the Supreme Court's implementing order was to refuse to adopt a 1955–56 budget; only the minimum required by the state law was at first appropriated. At the same time the county's leading citizens started a campaign to raise by popular subscription funds for the operation of private schools—for whites only. In July, however, a three-judge Federal Court gave the county a temporary reprieve by ruling that it was not practicable, as requested by the NAACP, to place the public school system on a non-discriminatory basis before the beginning of the school term in September 1956.

The year of grace will soon expire and it is clear that the NAACP will fight its renewal. The Prince Edward County Educational Corporation has $190,000 in pledges made a year ago for the support of a private school system in case it decides to close the public schools rather than desegregate them. Quite possibly it will do just that. In the November 22, 1955, issue of the Farmville *Herald*, editor Wall concluded his strictures . . .

"The schools have been chosen as a battlefield by those who would finally and ultimately crush the sovereignty of the states of this union, and centralize all power in the Federal government. Upon this decision rests the future of the United States—its rise or fall. . . .

"The price of expediency on this issue is the ultimate loss of individual liberties and the last vestiges of state sovereignty. Will Virginia submit?"

The answer, in somewhat less dramatic terms, is that Virginia is not the South Side, and that if it is permitted to do so by the Byrd machine, most of Virginia will proceed to desegregate its schools—not happily or hurriedly— but with "all deliberate speed," just as the Supreme Court has ordered.

Meanwhile, Prince Edward County stands adamant, with the South Side solidly behind her. The position of these intransigent Defenders at first glance seems to be like that of the man on the cliff who can see no way either to climb up or back down, but who will die if he stays where he is. People standing below shout and point impatiently to a path of escape, but the man on the cliff cannot see, and will not believe or heed. . . .

It is unlikely that the courts will grant the County another postponement, and it is equally unlikely, despite the fears of the segregationists, that gradual desegregation of the schools will cause serious disturbances in the community. In Norfolk and elsewhere, the Catholics have already proved that it is possible to begin integration in Virginia, even in communities where Negro pupils equal or outnumber the white ones, without experiencing violence or even major difficulties. To say that Prince Edward County can't adjust to an integrated society is in fact to underestimate the authority and capacity of the county's leadership. Here, as elsewhere in Virginia, the Defenders will evade and delay as long as it is practicable—within the law. But, a century after the Civil War, secession has no place in their thoughts, and they are much less likely than in the Deep South to practice or condone nullification by violence of the Supreme Court's decree. They don't like being shouted at. But in the end these men on the cliff will show themselves quite capable of finding their way down, and "the lower strata of the whites" will almost certainly follow them.

Commentary, May 1956, 431–38. Reprinted from *Commentary* with permission; copyright 1956 Commentary, Inc.

QUESTIONS

1. James Rorty wrote that Southside Virginia's history and race relations differed from that of the remainder of the state. How were race relations different, and why might this have been the case?
2. Who were the leading figures in the school integration battle in Prince Edward County described in Rorty's account?

Declaration of Convictions

Defenders of State Sovereignty and Individual Liberties
March 22–23, 1957

Following the *Brown v. Board of Education* decision, organizations committed to pre-serving school segregation quickly arose across the South. The Defenders of State Sovereignty and Individual Liberties was formed in Southside Virginia in 1954. J. Barrye Wall, publisher of the *Farmville Herald*, was a founding member. The organization's name came from a Confederate memorial in Farmville located just two blocks from the offices of the newspaper. Farmville businessman Robert Crawford, who had served on the county school board from 1932 to 1947, was the group's first president. Numerous local and state officials, including at least three members of the county Board of Supervisors, were also part of the group. The Farmville chapter of the Defenders, a strong and active one, included approximately six hundred members. For the next decade, the Defenders of State Sovereignty and Individual Liberties was the largest and most influential segregationist organization in Virginia.

The Defenders of State Sovereignty and Individual Liberties in convention assembled at Richmond, Virginia this the 23rd day of March, deem it appropriate that we should declare and affirm our convictions.

We first affirm our deep and abiding loyalty and devotion to our country and its institutions. We acknowledge the Constitution to be the bulwark of our liberties, ever subject to the sovereign powers reserved by it to the states and to the people. We know that the liberties of all Americans of all races rests upon the Constitution and the division of powers ordained therein. We deem it the obligation of free men to preserve the powers reserved under the Constitution to the states and to the people and to preserve the constitutional separation of the powers of government in the legislative, executive and judicial branches separately.

We believe that a policy which undertakes to force the association of one race with the other against the will of either, by court decree under threat of fine or imprisonment, is destructive of mutual good will and respect, breeds resentment and animosities, and is injurious to the true interests of all the people. We believe that the molding of the minds and characters of our children is the sacred duty and the priceless natural right and obligation of parents.

Freedom of decision with respect to these considerations touching as they do the most intimate relations of the people and the most cherished natural rights and duties of parenthood is absolutely essential to the maintenance, operation, management and control of our public schools. We conceive this freedom to be among the sacred rights "retained by the people" under the Ninth Amendment of the Federal Constitution.

Among the reserved rights and powers of the states, guaranteed to the State of Virginia under the Tenth Amendment, is the power to maintain racially separate public schools. We do not perceive that the exercise of this power has ever been prohibited to the states by any provision of the Federal Constitution. We believe that this power can be prohibited to the states only by the states themselves. To concede the right of a Federal Court to withdraw this power from the individual states is to concede that all the rights and powers of the states and of the people are enjoyed at the sufferance of the judiciary and that the guarantees of the liberties of the people are no longer fixed in the Constitution itself. Therefore, Federal Courts having refused to recognize these most fundamental, intimate and sacred rights and the profound necessity that they be respected, Virginia has been compelled to fix its course in defense of these rights of her people. We do most solemnly commend his Excellency, Governor Thomas B. Stanley and the members of the legislature of Virginia for their patriotic devotion to the liberties of their people and for the leadership they have given the people of Virginia in this crucial time. We pledge our support of the policy implicit in the measures adopted by the General Assembly of Virginia in its Special Session of 1956. We declare our conviction that these policies founded as they are upon that first American tenet of liberty—that free men should not be taxed against their will and without their consent for a purpose to which they are deeply opposed—to be both sound and in the finest patriotic tradition of the Commonwealth.

We do most solemnly commend our great senior Senator from Virginia, Harry Flood Byrd, for his recent clarion call for all Virginians to stand staunch and firm where Virginia has always stood in ages past in opposition to tyranny from whatever quarter it may come. We do likewise salute the entire Virginia delegation to the United States Congress and Senate, both Democratic and Republican, for the stalwart fight which even now they wage against the vicious assault upon the liberties of all Americans being made in the United States Congress through the proposed pernicious Force Bills, sometimes called Civil Rights Bills, now pending before that body.

The threat to the liberties of our people is mortal. The course of Virginia has been set. The contest is for eternal values. We call upon all local legislative bodies of the counties and cities of Virginia in the sacred name of the liberties of our people to stand firm and united in support of the policy and the course which has been fixed for Virginia in this crucial hour. . . .

These measures conceived and nurtured in the cynical greed of politicians for power, are directed against the people of the South, but they hold within themselves a deadly and mortal threat to the most sacred and essential constitutional safeguards to the liberties of all Americans of all generations. We appeal to Americans everywhere to arouse themselves from their lethargy and unite with us in the condemnation of these iniquitous measures.

While the immediate issue in the great contest that is presently being waged is brought into focus for Virginia and the people of the South in the unconstitutional usurpation of power exemplified in the school segregation decision by the United States Supreme Court and the threat of fine or imprisonment of our school and state officials, and through the denial of freedom of speech and trial by jury by Federal injunctive decree, nonetheless we are deeply convinced that the sinister attack upon the fundamental liberties of Americans and upon the basic constitutional system itself, manifests itself in many other facets of our American life.

Therefore we do further declare:

It is essential that those responsible for the administration of our schools should be alert, that the fundamentals of a sound education are taught to our Virginia children, including and understanding of the fundamental constitutional system under which we live, the blessings of liberty which it alone bestows, the part played by great Virginians of the past in the struggle for the establishment and preservation of these liberties.

It is essential that the molding of the minds, characters and spiritual lives of our children should remain under the control of Virginia parents. We do, therefore, urge our representatives in the Congress and the United States Senate to oppose all legislation designed directly or indirectly to repose control of our educational system in the Federal government. We specifically condemn the wholesale expenditure of Federal funds in support of the public schools of Virginia, knowing full well that the acceptance of such support requires the submission of our schools progressively to ideologies and influences alien to our people. ...

Wherefore, since Virginia, as so often in the past, is again in this generation the battle ground upon which the struggle for the eternal liberties of America must be waged, let us not falter. Let us conduct ourselves with dignity, with self-restraint, without violence and without hatred or ill-will toward any man or group of men. But withall let us conduct ourselves as worthy heirs of those who have gone before.

Adopted at the First Annual Convention, Hotel Jefferson, Richmond, March 22–23, 1957.

QUESTIONS

1. The Defenders of State Sovereignty and Individual Liberties declared their deep and abiding patriotism and loyalty to the United States yet encouraged opposition to the decision rendered by the nation's highest court. How did they justify this apparent contradiction?
2. The Defenders argued that individual rights and liberties were under attack in ways that extended beyond the school integration issue. In what other facets of life did they claim this attack on liberties was occurring?

Integration in Virginia

Edwin B. Henderson
May 1957

Edwin B. Henderson was born in Washington, D.C., and worked as a public school-teacher there for over fifty years. Henderson helped organize an NAACP branch in Fairfax County, Virginia, in 1918.[1] By the 1950s, the Virginia State Conference of the NAACP had more than a hundred branches, the largest collection in the South. In October 1955, Henderson was elected president of the state conference.

Because of its role in the *Brown* decision and its continuing efforts to end segregation, the NAACP was detested by many white southerners. By the mid-1950s, the organization was under attack from both segregationist groups and southern state governments, and was portrayed as subversive, anti-American, or communist. Journalist Benjamin Muse wrote, "It is difficult to describe the intensity with which the NAACP was hated by white Virginians."[2]

Henderson's essay on school desegregation was published in the "Jim Crow Issue" of the *Virginia Spectator*, an undergraduate monthly magazine at the University of Virginia.

Most Virginians find themselves somewhere between the extremes of two camps on the issue of integration vs. segregation. On the one hand are the seg-regationists typified by White Citizens Councils, and on the other, those who believe in complete public de-segregation. Segregationists believe in a dual citizenship, in restriction of the ballot to exclude most Negroes, and in forced separation of the races in schools, colleges, churches, transportation, employment, public parks and libraries and in all public assemblages. . . . Segregationists in the words of Senator James O. Eastland referring to the Supreme Court school desegregation rulings, advise: "You are not required to obey any court which passes out such a ruling. In fact, you are obligated to defy it." Segregationists counsel massive resistance to the Supreme Court edicts, and foster laws and law suits to delay compliance. . . .

True integrationists, on the other hand, hold literally to the fundamental principles of democratic government and of religious freedom as these principles have been universally interpreted. They believe all men are equal in the sense of the oneness of humanity despite physical differences. The sources of their philosophy lay in the Bible, the Bill of Rights and the Constitution of the United States.

In and between these two camps will be found a majority of Virginians. Practically all negroes favor complete de-segregation but like the NAACP people, they would be sympathetic to adjustments in some areas where there was honest forthright effort to comply with the de-segregation decisions of the Supreme Court. Many thousands of white citizens also suffer guilt complexes of reason of the conflict between devotion to ideals and practices of expediency. Some have the courage of their convictions; others keep quiet for fear of social ostracism, or because they fear some of the overt and violent acts of the hoodlum element of the 20th century crusaders for race supremacy.

Some racists justify segregation on the grounds that the laws and customs have lasted so long that they fall within the definition of social mores. This is not true, since most of the segregation laws are approximately less than a half century old. . . .

What, then, have been the causes for so much controversy over the Supreme Court mandate [on] segregation in public schools? The real cause is the fear of politicians that with the advent of negro children in schools hitherto for whites only, negroes will sense the differences that have existed under segregation, and will begin to challenge these politicians through a more enlightened use of the ballot. Once segregation is outmoded educated and intelligent Negroes will become competitors in a free society for positions and jobs now held by their inferiors. The politician, the rabid race-baiter and the opportunist, playing on the fears and ignorance of the masses dwell on the great scare, miscegenation, and the sub-scares, increased health hazards, morals contamination, and lowered educational standards. Most of these same arguments have been used from the beginning to object to public schools for the masses from the colonial governor down to some quarters today. For centuries aristocratic Virginians sent their sons and daughters to private schools, schools for the governing classes.

Two major reasons given for opposing "mixed" public schools are the fears of increasing health hazards and of lowering educational standards. Health department statistics do show that negroes bear a large share of certain infectious diseases, but these statistics come from clinics and free hospitals which the poor are obligated to attend. For many years no private physician listed his venereal disease patients by name or race in the public records. Many who oppose children attending the same school will employ the mothers or sisters of colored children all day in the closer contacts of the homes as domestics.

Negro children, the products of segregated education, do on tests show less achievement per upper grade than white children. For years negro teachers had larger classes and shorter periods to teach. Only recently have facilities for negroes approximated those for whites. When negro children approaching high school realized that only a few job opportunities outside the veil of segregation would be open to them, does anyone wonder that they would lose motivation for high grade achievement? It may take a few years to overcome the blight of segregation but there are educational methods which can remedy retardation caused by faulty facilities and poor environment for learning but by the time Virginia accepts fully the inevitable integration of public schools, negro children will, like others, be achieving in proportion to their native intelligence quotients.

This trumped up fear of mongrelization of the races as a real danger can be dismissed as a consequence of integrated schools. Millions of Negro-Americans are unrecognizable as negroes by skin color, texture of hair or other features. There are few pure African types in the United States today due to the fact that so-called mongrelization has come about not through school contacts, but by many of the same people or their ancestors who cry out so loudly about the scare crow, miscegenation. Segregation laws have favored miscegenation in that they were meant to protect the white male while affording no protection to the colored female.

We hear much about the breaking down of "good race relations" that presumably existed before the Supreme Court decisions. These "good relations" are the same kind that exist today in colonial nations, in Russia and its satellites between those who rule by power and those who must submit without effective means of protest. Good race relations existed between slave and master before 1865, and a similar deception is fostered by economic dependence today. But even during the period of slavery there were over 800 recorded uprisings and rebellions usually aborted by patrols of a police state. "Good relations" have existed only as surface indications. Negroes have been willing to trust to their supreme faith in God and justice and are seeking their legal and civil rights through process of petition to the courts of law.

The attempt to stifle the protest and aspirations of a beleaguered people by outlawing the National Association for the Advancement of Colored People is doomed to failure because the only way to destroy it is to destroy all of the sacred rights vouchsafed by the constitutions of Virginia and of the United States. The NAACP has been charged with being subversive and revolutionary. Yet its national board of directors include some of the great patriots of America, both white and negro. J. Edgar Hoover, a Southerner, Director of the F. B. I., is on record as in these words, "Equality, freedom, and tolerance are essential in a democratic government. The NAACP has done much to preserve these principals and to perpetuate the desires of our founding fathers." The NAACP has never been listed by the Department of Justice among subversive organizations. Its methods and its objectives are in every sense truly American. It is possible that here and there under false cover some communist may have joined, just as some may have infiltrated our churches, our government, the Klan and even possibly the F. B. I.

The laws passed in Virginia and other southern states to hamstring the organizations seeking to bring about brotherhood and tolerance show how easily otherwise intelligent people can be goaded into action that defies reason and common sense. As presently worded these acts negate some of the fundamental principles of our free society. . . . Laws have been passed that militate against individuals or organizations whose function may be to ameliorate injustices against citizens caused by reason of their "race or color." The requirement that the names of members of such organizations be made public is solely for the purpose of submitting these members to social or economic reprisals, just as the late Senator Glass said the poll tax was intended, to get rid of the Negro vote without "materially impairing the numerical strength of the white electorate." . . .

Virginia ranks near the bottom of the ladder in the money allotted by states for public schools. Although much progress has been made in the last few years, illiteracy is still high and is evidenced by the speech and actions of most of those who join the ranks of bigotry. As late as 1837, Governor Campbell of Virginia reported that one-fourth of all white persons applying for marriage licenses in 93 Virginia counties could not sign their names. In 1850, whereas New England states had an illiteracy ratio among the native white population over 20 years of age of only .42 percent, and in the Middle Atlantic States of only 3 percent, Southern states had an illiteracy ratio of 20.3 percent. Under such conditions demagogues and opportunists . . . can incite the more ignorant masses.

Many Virginians seem unconcerned or unaware that great statesmen like Jefferson and Mason warned of tyranny against the Negro. Once, in writing against deprivation of Negro slaves of liberty, he wrote, "I tremble for my country when I reflect that God is just, and that his justice cannot sleep forever." Chancellor Williams in his book, *The Raven*, quotes Edgar Allen Poe, then a student at the University of Virginia, as asking Jefferson, "Are All Men Equal, Did you founding fathers mean just that?" Jefferson was quoted as replying, "Yes, we meant exactly that. All men are created equal. . . . Some men are born deformed. Some with defective minds, some deaf, dumb and blind. Others like the colored people, for example, differ from us in the color of their skins and the texture of their hair, but the doctrine of equality stands steadfast and immovable, for it rests upon the fundamentals of human existence. . . . We poke fun at our African slaves, at their ignorance and insist they are an inferior people. Of course they are. We keep them that way. But I dare you free them and give them equal opportunities. They will rise as high as the white man as surely as God reigns."

This writer has long hoped for the day when the conscience of Virginia would seek to make amends for the years of bad treatment of its Negro citizens who have done so much by their work and in defense of our nation to deserve full citizenship. The only time in more than three score years that I have ever been able to appreciate the full blessings of American citizenship has been when I travelled in a foreign country where race nor color were barriers. I know no other country. My great grandfather was a proud member of Powhatan's dynasty. My mother's father was one of Williamsburg's aristocratic slave holders. My ancestors for hundreds of years were Virginians. My entire life has been subjected to the indignities suffered by every Negro citizen who lives where the practices and laws discriminate against him by reason of the accident of birth. Now that at long last the highest court in the land has declared state imposed discrimination unconstitutional, I and every other liberty loving Negro will continue to fight against segregation even in the face of violence. We shall do this in the faith that sooner or later more southerners will realize how silly are some of the fears that bigots have imposed upon them. When the South complies with the supreme law of the land an era of progress will take shape and many of our social and economic problems will be on the way to solution. More important sectionalism will disappear and our nation will become unified and stronger to meet the challenge to democracy by our national enemies. By eliminating these laws that insult people of color in America we will win friends among the non-white races of mankind around the world and add them in the struggle against Godless communism.

Virginia Spectator: Jim Crow Issue, May 1957, 19, 30–33.

NOTES

1. Beverly Bunch-Lyons and Nakeina Douglas, "The Falls Church Colored Citizens Protective League and the Establishment of Virginia's First Rural Branch of the NAACP," in *Long Is the Way and Hard: One Hundred Years of the NAACP*, ed. Kevern Verney and Lee Sartain (Fayetteville: University of Arkansas Press, 2009), 94–95.
2. Muse, *Virginia's Massive Resistance*, 48.

QUESTIONS

1. What is Edwin B. Henderson's response to arguments justifying segregation? Are Henderson's arguments convincing?
2. Henderson refuted the much-touted "good race relations" that supposedly existed in Virginia before the *Brown* decision. How did he describe race relations during the Jim Crow era? How does this contrast with *Farmville Herald* editor J. Barrye Wall's description of race relations in "A Problem Becomes an Issue" (see p. 49)?

School Integration—Four Years After

James J. Kilpatrick
May 12, 1958

James J. Kilpatrick, a native of Oklahoma, began his career as a journalist in 1941 at the *Richmond News Leader*, a daily evening newspaper and sister paper to the *Richmond Times-Dispatch*. Ten years later, Kilpatrick was appointed editor of the *News Leader*.

Kilpatrick was an ardent segregationist, and his strident opposition to racial equality permeated his writings. "The reality that the South has had to cope with most constantly, beyond the realities of defeat and poverty," he observed, "is the reality of the Southern Negro. . . . Instead of ambition, we have witnessed indolence; instead of skill, ineptitude; instead of talent, an inability to learn."[1]

Kilpatrick's advocacy of interposition in the mid-1950s greatly influenced southern political leaders and the public. This article was published in *Human Events*, an influential, conservative national magazine.

It has been four years now, come May 17, since Chief Justice Warren gazed upon a packed courtroom and began reading the brief opinion we have come to know as *Brown vs. Board of Education*. In the whole history of the Supreme Court of the United States, no single decision has had an immediate impact more profound than this one, or created more controversy over a wider area, or fostered more bitter resentments. Those who support and defend the Court's opinion might accept those superlatives, but would contend that no decision ever has accomplished greater social good. However the School Cases are viewed, pro or con, few persons would question their surpassing place in the judicial history of the United States. . . .

The ruling struck down the school segregation laws of 17 states and the District of Columbia; it immediately, personally and directly affected the lives of millions of school children and their parents. And the Court accomplished all this not on the basis of law, but upon "the extent of psychological knowledge." Members of the Court, agreeing to the *Brown* opinion, jettisoned some of the oldest rules of judicial construction; they usurped the power reserved to the states to amend the Constitution, and they substituted their own notions of desirable public policy for the plain meaning of the Constitution they were sworn to uphold.

So violent an explosion must cause vast changes. It is entirely too soon to appraise these consequences fully; and those of us in the Old South, attempting to cope with what is seen as the devastation of a social order, are doubtless the wrong ones to attempt an appraisal anyhow. For the South, these four years have been like the day after an earthquake: the ground still trembles, and the damage may be more or less severe than it seems. . . .

The 17 states and the District of Columbia affected by the School Cases have a public school enrollment of some 9,431,000 white pupils and 2,922,000 Negro pupils. Their school systems are subdivided into school districts, of which 3,000 districts are biracial. The fourth anniversary of the opinion finds approximately 760 of these districts "integrated," and 2,240 not integrated. I put the word "integrated" in quotation marks to suggest that, in some of these districts, integration has been accomplished in the barest token degree: one Negro pupil among 6,800 in Winston-Salem, N. C., four among 7,700 in Charlotte.

The statistics on this whole subject are deceptive, and need to be examined with care. When it is said that two million white children and 350,000 Negro children are now in "integrated situations," it should also be said that except for nine districts in Arkansas, three in North Carolina and three in Tennessee, all these integrated situations are in border states and in the District of Columbia. Four years after the decision, not a single public school is racially integrated in Virginia, South Carolina, Georgia, Florida, Alabama, Mississippi or Louisiana.

What carries perhaps the greatest significance is the fact that the trend toward voluntary integration has all but stopped. Of the 760 school districts now classified as integrated, 537 were integrated by the fall of 1955, and 723 were integrated by the fall of 1956. The movement now has stalled. Except for a few mop-up districts in fringe areas, the advance of integration will move henceforth an inch at a time. Court orders, directed at resentful defendants and backed by Federal force, will be required, and these will have to be carried out in an atmosphere not of acceptance but of active or passive hostility. There is a maxim that no law can be effective when it is imposed upon a community against its will; and when such imposition is attempted, it is not called law; it is called tyranny. It is in this light that the Court's decrees are viewed over most of the remaining unintegrated districts.

How well has integration succeeded in the 760 districts where it now obtains? In some areas, surely, it appears to have worked quite well indeed. For the most part, these are border areas in which the Negro school population is relatively small, or they are areas having relatively little identification with a peculiarly Southern way of life. In other areas, such as Washington, D. C., it is difficult to weigh the picture because the picture changes so rapidly; the District's schools are now more than 71 per cent colored, and in lower elementary grades the figure approaches 80 per cent. Many of the District's schools, for reasons of residential geography, thus are virtually segregated all over again.

Elsewhere, in some of the more critical areas, the Court's social experiment is not going too well. Correspondents of the *Southern School News*, interviewing white parents and teachers in integrated localities in Arkansas, Tennessee and North Carolina, found opinion still resentful, still unchanged. Even the minute degree of race-mixing that now obtains in these areas has been accepted with reluctance and with a helpless sense of resignation to a distasteful inevitability.

It will be recalled that two of the school districts that figured in the original School Cases were Clarendon County, S. C., and Prince Edward County, Va. Notably, both districts remain fully segregated to this day, and for the same reason: if Negro plaintiffs wish to push their victory at court to a showdown at the schoolhouse, all public schools in the two localities will be abandoned. In each case, plans are far advanced for the establishment of private schools for white children. What would become of the Negro children is uncertain. The implications of so drastic a decision can merely be acknowledged here; it must suffice to say that the prospect of closing deeply cherished schools is a miserably unhappy one all around, and represents to the white parents and taxpayers only a final desperate choice between evils.

This willingness to abandon a public facility, as a last resort, in preference to seeing it integrated, is reflected elsewhere in the South today. I am advised that few municipal swimming pools, if any, have been constructed in the unyielding South in the past four years. No new municipal golf courses have been opened in these states, and several municipal courses, indeed, have been abandoned and sold. Greensboro, N. C., is the most recent city to take this step, and the decision is all the more notable in Greensboro because of the generally "liberal" political climate that obtains there. To replace such public facilities, private recreational clubs are multiplying across the South at a phenomenal pace. Instead of calling upon government for a swimming pool and a tennis court, these groups are providing their own, at their own expense. Wholly apart from the integration issue, this is a marvelously healthy trend.

What is not healthy at all, and is to be most keenly regretted, is the palpable decline in white and Negro relationships across much of the South. This decline is not to be charted in anything so measurable as interracial violence. We have experienced, thankfully, very little of this so far. Indeed, I would imagine there are more incidents of interracial violence on any Saturday night in Brooklyn than the whole of Virginia would experience in a year. We are too far apart down here for that. And this apartness is growing. The *Brown* decision served to snap old lines of communication; it swept away the social foundation on which white and Negro could dwell tolerably together.

Prior to May 17, 1954, the Negro's status in the South was that of a subordinate. Now, it may have been wrong for the white Southerner to have thought of the Negro in such terms—probably it was; you grow up with such things—but at least a subordinate relationship is a familiar and normal relationship, known to every man who has a boss over him. There are ground rules in such a relationship; men know where they stand. In the South, that status has abruptly shifted; the Negro is seen now as plaintiff in a lawsuit, as party litigant, an antagonist. Where once we had thought of our society as Negro and white, now the judicial earthquake has tumbled up a new relationship of Negro versus white, as if we met in pleadings only. In individual cases, of course, a warm affection still binds countless whites and countless Negroes, but class-wise, or group-wise, the dividing gulf grows wider. . . .

These have not been happy years for the South—not for the white Southerner, and I suspect, not for his black brother either. But we survive. Both races in the South fortunately are characterized by a vast and almost boundless patience; we share a certain genius for procrastination, and facing what often seems to be a crisis, we sometimes are able to resolve the urgency by what John Randolph called a policy of judicious neglect. It may be, in time, that a new relationship of agreeable stalemate will provide us an acceptable *modus vivendi*. Each race needs the other, at least in terms of the Southern economy, and one day the process of gradual adjustment halted by the Court will have to be resumed.

But on this particular issue of public schools, the white South has not the slightest intention of yielding; and the Negro leadership seems determined to press its legal advantage at any consequence. Both sides, looking to the autumn, are a little apprehensive. We do not know what will happen, but we do know this: over the past four years, the apostles of integration have won the easy ground; and now, for good or ill, the easy ground is about used up.

Human Events, May 12, 1958, 56–60.

NOTE

1. Kilpatrick, *Southern Case for School Segregation*, 35.

QUESTIONS

1. James Kilpatrick stated that before 1954, the status of African Americans in the South was that of a "subordinate." How did he justify this social divide? How could that have been the case if segregated facilities were supposed to be "separate but equal"?

2. In his conclusion, Kilpatrick looked ahead to the fall of 1958. How was school integration in the South proceeding? What potential conflicts did he foresee?

NO WHITE MAN TO LOSE HIS VOTE IN VIRGINIA.

This Assurance Given by Men Who Are Most Competent to Speak with Authority.

A Meeting was Held in Richmond on October 17, 1901, at which Chairman Ellyson Presided and Hon. John Goode and Mr. Montague Made Speeches—All Three Declared the Policy of the Convention in Language That Cannot Be Mistaken. Great Enthusiasm Aroused.

STATE CHAIRMAN ELLYSON.

" The best men in this Commonwealth have been selected as the representatives of their people in the convention. They will not fail to be responsive to the wishes of their constituents, for every Democrat in that convention knows that the convention would never have been held but for the desire of the white people of this Commonwealth to have enacted such a constitutional provision as would take away from the negro the right to vote, and, at the same time preserve to the white men of the Commonwealth their right of suffrage.

" I have enjoyed the best opportunities for frequent conferences and consultation with the members of the convention on this question. I think I know their views as well as any other man in the State, and I do not hesitate to give to you and through you to the white men of this Commonwealth both my personal and official assurance that that convention has the fixed and unalterable intention of enacting a clause which will accomplish the end I have just mentioned and which will forever remove the negro as a factor in our political affairs and give to the white people of this Commonwealth the conduct and control of the destinies which they have the right to shape and determine.

" The Democrats of Virginia have always kept the pledges made to the people and they will not fail to do so in this instance."—Hon. J. Taylor Ellyson, Chairman of the State Democratic Committee.

HON. JOHN GOODE.

" The Democratic party is pledged in its platform to eliminate the ignorant and worthless negro as a factor from the politics of this State without taking the right of suffrage from a single white man, and, speaking for my colleagues in the convention, I solemnly declare to you that they will keep that pledge to the letter."—President Goode of the Constitutional Convention.

HON. A. J. MONTAGUE.

" The Democratic party, through its representatives in the convention, is slowly, but surely, framing a law that will so effectually exclude the idle, shiftless and illiterate of the negro race from the suffrage that the gates of republican wrath cannot prevail against it. The trouble with our opponents is that they realize now that we will accomplish this and keep the pledge that no white man will be disfranchised. I stand here and declare it, for I do know it is the truth."—Hon. A. J. Montague, Democratic nominee for Governor.

Political broadside promoting a new constitution for Virginia with the promise "No White Man To Lose His Vote," while also pledging the disenfranchisement of black voters, 1901. (Courtesy of Special Collections Library, University of Virginia)

VIRGINIA

HEALTH BULLETIN

Vol. XVI.   MARCH, 1924.   Extra No. 2

The New Virginia Law

To Preserve Racial Integrity

W. A. Plecker, M. D., *State Registrar of Vital Statistics, Richmond, Va.*

Senate Bill 219, To preserve racial integrity, passed the House March 8, 1924, and is now a law of the State.

This bill aims at correcting a condition which only the more thoughtful people of Virginia know the existence of.

It is estimated that there are in the State from 10,000 to 20,000, possibly more, near white people, who are known to possess an intermixture of colored blood, in some cases to a slight extent it is true, but still enough to prevent them from being white.

In the past it has been possible for these people to declare themselves as white, or even to have the Court so declare them. Then they have demanded the admittance of their children into the white schools, and in not a few cases have intermarried with white people.

In many counties they exist as distinct colonies holding themselves aloof from negroes, but not being admitted by the white people as of their race.

In any large gathering or school of colored people, especially in the cities, many will be observed who are scarcely distinguishable as colored.

These persons, however, are not white in reality, nor by the new definition of this law, that a white person is one with no trace of the blood of another race, except that a person with one-sixteenth of the American Indian, if there is no other race mixture, may be classed as white.

Their children are likely to revert to the distinctly negro type even when all apparent evidence of mixture has disappeared.

The Virginia Bureau of Vital Statistics has been called upon within one month for evidence by two lawyers employed to assist people of this type to force their children into the white public schools, and by another employed by the school trustees of a district to prevent this action.

Entered as second class matter July 28, 1908, at the Postoffice at Richmond, Va., under the Act of July 16, 1894.

Above: Interior of a Very Poor Colored School in Prince Edward County, Virginia, photograph by Jackson Davis, circa 1915. (Jackson Davis Collection, Albert and Shirley Small Special Collections Library, University of Virginia; reproduced with permission)

Right: Robert Russa Moton. (Alabama Department of Archives and History; reproduced with permission)

Helen Guerrant, mathematics teacher at Moton High School, and Barbara Rose Johns, circa 1951. (Photograph by John A. Stokes, copyright 2001; reproduced with permission)

School strike sign, Moton High School, April 1951. (Copyright *Richmond Times-Dispatch*; reproduced with permission)

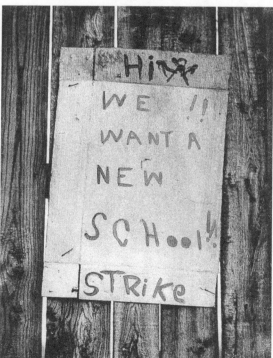

Robert R. Moton High School and the "tar paper shacks," Farmville, Virginia, 1952. (Plaintiffs exhibit in Civil Action no. 1333, *Dorothy E. Davis et al. v. County School Board of Prince Edward County et al.*, Civil Case Files, 1938–12/31/1990, Records of District Courts of the United States, Record Group 21, National Archives, Philadelphia)

Farmville High School for white children, 1952. (Plaintiffs exhibit in Civil Action no. 1333, *Dorothy E. Davis et al. v. County School Board of Prince Edward County et al.*, Civil Case Files, 1938–12/31/1990, Records of District Courts of the United States, Record Group 21, National Archives, Philadelphia)

Dorothy Davis, at center, and fellow students at Robert R. Moton High School. The "tar paper shacks" are seen in the background. Davis was the lead named plaintiff in the school desegregation lawsuit that became part of the *Brown v. Board of Education* Supreme Court case. (Photograph by Hank Walker, March 1953, the LIFE Picture Collection, Getty Images; reproduced with permission)

Right: Supreme Court docket, Brief for Appellants, October Term, 1953. Case no. 4 is *Dorothy E. Davis et al. v. County School Board of Prince Edward County et al.* These cases would be joined to become *Brown v. Board of Education.*

Below: The *Farmville Herald* newspaper headline announcing the Supreme Court decision in *Brown v. Board of Education,* May 18, 1954. (Reproduced with permission of the *Farmville Herald*)

IN THE

Supreme Court of the United States

October Term, 1953

No. 1

OLIVER BROWN, ET AL., *Appellants,*

VS.

BOARD OF EDUCATION OF TOPEKA, ET AL., *Appellees.*

No. 2

HARRY BRIGGS, JR., ET AL., *Appellants.*

VS.

R. W. ELLIOTT, ET AL., *Appellees.*

No. 4

DOROTHY E. DAVIS, ET AL., *Appellants,*

VS.

COUNTY SCHOOL BOARD OF PRINCE EDWARDS COUNTY, *Appellees.*

No. 10

FRANCIS B. GEBHART, ET AL., *Petitioners,*

VS.

ETHEL LOUISE BELTON, ET AL., *Respondents.*

APPEALS FROM THE UNITED STATES DISTRICT COURT FOR THE DISTRICT OF KANSAS, THE EASTERN DISTRICT OF SOUTH CAROLINA AND THE EASTERN DISTRICT OF VIRGINIA, AND ON PETITION FOR A WRIT OF CERTIORARI TO THE SUPREME COURT OF DELAWARE, RESPECTIVELY

BRIEF FOR APPELLANTS IN NOS. 1, 2 AND 4 AND FOR RESPONDENTS IN NO. 10 ON REARGUMENT

CHARLES L. BLACK, JR.,
ELWOOD H. CHISOLM,
WILLIAM T. COLEMAN, JR.,
CHARLES T. DUNCAN,
GEORGE E. C. HAYES,
LOREN MILLER,
WILLIAM R. MING, JR.,
CONSTANCE BAKER MOTLEY,
JAMES M. NABRIT, JR.,
DAVID E. PINSKY,
FRANK D. REEVES,
JOHN SCOTT,
JACK B. WEINSTEIN,
of Counsel.

HAROLD BOULWARE,
ROBERT L. CARTER,
JACK GREENBERG,
OLIVER W. HILL,
THURGOOD MARSHALL,
LOUIS L. REDDING,
SPOTTSWOOD W. ROBINSON, III,
CHARLES S. SCOTT,
Attorneys for Appellants in Nos. 1, 2, 4 and for Respondents in No. 10.

The Farmville Herald

AND FARMER-LEADER

FARMVILLE, VIRGINIA, TUESDAY, MAY 18, 1954

Unanimous Decision

United States Supreme Court Outlaws School Segregation

The United States Supreme Court today (Monday) declared segregation in the public schools unlawful in a 12-page, unanimous decision. It was read shortly before noon by Chief Justice Earl Warren, in Washington.

The highest tribunal in the nation said that education must be available to all on an equal basis, and that seperate educational systems prevents this.

Direct conflict with the nation's law was tied, in the opinion, to the 14th Amendment, which declares for equal rights to Negroes.

The court's ruling, awaiting by an anxious nation, will affect nine million white school children and two and one-half million Negro children in 17 southern and southwestern states and in the District of Columbia.

Virginia's state officials received the verdict in a silence, thus far unbroken. Governor Thomas Stanley, according to press dispatches has already begun, conferences with government officials.

Drenching rains to east their ballots referendum Friday. This picture was at Cumberland Court House.

npen ABC Store

Almond Opinion Rules Out Merger For Dillwyn Bank

J. H. Spessard 'Surprised' By Adverse Ruling

A legal snarl, concerning the question of just where Charlottesville is located, has blocked the proposed merger of the Buckingham County Bank, at Dillwyn, with Peoples National Bank of Charlottesville.

From Dillwyn, to Charlottesville, to Richmond and Washington attempts to get final approval for the merger have been unsuccessful. A final appeal to Attorney General J. Lindsay Almond, Jr., in which he upheld the opinion of the State Banking Commission attorneys, against the proposal, has now been received, putting an air of finality to the matter.

Parties to the proposed merger have expressed surprise at the final ruling since original negotiations were started only after preliminary approval by the State

Green Bay Elementary School, a typical grade school for white children in Prince Edward County in the 1950s, with indoor plumbing and central heating. The school was abandoned in 1959 when the county closed its public schools. (Photograph circa 1962–63 by Edward H. Peeples; Edward H. Peeples Prince Edward County. (Va.) Public Schools Collection, Virginia Commonwealth University Special Collections and Archives; reproduced with permission)

Levi Elementary School, a typical grade school for black children in Prince Edward County in the 1950s, with no indoor plumbing, running water, or central heat. The school was abandoned in 1959 when the county shut down its public schools. (Photograph circa 1962–63 by Edward H. Peeples; Edward H. Peeples Prince Edward County. (Va.) Public Schools Collection, Virginia Commonwealth University Special Collections and Archives; reproduced with permission)

Phyllistine Ward, Jimmy Allen, and an unidentified third student outside the new Robert Moton High after the closing of the public schools, 1960. (American Friends Service Committee Archives; reproduced with permission)

NAACP lawyers Oliver Hill and Spotswood Robinson with Reverend L. Francis Griffin at an NAACP Rally at the Prince Edward County Courthouse on May 21, 1961, for the seventh anniversary of the Supreme Court school desegregation ruling in *Brown v. Board of Education*. (Copyright *Richmond Times-Dispatch*; reproduced with permission)

Dr. Martin Luther King Jr. visiting Farmville, Virginia, March 28, 1962, speaks with three students who are without schools, Dorothy May Logan, Naja Griffin, and Shirley Wiley (L to R). (Photograph by Scott Henderson, Scott Henderson Collection, copyright Virginia Union University; reproduced with permission)

Student protest, Farmville, Virginia, July, 1963. (Copyright *Richmond Times-Dispatch*; reproduced with permission)

Virginia governor Albertis Harrison announces opening of Prince Edward Free Schools Program with Reverend L. Francis Griffin, state NAACP president; William vanden Heuvel, U.S. Department of Justice; and NAACP attorney Henry Marsh, August 14, 1963. (*Virginia Pilot* photograph; reproduced with permission)

Prince Edward County students in the March on Washington for Jobs and Freedom, August 28, 1963. (Photograph by Thomas J. O'Halloran, *U.S. News and World Report* Collection, Library of Congress; reproduced with permission)

Opening day of the Prince Edward Free Schools, September 16, 1963. (Photograph by Thomas J. O'Halloran, *U.S. News and World Report* Collection, Library of Congress; reproduced with permission)

Robert R. Moton High School, site of the 1951 school strike, was designated a National Historic Landmark on August 31, 1998. (Photograph by Brian Grogan, copyright 1997)

Above: Virginia Civil Rights Memorial, located on Capitol Square, Richmond. (Photograph by Brian Grogan, copyright 2017)

Left: Barbara Johns statue, detail view of the Virginia Civil Rights Memorial. (Photograph by Brian Grogan, copyright 2017)

4

"With Profound Regret"

Although Virginia's massive resistance policies had been defeated in the courts, white resistance remained strong. In the spring of 1959, the Virginia General Assembly passed new legislation aimed at minimizing school integration as Virginia's political leaders shifted from a strategy of outright resistance to a new strategy of delay. In addition, local officials were granted greater authority to address the threat of school desegregation through a program of pupil placement and revised tuition grants.

On May 5, 1959, the U.S. Fourth Circuit Court of Appeals issued an order for Prince Edward County to begin school desegregation by September of that year. The county Board of Supervisors responded on June 2 with a unanimous decision to cut off all funding for the public schools: "It is with the most profound regret that we have been compelled to take this action. We do not act in defiance of any law or any court. Above all we do not act with hostility toward the Negro people of Prince Edward County."[1] Rather than desegregate its schools, county leaders chose to abandon public education entirely.

The educational crisis in Prince Edward County touched the lives of both black and white children when the public schools closed. The entire social fabric of the county was disrupted. Every parent wanted their child to be in school. The intractable question was where and with whom, or if they would go to school at all. As stated by historian John Egerton, "No other political jurisdiction in the United States had taken the extreme step of closing its entire public school system to avoid desegregation. It was a reactionary step taken with deliberation by mild-mannered whites against mild-mannered blacks, and it was ultimately fruitless and destructive."[2]

The pledges made at the mass meeting in June 1955 to guarantee white teacher salaries were now called on to provide funding for a private school program under the auspices of the Prince Edward School Foundation. These donations provided the operating funds for the first year of the newly formed Prince Edward Academy.

In September 1959, the county Board of Supervisors cut the local tax rate by 53 percent, the amount normally dedicated to public education.[3] The tax cut provided local citizens with additional funds that could be used to support the new private school. This move, however, primarily benefited the large landowners and business leaders of the county, who also controlled the county government, the Prince Edward Academy, and the local chapter of the Defenders of State Sovereignty and Individual Liberties. A driving motivation of the private school leaders, charged Dr. C. G. Gordon Moss, a white opponent of the school closings (see p. 161), was to end public education entirely both to relieve the white county elite of the tax burden of paying for those schools and to maintain a supply of cheap, unskilled labor for their businesses.

By 1960, state and local authorities had implemented a system of tuition grants that was used in the county to fund private education. These grants, combined with tax relief and private donations, funded Prince Edward Academy during the 1960–61 school year. In August 1961, however, Judge Oren Lewis of the federal district court invalidated the use of public funds and tax credits in a ruling that also called for the reopening of the public schools. Although Lewis's decision was appealed, and the schools remained closed in the interim, the judge's ruling meant that white parents would henceforth bear a financial burden for their children's education at Prince Edward Academy. The penalty of the closed public schools now also fell on poor white children, who could no longer afford the private school. Historian Jill Ogline Titus notes, "Education shifted from a fundamental right to a privilege for those whites who could pay."[4]

When the public schools first closed, white students moved from the public schools into makeshift classrooms of the Prince Edward Academy, which were located in church basements, civic clubs, private homes, and the town movie theater. Academic programs were abandoned in arts, music, and languages, as the academy promoted an educational emphasis on fundamentals. The school quickly became a model for the rapidly expanding private school movement in the South and attracted hundreds of visitors to observe the school in operation.[5]

The academy could not use the former public school buildings and facilities; nonetheless, the public schools were used as a source of materials to outfit the private school. "Truth of the matter is we went down there and got all the damn books, even charts off the wall," stated Robert Taylor, a local building contractor and segregationist leader.[6] Taylor's company would later help construct the county's all-white, segregated private school, which opened in September 1961.

In December 1959, segregationist leaders that had closed the public schools and established the academy now announced the formation of Southside Schools, Inc. This initiative proposed to assist the black residents of the county in forming their own private schools. The proposal was rebuffed by the black community, however, which regarded the offer merely as a ploy that would validate the state tuition grants if they were accepted by both black and white students, and would help the white community gain control of former public school buildings for use by the new private academy.

Approximately 1,700 African American children were shut out of school in September 1959. The education of an estimated 2,700 black children would be affected during the years the public schools were closed. Black families struggled to find any educational opportunity. Many families were forced apart as children left the county to live with relatives, friends, or caring strangers in order to attend school. One mother later recalled the anguish of the choices forced on them. When her seven-year-old son went to live with relatives so he could attend school, "My husband cried for two weeks after our boy left home."[7] One student forced out of school was later drafted into the U.S. Army where he was awarded the Bronze Star for his military service in Vietnam. "I could go to war for my country," stated Charlie Taylor, "but I could not go to school in Prince Edward County."[8]

The African American community attempted to educate its children by any means possible. Former teachers and parents organized fledgling educational efforts. An initial focus was on rising high school seniors, to ensure they could graduate without disruption. The Prince Edward County Christian Association (PECCA) was formed and, with the assistance of the NAACP, operated "training centers" in the county that offered rudimentary classes to keep children engaged in basic reading and math. PECCA and the NAACP arranged for sixty-one students to enroll in the high school program at Kittrell Junior College in North Carolina. The American Friends Service Committee (AFSC) organized the Emergency Student Placement Project, which found homes for sixty-seven Prince Edward students with volunteer families in the Midwest and Northeast.

The Virginia Teachers Association (VTA), the professional organization for African American teachers, helped establish emergency educational programs. The VTA Pupil Relocation Project temporarily placed approximately one hundred students in other Virginia communities to attend school. Support came from outside of Virginia as well, as both the American Federation of Teachers and United Federation of Teachers sponsored summer programs in the county. Students and professors from Hampton Institute, Union Theological

Seminary, Yale University, and Queens College provided assistance during the coming summers.

The inauguration of President John F. Kennedy on January 20, 1961, offered hope of federal government participation in resolving the schools crisis in Prince Edward County. Shortly after the new president was inaugurated, the U.S. Commission on Civil Rights convened a conference in Williamsburg, Virginia, focused on school desegregation, including the question of the closed public schools in Prince Edward County. President Kennedy sent a telegram to the conference: "This is no time for schools to close for any reason, and certainly no time for schools to be closed in the name of racial discrimination."[9]

Reverend L. Francis Griffin addressed the morality of closed public schools as a national issue in his own statement to the conference: "The tragedy is not in the fact that these children, white and black, are out of school. The real tragedy is that this could happen in America and arouse no more action than it has" (see p. 132).

NOTES

1. Minutes of the Board of Supervisors of Prince Edward County, Virginia, June 2, 1959, Office of the Clerk of the Court, Farmville, Virginia.

2. John Egerton, "A Gentleman's Disagreement in Prince Edward County," in *Shades of Gray: Dispatches from the Modern South* (Baton Rouge: Louisiana State University Press, 1991), 116.

3. Muse, *Virginia's Massive Resistance*, 150.

4. Titus, *Brown's Battleground*, 221.

5. Ibid., 36.

6. Robert Taylor, interview by Larissa Smith Fergeson, Longwood University, Farmville, Virginia, May 1, 2004.

7. Private, anonymous conversation between a Prince Edward County resident and Brian Grogan, Worsham, Virginia, June 2003.

8. Charlie Taylor, interview by Brian Grogan, Farmville, Virginia, May 15, 2004.

9. U.S. Commission on Civil Rights, *1961 U.S. Commission on Civil Rights Report, Book 2: Education* (Washington, D.C.: U.S. Commission on Civil Rights, 1961), 149.

First County to Give Up All
Its Public Schools

U.S. News and World Report
June 22, 1959

On May 5, 1959, the Fourth Circuit Court of Appeals ordered school desegregation in Prince Edward to begin the coming September. In June, the county Board of Supervisors voted to withhold funds from the county's public school system and closed the schools. That month, *U.S. News and World Report* sent an editor to the county to report on the first community in the nation to abandon public education.

Here, in Prince Edward County, Va., the nation is going to see, for the first time, what happens when an entire community abandons public schools and turns to private schools to escape integration.

In four other Southern communities, individual schools have been closed when facing integration. But Prince Edward is going further than that.

When a federal court last May 5 ordered Prince Edward to admit Negroes into its white high school next autumn, not only the high school was ordered shut down. The county board of supervisors acted unanimously on June 3 to wipe out the county's entire system of 20 public schools—by voting no funds at all for public education in the 1959–60 school year.

In place of the public schools, this county is preparing to set up private schools—for whites only.

This test of private schools is one that will be watched closely, not only by the South, but by the entire country.

What kind of community is this, where such a major test is to be made? How do the people feel about giving up their public schools? Can they make their private-school plans work? . . .

Public schools are scattered throughout the county. There are 13 schools for Negroes, including a $900,000 high school built in 1953. There are seven schools for whites, including a high school in Farmville and a smaller high school in Worsham.

Whites point out that the valuation of the Negro schools exceeds that of the white schools. They cite the Negro high as the county's most modern school.

Negroes point out that some of their elementary schools are frame buildings without plumbing—and say they didn't get a good high school until they started suing in federal court.

Most of the schools here are small. Total enrollment for the entire county is 3,192. Of this total, 1,715 are Negroes and 1,477 are whites. If schools were completely integrated, whites often would be outnumbered in classrooms.

Walk up to almost any white man—on the streets, working on a farm, or going to church—and he will tell you: "We are not going to integrate."

This is almost always said without heat. Integration has been the major issue here since 1951. Yet you find almost no signs of racial bitterness.

Robert M. Bradshaw, a merchant, landowner and former postmaster of the village of Rice, put it this way:

"Our relations with the colored people now are just as fine as ever. There are no hard feelings. But we are just not going to integrate, that's all there is to it. I think almost 100 per cent of the white people here would rather abandon public schools than submit to integration. We are more united on this than on any issue I've ever encountered in this county. I don't know how long we can maintain private education, but we sure are going to give it a try."

The Rev. L. Francis Griffin, pastor of the Negroes' First Baptist Church and a local leader in the National Association for the Advancement of Colored People, said:

"I don't know of one white person that is on our side. There used to be a minister here who made some statement about segregation being un-Christian. But he left for another pastorate soon after that. Now not even the white ministers speak up for us."

Three years ago, a statement that "we prefer to abandon public schools . . . if that be necessary to preserve separation of the races" was signed by 4,100 persons—the overwhelming majority of the county's white adults.

Of 110 white high-school pupils writing themes on the subject of public schools recently, a teacher reports only one pupil said he would rather accept integration than close public schools.

The graduating class of Farmville's white high school donated the $66.92 balance in its class treasury to the fund being raised for private schools.

About Negro attitudes, Mr. Griffin said:

"There have been some Negroes weakening on their integration stand. There are those who say the time is not ripe yet and they would rather go slow. But I think the majority of Negroes are still firm for integration—maybe 70 or 80 per cent of them."

Talk to Negroes and you get two views.

Fred D. Reid, a Negro worker in a railway freight depot, says: "I am 100 per cent for equal educational facilities, but I am not for integration at this time. We have pushed too fast."

Another Negro, who preferred to remain anonymous, said: "Most of the colored people here want integration. If we lose our public schools for a while, then this is a sacrifice we have to make, and most of us think it is worthwhile."

Are Negroes being intimidated? To this question, Mr. Griffin replied:

"Well, there's always that threat of intimidation, either real or unreal. But the intimidation is only in an insidious form here, not in an open form."

It is in this setting that the white people of Prince Edward County are preparing to try private schools. They have set up the Prince Edward School Foundation, and are raising funds. They estimate they will need about $300,000 for the first year.

B. Blanton Hanbury, head of the foundation, says, "We don't anticipate any trouble raising the money." He points out that a few years ago, when a court order to integrate appeared imminent, "we raised $12,000 in cash and pledges totaling $200,000." Those pledges have expired, but new pledges are being solicited.

Of the $780,600 school budget which the board of supervisors turned down, about half would have come from county funds, the rest from State and federal aid. Elimination of the county's $392,000 contribution is expected to make possible a reduction in the county tax levy from the present $3.40 per $100 of assessed property valuation to about $1.60.

White citizens are being urged to contribute their tax savings to the private-school foundation.

The plan is to use churches, halls occupied by fraternal organizations and perhaps other buildings as schools. Most of the 72 white teachers in the public-school system are reported available for service in the private schools.

Says Mr. Hanbury: "I can guarantee that every white child in the county will be offered an education, and a good one—an accredited education."

What about the Negro children? Negroes say they have no plans yet for private schools. Their hope is that some court or a governmental agency higher than the county supervisors will step in to keep public schools open. If not, some say they will send their children away to school in other communities where they have relatives or friends. There are four public high schools for Negroes in neighboring counties within 25 miles of Farmville.

For most Negro youngsters, however, the prospect admittedly is that there will be no schools—and for the 70 Negro teachers, no jobs unless they move to other communities.

How long will Prince Edward go without public schools? The board of supervisors expresses the hope "that we may in due time be able to resume the operation of public schools in this county upon a basis acceptable to all the people of the county." But the board adds that, "knowing the people of this county as we do, we know that it is not possible to operate the schools" on an integrated basis.

QUESTIONS

1. In what ways was Prince Edward County making history in 1959? Why was Prince Edward the first county to abandon public education rather than integrate?
2. How are race relations in Prince Edward County described by those interviewed in this article?
3. What was the role of religion in the civil rights struggle in Prince Edward County? How did the white churches in the county respond to the school integration crisis?

Letter to President Eisenhower and Response

L. Francis Griffin
August 20 and 29, 1959

Reverend L. Francis Griffin, president of the newly formed Prince Edward County Christian Association, wrote an appeal to President Dwight D. Eisenhower for federal support for public education in the county. A little over a week later, an Eisenhower administration official sent a reply that offered no consolation to Reverend Griffin.

My dear Mr. President:

As Americans who believe in the authority and dignity of the law, we the members of the Prince Edward County Christian Association, appeal to you for whatever help you can offer in a tragic situation involving our county, state and nation.

We are citizens of a county involved in the now famous May 17, 1954 United States Supreme Court decision declaring racial segregation in public education to be unconstitutional. Five years after this decision, and nine years after legal action was instituted, Federal Court orders remain unobeyed. We submit that in a Christian democracy this is deplorable.

When the Supreme Court declined to grant a stay of the lower court's order requiring integration of the county public schools beginning September, 1959, the Prince Edward County Board of Supervisors (the law-making body of the county) declined to appropriate funds to operate any public school. No tax was levied for public school purposes.

As a result of this defiant and undemocratic action by the Board of Supervisors, approximately 3,300 children of both races are confronted with educational malnutrition.

The segregationists of the county are proclaiming in strong terms, "There will be no racial mixing in the public schools, regardless of cost." These benighted and confused people are attempting to operate private schools to circumvent the law encouched in our constitution. We do not believe this should be permitted.

We realize that in a representative democracy such as ours our governmental processes will become stagnant unless the education of citizens is broad enough to encourage maximum interest and participation according to one's ability without being hampered by artificial barriers and restrictions. Our advocacy of public education is strengthened when we realize that we no longer live in a provincial society. Today, we are part and parcel of a space age society and being such, if we expect the youth of Prince Edward County to compete with the youth of this nation and of the world as equals, we must provide for them the strongest system of public education possible. To rely on private education to fill these modern day needs is utter folly.

We believe that segregation in any form is morally and legally wrong, therefore, we prayerfully request that you use the full extent of your good office in the alleviation of our conditions in Prince Edward County, Virginia.

> Respectfully yours,
> L. Francis Griffin
> President
> Prince Edward County Christian Association
> Farmville, Virginia

Dear Mr. Griffin:

The President has asked me to acknowledge your letter to him of August twentieth. He appreciates your interest in writing concerning the difficulty being experienced in respect to the integration of the public schools of Prince Edward County.

The Supreme Court decision did not, as some suppose, require the States to have public schools. It merely held that if a State or locality did operate public schools, it could not deny admission to such schools solely on the ground of race or color. While the President deplores the action of the Board of Supervisors in depriving the children of Prince Edward County of opportunity for public education, he is powerless to take any action since public education is exclusively within the jurisdiction of the States—subject only to the requirements of the United States Constitution.

The President is fully sympathetic with the reasons that prompted your letter.

Sincerely,
Gerald D. Morgan
The Deputy Assistant to the President

Dwight D. Eisenhower: Records as President, White House Central Files, 1952–61, General File, box 917, 124-A-1, Negro Affairs, School Decision, Pro (5), Dwight D. Eisenhower Presidential Library, Abilene, Kansas.

QUESTIONS

1. Reverend L. Francis Griffin discussed the importance of a good education in his letter to the White House. What points did he make to increase the persuasiveness of his letter?
2. In his response to Griffin on behalf of President Dwight Eisenhower, Gerald Morgan noted that the president had no authority to reopen the schools. Why was this the case, and how did that contradict the position of Griffin and the NAACP?

A Good Example

Citizens' Council
October 1959

The Citizens' Council was a segregationist organization formed in Mississippi in July 1954 to oppose civil rights activism and the *Brown v. Board of Education* decision. The organization grew rapidly across the South and became one of the most influential segregationist organizations in the country.

In the fall of 1955, the Citizens' Council began publishing the *Citizens' Council* newspaper. The organization used the newspaper to promote a racist, segregationist philosophy, and provided political voice in the fight against civil rights and racial integration. By 1960, the circulation averaged fifty thousand copies per issue. Its editorial board included members of other southern segregationist groups, including the Defenders of State Sovereignty and Individual Liberties from Virginia.

The *Citizens' Council* newspaper reported on the Prince Edward private school program in October 1959. Editor William J. Simmons was a strong supporter of the county and helped to raise funds and obtain supplies for Prince Edward Academy.

Prince Edward County, Virginia, is showing the nation how a determined community can maintain segregation by turning to private schools.

The county, with a population of 8,600 whites and 6,500 Negroes has become the first county to close all its public schools rather than submit to "token" integration.

Determined white citizens have set up the Prince Edward School Foundation, an organization which has established a county-wide private school system for all school-aged white children.

While the 21 fully-equipped public school buildings remain vacant, the Foundation has found sufficient classrooms, teachers, books, and other physical supplies to assure every white child in the county an adequate education.

The Negro community, on the other hand, has shown a complete lack of concern over whether or not their children go to school, since the white citizens have demonstrated that Negroes definitely cannot go to white schools.

The NAACP has not offered to help, and has even persuaded the Negroes not to accept the help of the Foundation, which offered to set up a system of private schools for Negroes as well as for white students. The only conclusion to be drawn is that the NAACP has no real interest in the welfare and future of the Negro children. Obviously, the NAACP is agitating only for integration, not education.

Most of the schools operated by the Foundation are housed in churches, with the largest, the Prince Edward Academy, meeting in the Sunday School rooms of the Farmville Presbyterian Church.

The library has over 7,000 books contributed by persons and organizations in and out of Virginia and collected by the Richmond chapter of the United Daughters of the Confederacy.

Other classes are held in the local Moose hall and in privately owned buildings, including a movie theater which serves as an assembly hall.

More important than these physical facilities are the teachers, textbooks, and finances.

The private system has 66 teachers, all fully qualified according to standards set up by the state department of education. As for textbooks, Roy Pearson, superintendent of the private school system, says it "appears as though adequate books, old and new, are on hand."

The Foundation was reported by Louis Dahl, treasurer, to have $100,000 on hand, with pledges of over $200,000 more received from Virginia, and from such places as Massachusetts, California, Texas and New York.

Dahl told a news conference that contributions from out of the state have been coming in from people who think "we are fighting their battle."

Some equipment is still lacking. The system is in need of gym equipment, industrial arts and shop equipment, and some science laboratory equipment, but, as a whole, financing has been no problem to the people, who are willing to pay any price to keep their schools segregated.

To doubters who say that the sources of finance might dry up in future years, Pearson says that "Prince Edward will have private schools as long as public schools are required to be integrated."

If the NAACP thought the people of Prince Edward were bluffing, it knows differently now, as the white children continue their segregated education while the Negroes roam the streets.

The NAACP won its lawsuit to "integrate" in Prince Edward County. But the Negroes have lost their schools.

Citizens' Council: Official Paper of the Citizens' Councils (Jackson, Mississippi), October 1959. Reprinted courtesy of Edward H. Sebesta and the *Citizen's Council* newspaper website, http://www.citizenscouncils.com.

QUESTIONS

1. How did the *Citizens' Council* portray the white residents of Prince Edward County? How did the newspaper portray the black residents, and the actions of the NAACP?
2. Why do you think whites elsewhere in the South supported the county's decision to close its public schools?

The Prince Edward County Virginia Story

John C. Steck

March 15, 1960

When Prince Edward Academy opened in the fall of 1959, nearly 1,500 white children attended, only 100 fewer then the number that had been enrolled in the public schools.

Near the end of the first school year, the *Farmville Herald* published a pamphlet on the school situation written by John C. Steck, managing editor of the newspaper. Steck was also a member of the county Board of Supervisors from 1958 to 1977. Based primarily on the *Herald*'s coverage of events, "The Prince Edward County Virginia Story" offers the perspective of the white leadership on the closing of the public schools and the rise of the private school movement.

The story of Prince Edward County, Virginia, is essentially the story of a determined, united people and their arduous, but devoted labors, to preserve, by every legal and honorable means, a cherished institution, the education of their children.

It is a story without precedent, for these people lived in a period of historic crossroads for public education. They were the first to see this institution tormented and, finally after six agonizing years, toppled, from without.

It is a story of courage. The courage, first of all, of conviction, then of determination and, not the least, the courage of uncharted invention. To many it has meant consuming sacrifice of time, pleasure and normal pursuits as shock and dismay in the spring of 1954 have given way to dauntless action.

It is a story without hate for any man or any race. From almost the very beginning, these people enunciated, simply and without equivocation, that the education of their children must be left to them. Was it too much, they asked, that they be allowed to conduct it as they believe wise, best and profitable for white and Negro children alike? It was not, they maintained, and, if that could not be possible, then they would withdraw from public education.

The story hasn't the slightest trace of deceit, or of threat, or of mistreatment. Within two months of the United States Supreme Court's May 17, 1954 desegregation mandate, the county governing body had declared that it was "unalterably opposed to the operation of non-segregated public schools." In ensuing expressions of that body and of the white public, always given wide and honest dissemination, it would be declared down through the years of litigation:

The mixing of the races at the insistence of voices we cannot sanction, by means which we deem illegal, is not something to be lived with; not a pill to be swallowed. It simply cannot be tolerated. That, they made crystal clear quickly. Time has demonstrated that they have not tolerated it.

Today, nearly six years after the United States Supreme Court's historic decision, Prince Edward County, Virginia, has no public school system. It levies no taxes, it appropriates no funds—other than to pay the debt on its finest school, $850,000 R. R. Moton High School for Negroes—for public schools. Its $2,000,000 investment in three high schools, 17 elementary schools, busses, athletic fields and laboratories, faithfully accumulated despite limited economic resources, is idle. Not a room, or a single piece of equipment, touched.

Yet six months after taking this unprecedented American way to the only freedom they can tolerate, 1,500 of their white children, or 98 per cent of the eligible school population of that race, are attending accredited schools. They assemble from homes throughout the county in community corporation busses, driven by volunteers with a concern for freedom and honor. The high school athletic teams perform on a people-built and people-owned gridiron, grassed, lighted and pine forest encircled.

The transition from one to the other is the story of Prince Edward County, Virginia. Its chapters describe how the people negotiated the swift and tortuous rapids of federal intervention, to this point, at least, safely. Six years of harassing uncertainty has become a humble, but satisfying certainty with a bright horizon beyond.

Thus, it is a story of hope. These people have not succumbed to pressure. These people believed a certain thing, felt its accomplishment necessary, and now possess it. Perhaps, as well as anything else, the words of the address made to the last graduating seniors of Farmville High School in June, 1959, tell the story. The words are those of James Jackson Kilpatrick, editor of *The Richmond News Leader:*

"Yours is a small voice, crying boldly to a suddenly and soberly attentive land, that here in Prince Edward, free men survive who face an oligarchy unafraid.

"I suppose that all of us regret the necessity for the decision your county has at long last found inescapable. You who have known the value of public free schools will regret the suspension of these public school values most keenly; their replacement will demand of you sacrifice, and years of effort and a devotion to principle not many men are capable of sustaining.

"Yet by this action a great part of the South has said through Prince Edward, 'Yes, we believe in public schools, but we do not believe in public schools at any price.' You have said, as man has almost forgotten how to say, that you will provide for yourself, as free men, a better, happier life than the super-state hungers to thrust upon you from above."

The story has one unfinished chapter. It concerns the 1,700 Negro children without schooling. Regardless of the fact that certain Negro leaders precipitated this problem in Prince Edward County, the circumstances of these youngsters is not overlooked. They will not be forgotten, nor forsaken to their own people's dim, faint, undisciplined groping.

An arrogant, misguided and uninformed outside Negro leadership, that of the National Association for the Advancement of Colored People, particularly its Virginia leaders, still cries blatantly, at their people within the county, as did Oliver W. Hill, Richmond Negro and chief of the NAACP's Virginia legal staff, in June, 1959:

"The people who control Prince Edward County are a type known as reactionaries, who must rule or ruin, and never exercise any intelligence to a new situation." Within the very confines of the county, he told the same Negro rally it was reactionaries who crucified Jesus Christ, who were responsible for the unfair taxation practices that led to the American Revolution, and who caused the Civil War.

No, the voices like that of Oliver W. Hill will not bring back schools for the Negroes. The white peoples' efforts to help them restore education this winter of 1960 were ignored under top-level NAACP pressure, which brought Roy Wilkins, national executive secretary, to the county to defeat the move.

But Prince Edward's indigenous store of determination, of conviction, of courage and invention will complete the unfinished chapter, too—in her people's own way.

Southern States' Pamphlet Collection, box 25, no. 15, Albert and Shirley Small Special Collections Library, University of Virginia, Charlottesville.

QUESTIONS

1. John C. Steck argued that the Prince Edward story was a "story without hate for any man or any race." Do you agree with this assessment?
2. How did Steck portray the NAACP? Did you find his argument convincing?

Resignation of the School Board of Prince Edward County

April 26, 1960

The federal court order requiring desegregation and the Board of Supervisors' decision to close the public school system placed the Prince Edward County School Board in a difficult situation. Following the *Brown* decision, the school board supported both continuing segregation and maintaining public education. With the public schools now closed, local residents debated what to do with the school facilities and questioned the need for a board.

The Prince Edward School Foundation had been formed to establish a white, private school program to replace the closed public schools. The board of directors included J. Barrye Wall, publisher of the *Farmville Herald*; former Virginia governor William Tuck; Congressman Watkins Abbitt; attorney William Old, a leading proponent of states' rights (see p. 73); and various other political and business leaders from across Southside Virginia. Many of these men were members of the Defenders of State Sovereignty and Individual Liberties.

The foundation leadership attended the county school board meeting in January 1960 and requested that the closed white high school be declared surplus property, which would allow the county Board of Supervisors to sell the building to the private school foundation. The school board declined the request and instead recommended a county-wide referendum be held to address the issue. Shortly thereafter, five of the six men on the school board resigned. To explain their decisions and resignations, the board issued the following statement.

To the people of Prince Edward County, Virginia:

The members of the School Board of Prince Edward County have been the targets for much criticism in recent months. We do not expect all the actions of the Board to be completely acceptable to all our citizens. We do feel that many who have criticized our actions have done so because they did not fully or accurately know many of the facts which were available to the Board and on which our decisions were based. We fear also that some of our critics have not fully considered the many problems which we feel must be resolved by any new system of education that takes over the job done by the public schools throughout the 90 years that they have operated in our State. . . .

We make this report to our people without any intention to blame anyone. This is a report to the citizens of Prince Edward County—nothing more.

We desire to start with a brief summary of the events that have taken place. Surely it must be well known in Prince Edward County that the School Board for nearly ten years has used every legal means to avoid integration of our schools. All the way through the lower courts up to the Supreme Court three times the School Board has taken the fight to resist integration in our schools. In this fight we have been assisted by one of the ablest legal firms in Virginia. . . . We also have been tremendously aided by competent local counsel. Incidentally, early in this long legal battle we were advised by our lawyers to say as little as possible about what we were doing or planned to do. It was felt that any statement might be turned against us in court. We make this explanation simply to answer any of our citizens who may feel that members of the School Board should have been more outspoken.

We fought this legal battle because we believed and continue to believe that education can best be provided in this County for the children of both races in segregated schools. Moreover, we fought this battle because we believe in public schools and that every possible effort should be made to operate them in a manner acceptable to our people. As members of the School Board, we are your trustees. In this capacity you gave us a moral obligation to provide education for your children through a system of public education so long as it is possible to do so.

It is well known by now that the School Board can operate schools only if the Board of Supervisors appropriates the necessary money. It has always been necessary for the School Board to go before the Supervisors each year with a budget and present its requests for funds with which to operate the schools. Recognizing this point, the Board of Supervisors decided in 1955 to appropriate money to the School Board only one month at a time. We gave our whole-hearted support and fullest cooperation to the Board of Supervisors in this method of financing. We do not know of any seriously unsatisfactory results of this procedure. Moreover, we know that the same system is now being following in several other Virginia counties.

Then in June 1959, the Board of Supervisors refused to appropriate any money for the operation of schools, for administration or for maintenance and insurance of buildings. This action was taken in spite of the successful operation of schools on a month-to-month basis; in spite of an appeal pending in the courts which had not been finally settled; and in spite of the fact, known by the Supervisors, that there was not a single application before the School Board for the assignment of a Negro pupil to a white school. Furthermore, there was already in the hands of the School Board a 100 per cent return of Negro registration applications for assignment to the R. R. Moton High School in 1959–60 . . .

When the Board of Supervisors denied any funds for schools, the School Board was faced with many new problems. It had a four-year contract for the employment of the Superintendent of Schools who had for 41 years rendered distinguished service to the County in that office. As trustees of the citizens of the County, we had the responsibility of preparing school properties for the winter and of keeping fire insurance in force. Incidentally, the obligation of making payments on the bonded debt of the County for schools is a legal obligation of the Board of Supervisors. They made appropriations for these debt payments, but denied the requests of the School Board for funds with which to meet its obligations such as those mentioned above. . . .

Since the action of the Board of Supervisors in June of 1959, many people have asked: "Why do we need a School Board and a Superintendent since we no longer have any public schools?" Here are some of the things that simply had to be done by someone. The whole matter of winterizing the buildings and buses had to be handled. The same was true of the question of insurance on the buildings. Arrangements had to be made for preservation of the records of the pupils and others and for their use when needed. For example, transcripts of many of these records had to be sent to other schools upon request of the pupils. The State tuition grant law left with the School Board responsibility for receiving applications for these grants and for certifying eligibility to the State Board of Education. There have been some applications. An annual report on the operation of the schools for the year 1958–59 had to be prepared by the Superintendent after the close of the year on June 30, 1959. This report is required by the laws of the State. Many decisions had to be made as to what to do with property located in the schools and which was donated by some group or individual. . . . We remind you that the Superintendent, the Clerk and the members of the School Board continued to serve in these essential matters without any assurance of compensation. . . .

It will be recalled that representatives of the Prince Edward School Foundation appeared before the School Board at its meeting on January 11, 1960, requesting us to declare the Farmville High School property surplus and to make it available for sale. These representatives declined, however, to make further commitments for the Foundation at that time. We deferred action until the following week, January 18th, when a large number of citizens appeared at a meeting of the Board to discuss the pros and cons of this request. Following this open discussion, the Board passed the following resolution:

"After having thoroughly considered this request, on motion made and unanimously adopted, the following resolution was passed:

"At this time, the School Board does not feel that it should take the sole responsibility of selling the main white high school in the County. This school belongs to the people of Prince Edward County, and State law provides a procedure whereby the voters may require and approve such a sale. We believe this statute should be followed here."

The next day, the Foundation officials announced that they were not interested in purchasing the Farmville High School property.

It should be very clear that means exist whereby the people of the County can decide whether the property should or should not be declared surplus. We felt, and continue to feel, that so grave a matter should not be decided by six people when the State law provides a readily usable method of getting an expression of the will of all the people. That should be done, as the law contemplates, through a secret ballot referendum. We do not believe that the people should be bypassed.

Furthermore, there is a very practical side to this problem. Our counsel advise us that, in their opinion, the sale of a school building for an inadequate price to an organization that intends to continue to use the building as a school raises grave legal problems. Action to enjoin such a sale would be very likely. It would, in the opinion of our counsel, be much easier to defend a sale that resulted from a referendum approving the sale. We doubt whether it is in the best interest of the County for it to be embroiled at this time in further difficult litigation; we believe that the County should be put in the best position possible to defend further litigation. Sale after a referendum is much to be preferred from this point of view. . . .

In its decisions the School Board has been guided by the fundamental belief that education must be provided for all the school age children of the entire County. Anything short of this we regard as contrary to the best interests of all of us in the long run. We know that educated citizens are absolutely essential to the very existence of democracy in local affairs as well as in state and national ones. If a community leaves uneducated any large portion of its citizens, because they cannot afford its cost, or for any other reason, it inevitably creates for itself enormous problems in welfare, delinquency, crime and unemployment. It means numbers of illiterate laborers which are difficult to absorb in the labor force. Today business and industry are demanding a higher level of training of its employees than ever before.

We are aware that the Prince Edward Foundation has obtained contributions from those who have school age children and those who do not. No white child was denied admission to the Foundation's schools for the session 1959–60 because his parents could not make a contribution or because they could afford only a small gift. For this stand we are grateful. Yet the people of Prince Edward County must face the question of whether this method of voluntary support of schools can be depended upon year in and year out through good times and bad to pay the cost of education for all. Education must meet standards of quality over a period of many years and be conducted by teachers and administrators of dedicated purpose and training if it is to continue to be effective to meet the needs of our people.

Unless some new system of education for all can take over the whole job of the public schools and have its cost guaranteed in a reasonable manner, we fear the economic consequences to the County. This year, for example, when the people of the County have paid all of the cost of education in the County, we have seen at least a half million dollars not come into the economic life of the County which did come in earlier years. We refer specifically here to two items. In the past we have received approximately $400,000 from the State for operation of public schools. Also in the past the large taxpaying corporations in the County have paid approximately $100,000 in local taxes. This year, this money did not come to the County in any form.

We believe that the concerns expressed herein are sufficient to indicate some of the reasons why we six men were unwilling alone to declare the Farmville High School Property surplus. We cannot base our decisions in this crucial matter on a short term view. We must ask ourselves what are the consequences for the next five, ten or more years, before we completely and finally dispose of the two million dollars worth of school property our citizens have provided with considerable sacrifice. We believe that, if a referendum were called in which each voter would register his decision in a secret ballot, there could be a free and open debate of the issues. Only through such a free debate of possible courses of action for the future education of our children can we possibly chart the right course. But no effort has yet been made to initiate action for a referendum. A majority of us are unwilling at this time in good conscience to vote to declare the High School surplus, but we cannot sit idly by and see all our school buildings unused forever. Other people who are admirably qualified to be members of the Prince Edward School Board may reach, after consideration, conclusions entirely different from ours. We feel that we can no longer be useful members of the School Board and we are therefore submitting our resignations as members of the School Board.

But the people must know that a School Board is necessary in fact as well as required by law even though no schools are operated in the County. . . . The school records of the County are invaluable; people every day consult them for purposes that range from getting into college to obtaining social security benefits. These records must be preserved and it is the duty of the School Board to preserve them.

A School Board is necessary and a new Board will no doubt be promptly appointed.

"School Board Report," *Farmville Herald*, April 29, 1960.

QUESTIONS

1. Why did the school board resign in 1960, and how did this reflect its members' concern over the closing of the county's public schools?
2. In what ways did the school board believe that county residents were being misled by those who supported private school education in Prince Edward County?

Statement to the U.S. Commission on Civil Rights

L. Francis Griffin

February 25–26, 1961

The U.S. Commission on Civil Rights is a federal agency, established by Congress in 1957, that investigates, reports on, and recommends civil rights policy. Its 1961 annual conference, held in Williamsburg, Virginia, focused on the problems facing "schools in transition," and challenges related to school integration were central to the discussions.

Reverend L. Francis Griffin submitted a statement to the conference on behalf of the African American community of Prince Edward County. Griffin's statement addressed the black community's desire for better educational opportunities and the problems created by the closure of the public schools. Griffin harshly criticized the actions of Prince Edward County's elected officials.

Gentlemen, I am pleased to have this opportunity and means to address you on a subject of uttermost importance in my mind—the closed public schools in Prince Edward County, Va. The action of the board of supervisors in closing public schools represents a complete abdication of all that democracy stands for. It is very depressing, to say the least, to be constantly aware that we live in the only place in the United States that has no public schools.

I trust that the following report will give you a clearer insight into the shameful situation that exists in our county. Despite the constant threat of reprisals, some of us are determined to see democracy become an actuality in Prince Edward County and throughout America regardless of the attitude of diehard segregationists.

Prince Edward County is one of the several Virginia counties situated in the so-called Black Belt of Virginia. The Black Belt is a rather loosely defined geographical political area where the Negro population approximates or exceeds the white population.

Racial patterns evident in Virginia's Black Belt follow very closely the patterns found in similar densely Negro-populated areas of other Southern States, included among which are South Carolina, Georgia, Alabama, and Mississippi.

Prince Edward County, like many of her counterparts in many of the above-mentioned States, has traditionally been a strict adherent to the "separate but unequal" doctrine in all matters pertaining to race. Voting has been discouraged. Public employment offers only the most menial job opportunities to the Negro, and even in these he is the last to be hired and the first to be fired. In private employment the same discriminatory pattern follows. More than likely the few who satisfy the prejudiced whims of the white employer hold such privileged employment with tenure that is in direct proportion to the degree to which they are willing to forfeit their dignity, manhood, and citizenship rights as free Americans. Public educational opportunities at all levels (elementary, secondary, and collegiate) have followed the same pattern.

Negro parents, having been conditioned by the innumerable overt and subtle practices of racial discrimination, found themselves at the midcentury mark (1950) frustrated and in a position bordering on utter despair.

However, in April of 1951, the Biblical passage ". . . and a little child shall lead them," came into play. The Negro high school population, numbering 456, noting that their parents were either unable to, reluctant, or indifferent toward doing anything about the educational discrimination they and other Negro pupils were forced to suffer, startled the world with the now famous R. R. Moton High School strike.

The gallant young Americans of color appealed to their parents for support, and received it. The children and their parents appealed to the National Association for the Advancement of Colored People for assistance, and received it.

The Prince Edward County authorities refused to give any consideration to the requests of these children and their parents in their quest for nondiscriminatory public educational opportunities. To secure the constitutional rights of their children, action in the Federal courts followed.

Three years later, the Supreme Court of the United States, in its now famous May 17, 1954, decision, declared racial segregation in public education to be unconstitutional. The NAACP, heralding the Supreme Court decision as being the law of the land, was jubilant in its expectations that, at long last, democracy in education would find its way into the public schools of Prince Edward County. However, history has proved otherwise, for it has been made unmistakably clear that the Constitution of the United States and the Court's interpretation thereof mean little, if anything, when prejudiced southern whites such as those at the helm of authority in Prince Edward County are confronted by Negroes who seek and demand their basic constitutional rights.

Seven years after the historic May 17, 1954, U.S. Supreme Court decision, and 10 years after legal action was instituted, Federal court orders remain unobeyed.

When the Supreme Court declined to grant a stay of the lower court's order requiring integration of the county public schools beginning September 1959, the Prince Edward County Board of Supervisors (the lawmaking body of the county) declined to appropriate funds to operate any public school. No tax was levied for public school purposes that year, and none has been levied since.

As a result of this defiant and undemocratic action by the board of supervisors, more than 3,300 children of both races were and are confronted with the specter of educational malnutrition.

The segregationists of the county, waving the Confederate battle flag, proclaim in loud and uncouth terms, "There will be no racial mixing in the public schools regardless of the cost."

These benighted and confused people are attempting to delude the county's white population into believing that private schools are the answer to the white children's educational malnutrition. This same group has constantly appealed to certain elements of the Negro community to forfeit the Negro children's dignity and constitutional rights by the acceptance of a pre-1954 status quo (i. e., the Negroes of Prince Edward County will meekly and without complaint return to a rigid and completely racially segregated society).

We realize that in a representative democracy such as ours our governmental processes will become stagnant unless the education of citizens is broad enough to encourage maximum interest and participation according to one's ability without being hampered by artificial barriers and restrictions. Our advocacy of public education is strengthened when we realize that we no longer live in a provincial society. Today, we are part and parcel of a space-age society and, being such, if we expect the youth of Prince Edward County to compete with the other youth of this Nation and of the world as equals we must provide for them the strongest system of public education possible. To rely on private education to fill these modern-day needs is utter folly. . . .

We maintain that our action in pressing for relief through the courts was not the result of outside agitators, but, rather, the result of the vicious pattern itself. When one keeps before oneself the fact that resentment was being built up of gigantic proportions in the minds of Negroes through the years because of obvious maltreatment, it is not difficult for normal people to understand open rebellion on the part of Negro citizens of the county or any other oppressed people.

For an oppressed people to continue living under a system designed to relegate them to a subordinate role and a second-class citizenship and not seek all legal, moral, and democratic methods to correct the evil, they would have to be absolute degenerates. We are not ready to submit that all Negroes in Prince Edward County, Va., are degenerates.

We Negroes who live in the county are fully aware that all of the white children and their parents are not satisfied with present conditions in the county;

however, every white person who shows any sign of weakening or voices the mildest protest is promptly set upon by the "power interests" of the community. Subtle methods of harassment are being thought up daily to use against white persons who fall out of step with massive resistance.

At this very moment, a petition is being circulated against two members of the Longwood College faculty in Farmville, requesting their removal for expressing moderate views. The family of a prominent white businessman was socially ostracized for the same reason. There are any number of incidents of this type that we in the community know of; however, they are difficult at present to document because individual whites are fearful of further harassments and reprisals. Truly, the proverbial shoe is on the other foot, for, whereas at one time reprisals were against the Negroes of the county, it is now against whites to keep them in line.

These Iron Curtain tactics, whether practiced against white or black, should not be a part of the American way of life. Russia and her satellites allegedly would do things of this nature without any moral qualms, but, sirs, this is not Russia: This is America—a Christian, democratic nation.

Again, it is significant to note that in a Christian, democratic society the voice of the prophet has been stifled and hushed. All of the white ministers and their church congregations, without exception, and many of the Negro ministers and their congregations, have failed to raise their voices against this social evil. Thus, you can see that the community is being affected economically, politically, socially, and religiously. . . .

Now, sirs, I do not propose to know the law, but I know what the law ought to be in a democratic society. In every instance "human rights" should be above "State rights." If our minds and souls had kept pace with our technology we would know that law and human dignity are far more important than a people's prejudices, mores, customs, and traditions.

Will Prince Edward County become America's greatest disgrace? Will the well over 1,500 Negro boys and girls be the forgotten and lost ones in America? These are the questions that will have to be answered quickly if America is to maintain her position of world leadership. The tragedy is not in the fact that these children, white and black, are out of school. The real tragedy is that this could happen in America and arouse no more action than it has. . . .

This report cannot fully tell the story of all the problems created by closing the schools in Prince Edward. It is a story of frustrated adults and children, of families torn apart while children are in the formative, impressionable years, when they need the constant assuring love and guidance of both parents. This is a story of hatred, reprisals, harassments in which the principal characters are determined that stubborn wills are far more important than our inherited democratic way of life, and the preservation of a free public school system. It can only give an insight into a problem of vast proportions. We trust that it will in some way prove helpful to you gentlemen in your deliberations.

Written statement submitted to the Third Annual Conference on Problems of Schools in Transition, Records of the U.S. Commission on Civil Rights, Record Group 453, no. 1076669, 1953–78, National Archives and Records Administration, Washington, D.C.

QUESTIONS

1. What language here gives insight into the feelings of Reverend L. Francis Griffin in the spring of 1961?
2. How did Griffin describe the effects of the closed public schools in Prince Edward County?
3. What similarities do you note between this statement and Griffin's letter to President Dwight Eisenhower (see p. 119)? What is the essence of Griffin's argument?

Lessons from Prince Edward County

Helen Estes Baker
April 1961

When the public schools closed in Prince Edward County, several outside organizations offered assistance to the black community and its displaced students, including the American Friends Service Committee (AFSC), a Quaker organization established in 1917 to promote peace and justice. Members of the Philadelphia Quaker Meeting had run the first schools for African Americans in Prince Edward following the Civil War. Now, in 1960, the AFSC organized the Emergency Student Placement Project, which relocated dozens of black students to live with families outside of the county to continue their education. The AFSC also opened an office in Farmville, which served as its center for community development work in Prince Edward for the next five years.

From October 1960 to August 1961, Helen Estes Baker ran the AFSC's Farmville office. A devout African American Quaker, Baker worked with the county's displaced black students and sought to restore communication between blacks and whites in the county. In this article written for the Virginia Teachers Association, Baker explains the lessons of the school closing crisis for Virginia schoolteachers.

The major project of the American Friends Society in Prince Edward County involved what we considered to be the prior emergency—taking out of the county the older children who would be lost to education if they stayed out of school two years. Forty-seven Prince Edward children were selected at random to go to seven cities in the north and midwest. The children were not selected on the basis of any economics or standing in school—only on the basis of whether their parents said that they could go. (Kittrel College in North Carolina invited an additional 50 to enroll at that school—a magnanimous gesture.)

The children were placed in 47 Negro and white homes in these seven cities. A committee in each city was named to be responsible for the child in addition to the foster parents. Two tutors were also assigned to each child to help them overcome the difficulties they encountered in the northern schools.

The children were consistently weak in English and even more so in mathematics. I suppose that this is part of problem of separate but unequal schools which we inevitably encounter in the South.

The homes were carefully selected. None of them was in the top economic strata, but all were good homes operated on sound principles.

The 47 students sent to schools in the north and midwest had great difficulty settling down to doing homework. In these schools, children were required to do four to six hours of homework. The Prince Edward children had been accustomed to doing no homework. . . .

There was a notable lack of knowledge about themselves, their heritage, about the men and women of their race who had made outstanding contributions to America and to civilization. All knew about a few—maybe four or five—outstanding Negroes—Marian Anderson, George Washington Carver, Mrs. Bethune. But they did not have the facts about Negroes that would give them a sense of dignity—a sense of worthwhileness—that would permit them to move around in the majority society.

What then are the emphases which teachers must adopt in the light of all that we have learned from the Prince Edward situation? What must be the concern of teachers interested in building citizens?

1. We must recognize that the kind of citizenship we teach must be the kind that operates above the intra-racial strata. Teachers had not seen to it that there were enough voters to prevent the kind of action taken by the majority group in Prince Edward County.

2. The kind of citizenship taught must be one which teaches a love for the institutions and laws under which we operate in this nation. The actions of the white people in Prince Edward County in closing the schools do not

demonstrate that they have this love and respect for the principles, the laws, the institutions which are America's.

3. Token integration is not enough. We must either have desegregation, or where ghetto living makes that impossible, then we must have enough voters in order to have representation on the boards which control our destiny. If the school boards and other boards which control our lives are made up of people who have a concept of a master race, then we have no chance of getting a fair deal. A school board will not require the same thing of Negro teachers that they do of white teachers if they are going to preserve a master race. A school board is not going to seek the strongest principal—one who will put the needs of the children above all else—if the members of the board wish to preserve the concept of a master race.

4. The citizenship we teach must not emphasize being a Negro. We must teach that citizenship is an American property. Children must be taught to apply for jobs because they are capable people, and not to refrain from applying because they are Negroes. We must teach more about our government, how it operates. When we take children to Washington, we must take them to the White House, the Congress, the Department of Justice.

5. The catastrophe in Prince Edward County is not local. The March 23 and March 30 issues of the *Manchester Guardian*, published in London, England, carried full-page editorials on Farmville, Virginia. Prince Edward County has learned in the past two years that it is a part of the world. Our children must learn about the world. . . .

6. We have suffered a kind of loss in Prince Edward County for which we will never finish paying. Seven hundred American children—not white, colored—but 700 children have been lost forever to education. How many artists, physicists, potential presidents we have lost, we will never know.

7. "Prince Edward County" can happen in your county.

8. In spite of the seeming hopelessness and the pathos of the Prince Edward situation, we still live in a very good country. There is concern for the children of Prince Edward County all over America. The job of opening the schools in Prince Edward County is no longer Prince Edward's job. It is Washington's job. We have every reason to believe that the schools will open in October. Eighteen hundred white children and 1,700 Negro children have been deprived of education for two years. There's a tremendous job to be done and you have a part in it.

Virginia Teacher's Bulletin, April 1961.

QUESTIONS

1. What were Helen Baker's main points about the AFSC's Emergency Student Placement Project?
2. What advice did she offer to schoolteachers based on the experience of Prince Edward County?
3. Baker suggested that token desegregation would not be enough to bring about real change. Why did she feel this way?

5

"The Closed Schools"

John F. Kennedy began his presidency seeking to balance his concern for the rights of black southerners with his need to maintain the political support of white southern leaders. As chairmen of the Senate and House Finance Committees, respectively, Senator Harry F. Byrd and Congressman Howard W. Smith, both from Virginia and leading segregationists, wielded significant control on federal government policy and had the power to thwart any actions taken by the president to advance civil rights for African Americans.

Civil rights activities across the South, including the Freedom Rides in 1961, the desegregation of the University of Mississippi in 1962, and the Birmingham demonstrations in 1963, strongly influenced the president's evolving position on civil rights. In June 1963, Kennedy proposed new federal civil rights legislation that, following his death, was enacted as the Civil Rights Act of 1964.

President Kennedy appointed his younger brother Robert F. Kennedy to serve as attorney general of the United States. On May 26, 1961, in his first official speech, Robert Kennedy spoke about the public school crisis in Prince Edward County: "I cannot believe that anyone can support a principle which prevents more than a thousand of our children in one county from attending public school—especially when this step was taken to circumvent the orders of the court."[1] Robert Kennedy would later emerge as a key figure in finding a resolution to the closed public schools.

In August 1962, NBC News broadcast a half-hour television special on the closed schools of Prince Edward County, presenting the school crisis to a national television audience. Interviewed in the program was Dr. C. G. Gordon Moss, professor of history and dean at Longwood College, one of the few white citizens who publicly opposed the segregationist leadership of the county and the closing of the public schools. When asked about the effects of three years without education, Moss described a "crippled generation" of children.

In the same television program, Reverend L. Francis Griffin spoke of the heavy responsibility he felt for the out-of-school children: "It has always been a moral debate whether we had the right, or I as an individual had the moral right, to involve other people in this movement, but we believe that the ultimate end is worth the sacrifice that is being made on the part of negro children and negro parents in the community."[2]

Worn down by stress, Reverend Griffin spent a month in a Veteran's Administration hospital that spring, recovering from surgery that removed half of his ulcerated stomach. Upon returning home, he confided in a letter to a friend, "The school problem is a minor problem in comparison with what has been going on in this county over many years. Democracy is being crucified daily—both the middle class whites and the negroes are innocent victims—while races are clashing with each other over the school problem."[3]

The voices of white moderation in the county had been suppressed by social, political, and economic pressures. Few whites spoke up for public schools, and even fewer for integrated education. The white churches remained silent on the moral issues presented by the closed public schools. This silence gave the impression that the white community had fully united behind the actions of county officials and segregationist leaders.

In the face of these enormous challenges, Griffin's moral and spiritual leadership was praised in a telegram he received in the fall of 1962 from Reverend Dr. Martin Luther King Jr.: "Once every few generations God molds an unusual man. The long hard struggle in which you have been engaged in Prince Edward County manifests that he has used you in a unique way. America will never be able to calculate what your leadership will mean in the future to public education in our democracy. My prayers and best wishes are with you constantly. Martin Luther King Jr., President SCLC."[4]

NOTES

1. Attorney General Robert F. Kennedy, Law Day Address, University of Georgia, May 6, 1961, U.S. Department of Justice Archives, Washington, D.C.

2. NBC News Special Report, "The Crippled Generation," broadcast, August 3, 1962, NBCUniversal Archives, New York.

3. Reverend L. Francis Griffin to Sarah Patton Boyle, April 8, 1962, Papers of Sarah Patton Boyle, Accession #8003-a, -b, box 2, Albert and Shirley Small Special Collections Library, University of Virginia, Charlottesville.

4. Martin Luther King Jr. to Reverend L. Francis Griffin, October 8, 1962, telegram, Martin Luther King Jr. Papers, box 7, folder 3, Martin Luther King Jr. Center for Nonviolent Social Change, Inc., Atlanta.

A Defense of Prince Edward County

Harry F. Byrd

May 17, 1961

On the seventh anniversary of the *Brown v. Board of Education* decision, Harry F. Byrd delivered this speech about the Prince Edward County school crisis on the floor of the U.S. Senate. The public schools in the county had been closed for two years, and the anniversary of *Brown* brought attention to the county's actions.

Action by the National Association for the Advancement of Colored People resulted in withdrawal of Prince Edward County support of public schools. Under NAACP influence colored leaders in the county will neither provide for education of their children nor accept assistance from the white people of the county.

In short, the NAACP is more interested in the integration of public school children than it is in the education of colored children; and the NAACP, alone, is responsible for the fact that 1,700 colored children in Prince Edward County are not now attending good schools with qualified teachers.

White people of the county deplore the fact that colored children of the community are being kept out of school; but everyone should be aware that so long as this condition can be maintained, the NAACP and others can make propaganda use of it to discredit the county's efforts to restore full and complete educational facilities. This has been done and it is being done now.

White citizens of Prince Edward have successfully established a system of accredited schools for their children, and they have offered to do the same thing for colored children. This offer has been open and standing since December 1959, but parents of only one colored child have dared to submit an application for enrollment.

When Negro leaders did nothing to provide education for colored children in the county, white citizens formed a corporation in the name of "Southside Schools, Inc.," to provide educational opportunities for Negro students. Officers of the corporation communicated with parents of every potential colored student in the county.

In a letter to every Negro parent in Prince Edward, dated December 19, 1959, R. B. Hargrove, president of the corporation said:

"Southside Schools, Inc., has been formed to provide schools for those Negro children who have not been able to get an education since the public schools were closed this fall.

"It is our intention to set up good schools, get qualified teachers, and, so that the Negro children of this county will not lose time from school, to run these schools at least 180 days, which is a full school year. The actual location of the schools and the securing of the teachers will be determined after all applications have been received.

"There are funds available from the State of Virginia to pay tuition for children when public schools are closed. The board of this corporation has set a tuition charge of $240 per child. Therefore, each parent can apply for this money after enrolling, which will pay for educating your child. How to do this will be explained to you and help given by this corporation after your child is enrolled in school. . . ."

The letter enclosed a form for use in applying for admission to the school. The form consisted simply of blanks for the name; date and place of birth; grade completed, and last school attended; and the name and address of parent or guardian; signature and date. . . .

To this date there has been only one application for school enrollment in response to this letter.

Members of the board of Southside Schools, Inc., are well known, outstanding citizens of the community. The Negroes of Prince Edward County have every reason to trust them, and confide in them. . . .

When this letter, offering schools to colored children in Prince Edward, went out, Oliver W. Hill, the Negro lawyer representing NAACP in Richmond, and Roy Wilkins, NAACP executive director from New York, made a hurried return to the county. They showed up at a Christmas party for the county's colored children on December 23, 1959.

Hill used such an occasion as the Christmas party for colored children to tell their parents that:

"Some benighted individuals are trying to entice you away from your rights by promising you a private school.

"All you are losing is 1 or 2 years of Jim Crow education, but at the same time in your leisure you can gather more basic education than you would in 5 years of Jim Crow schools."

Accepting this kind of outside guidance for their "advancement," instead of the offers of assistance from their white neighbors who want to work with them for the establishment of schools, the colored people of Prince Edward County have ignored educational opportunities provided for them.

Noting the clear indications of intimidation by the NAACP—when only one application for enrollment was received—officials of Southside Schools, Inc., promised that the identity of applicants for enrollment would not be disclosed until the schools were open. But even this did not result in any more applications.

Later, members of the board of Southside Schools, Inc., personally visited their Negro friends in each magisterial district in the county, urging them to take advantage of the opportunities to get the schools open for their children.

After these visits they called an interracial meeting on June 30, 1960, for the same purpose. The proceedings of the meeting were not published, but the fact remains that all efforts to persuade Negroes in Prince Edward County to accept the educational opportunities offered to them have been totally unsuccessful.

Prince Edward supervisors have adopted ordinances to provide educational opportunities for all children, white and Negro. From the beginning the Prince Edward people have done all they could to encourage Negroes in the county to take advantage of the school facilities that were offered.

Great publicity has been given the Prince Edward case. Much of the publicity consists of more propaganda than fact. . . .

The white people of the county are still ready and eager to help, but the fact remains that the NAACP, which precipitated the problem in the first place, is still keeping 1,700 Negro children in Prince Edward County out of school.

Proceedings and Debates of the 87th Congress, 1st Session, Wednesday, May 17, 1961, *Congressional Record* (Washington, D.C.: U.S. Government Printing Office, 1961), 8194–95.

QUESTIONS

1. What were the principal arguments offered by Senator Harry Byrd? Do you find this speech convincing?
2. Why do you think the black community of Prince Edward County refused the offer made by Southside Schools, Inc., to create a private school for local black students?
3. How would the black residents of Prince Edward County have responded to Byrd's speech? On which points would they have disagreed with him?

Speech on the Seventh Anniversary of the May 17 Decision of the U.S. Supreme Court

Oliver W. Hill

May 20, 1961

Three days after Senator Harry Byrd delivered his speech, Oliver W. Hill responded with a speech in Farmville supporting the NAACP and its efforts for school integration. Hill, attorney for black plaintiffs in the Prince Edward school litigation since 1951, had recently resigned his position with the NAACP to accept a position in the administration of President John F. Kennedy.

It is most appropriate that we assemble here in Farmville, the political center of Prince Edward County, at this time to celebrate the seventh anniversary of the decision of the Supreme Court of the United States in which the constitutional provisions and the laws of the Commonwealth of Virginia requiring racial segregation in public schools were declared invalid.

There are things that need to be said to and heard by those whom Judge Gravatt fondly refers to as the "good people" of Prince Edward County, meaning, of course, the white segregationists, as well as things that need to be said to and heard by those whom I regard as the "good people" of this county, namely, those persons interested in the development, extension and orderly evolution of the principles and ideals set forth in the Declaration of Independence and guaranteed by the Constitution of the United States—the right of a person to be regarded and treated, publicly and privately, as an individual.

If I had to state a subject for my remarks, I would say that I am going to speak about "Common Sense, Tyranny, Love and Affection, and Hysteria."

The situation here requires calm reflection and plain talk—without rancor or malice—and hard, constructive work. From time to time, various segregationists have proclaimed that the responsibility for the failure of this county to provide any elementary or secondary educational facilities for over 1,700 Negro children of school age rests upon the NAACP and individuals who think as I do. These segregationists say that when the public schools of this county were closed in 1959, Judge Gravatt's "good people" offered to provide separate "private" schools for Negroes, but that the NAACP and those of us prominently identified with the NAACP advised the Negroes of this county not to accept this offer. These segregationists are right on one count—I certainly did, and still do, advise Negroes in this county and elsewhere not to voluntarily accept racially segregated public school facilities or any other racially segregated facilities.

Let us put aside for the moment all questions relating to the legality or morality of the actions of the county officials in closing the public schools and simply look at the matter from the point of view of ordinary common sense.

At the great personal and financial sacrifice of a large number of persons, the Prince Edward School Case was carried all the way to the United States Supreme Court. The Justices of that Court unanimously determined, as we had contended, that the doctrine of "separate but equal" has no place in the field of public education and that "separate educational facilities are inherently unequal." We need not even add to this the passage of years in time; or the numerous District Court hearings and two additional appeals to the United States Court of Appeals for this circuit; or the decision of our own Virginia Supreme Court of Appeals invalidating the school-closing laws enacted by the General Assembly of Virginia; or the successful experience with desegregation in public schools in communities within this Commonwealth, as well as in the surrounding states and the District of Columbia.

In light of these facts, how could any sensible person expect anyone with an ounce of common sense to voluntarily accept an arrangement designed solely for the purpose of perpetuating "inherently unequal" school facilities simply because the public officials of this county, in the exercise of an overabundance of obstinacy and self-aggrandizement, had closed the public schools?

Let no one be deceived. The onus for the despicable action of the public officials of Prince Edward County in depriving the Negro children of this county of an opportunity to secure a public school education rests upon the county officials and the so-called "good people" of this county. In my opinion, they are guilty of "a crime against humanity" no different than the crimes perpetrated by Eichmann and his Nazi cohorts except in the matter of the degree of the offense. . . .

The contention of the Prince Edward officials that their action is permissible under Virginia law does not alter the situation, for I remind these "good people" that Eichmann's actions were permissible under the laws of Nazi Germany, but that did not alter the nature of his offense, nor does it alter the nature of theirs.

Let us explore one step further this contemptible action of the deprivation of Negro children of educational facilities. If the General Assembly of Virginia, in the exercise of the same kind of wisdom that prompted the school-closing laws, enacted a statute permitting local governing officials to bind children in order to retard their physical growth, and the public officials of this county, in the exercise of their discretion under such a law, decided to bind white children loosely with ribbon and to bind Negro children tightly with steel bands and the state officials failed or refused to intervene, would any reasonable person consider it an act of tyranny for the Federal Government to step in and protect its citizens?

In this day and age, to say nothing of what the requirements of the decades beyond will necessitate, when a person has to have a good education to secure ordinary jobs, is physical restraint any less serious than educational deprivation? I think not. Nor is the comparison unfair, because the difference between the opportunities afforded Negro children in Jim Crow facilities and the opportunities afforded white children is equivalent to the difference between ribbons and steel bands. The best proof is that in every instance in which an objective survey has been conducted, the inferiority of the Jim Crow facilities has been established.

Yes, there is tyranny in Prince Edward County, but it is high time that the people of this county—"good" and otherwise—recognize the fact that the tyrants are the bigots who are more concerned about maintaining political and economic power than they are about the welfare of human beings or the prosperity of this community. How can it possibly contribute to the future growth and prosperity of this county for more than one-half of its future citizens to grow up in ignorance? What are the adverse effects on the economy of this county going to be five, ten, and fifteen years from now when these deprived school children will be adults? The plain fact is: these education robbers don't care, because it is inconceivable by any stretch of the imagination that this act is calculated to improve the future economy of this county.

It has been said that the "good people" of Prince Edward County have the greatest love and affection for the colored people of this county and that, but for the NAACP and a few radicals, everything would be "just fine." How do they demonstrate that love and affection in Prince Edward County other than by closing the public schools?

In ever increasing numbers, opportunities in employment are being opened up to Negroes—positions requiring ability, training and experience....

The same is true in business and industry. More importantly, employment opportunities affecting the masses of people are available in these areas with increasing opportunities for advancement in both public and private employment. This is the kind of "love and affection" I can understand. Do the "good people" of Prince Edward County have that kind of love and affection for Negroes? What opportunities do they afford Negroes in Prince Edward County beyond the level of tenant farmer, broom guider or domestic servant?

I am not implying that there is anything wrong with earning an honest dollar in those occupations if that is the extent of one's ability, but I do say that it is an evil thing to limit a person to these occupations if he is capable and wants to do better. How do these "good people" demonstrate that love and affection for faithful and competent employees in matters of advancement and upgrading?

Open occupancy in housing is on the increase in the north, east, west and even in parts of the south. Does the Prince Edward brand of love and affection include the right of a Negro to purchase and occupy a home or to purchase and conduct a business wherever he chooses? What becomes of this great "love and affection" when a Negro seeks to avail himself of the services afforded in places of public accommodation and entertainment?

"Good people" of Prince Edward County, don't tell us about your great love and affection—demonstrate it by according us the ordinary courtesy and civility to which every free man or woman is entitled.

Of course, the things we are requesting in some instances and demanding in other instances will produce a change in the customs and mores of the people of Prince Edward County. Change is inevitable. Sensible people consider proposals and trends leading to changes on the basis of factual information, reason, convenience and utility, but the segregationists oppose the evolution of the Negro into the main stream of American life purely because of hysteria based upon superstition.

It is important that those of us who are seeking to promote this social change recognize that most segregationists are suffering from hysteria and to a certain degree are emotionally unbalanced. No wholly rational human being could possibly reach the conclusion that a person designated as a Negro is unfit to associate with another person designated as a white person, solely because at some time—one, two or even three hundred or more years ago—some of the Negro's ancestors lived in some part of Africa. The absurdity of the proposition speaks for itself and only a person suffering from delusions generated by hysteria would try to justify any such proposition. . . .

Segregationists do a great deal of talk about freedom of association. Well, I am all for freedom of association, but I want the right to choose with whom I will associate in my private affairs and not have some one else to do it for me. That is freedom of association, and I respect everyone else's right to do the same. The difficulty is that the minds of the segregationists are so twisted and warped that they are unable to distinguish between public and private association or even as to what is public and what is private. That is the reason they regard public funds as their private funds, and public institutions as their private institutions. . . .

Just as it is important that we fully understand the segregationist in bringing about this social change, it is equally as important that we understand and make explicit our own role in these changing times.

We want to see the emergence of a new day—then it is imperative that we think and act accordingly. We must stop thinking and acting within the limitations characteristic of a second class citizen. All of our actions, attitudes and thoughts should be focused not upon ourselves as colored Americans, but simply as Americans. . . .

There is more at stake than the mere improvement of our individual condition, important as that is. The survival of democracy is at issue. A good fifty per cent of the world's problems of today were caused by mistakes made in yesteryears, predicated upon the false philosophy of white supremacy. The faster we break down notions of racial segregation, the more rapidly we build bulwarks to strengthen democracy.

The pitiful little white children presently being miseducated in the schools here in Prince Edward County are simply being molded into grist for a totalitarian mill. . . . How can a child who is taught that a person with a black face, or even a black ancestor, is for that reason unfit to study with him in school, to eat at the same lunch counter he does, or to occupy a room in the same hotel, or to engage with him in any of the ordinary functions of life—I say, how can such a child be expected, when he grows up, to deal successfully with black men and women on affairs of government or matters of commerce and industry? How can he be expected to meet and accept the dark peoples of the world as equals after his mind has been twisted and misshapen by the present day thought controllers of Prince Edward County and their counterparts elsewhere?

So, every day that we contribute to the delay of the end of segregation, we not only handicap Negro children, but we also aid the totalitarian enemies of our government, because with each passing day additional white children are being debilitated as supporters of democracy.

One final statement. We hear a lot of talk today about new frontiers in different areas of our conventional life and of space. But, in order to reach new frontiers, there must be pioneers. Destiny has afforded us an opportunity to lengthen the frontier in one of the greatest experiments ever undertaken by man—his individual freedom. The enemies facing us are powerful only because they are well entrenched—actually they are decadent and ill—so let us demonstrate that we possess the skill, the tenacity and the moral fortitude to meet the challenge. So let us be up and moving—determined, but without rancor or malice.

C. Brian Kelly Papers, box 7, Albert and Shirley Small Special Collections, University of Virginia, Charlottesville.

QUESTIONS

1. Describe the principal points Oliver Hill made in this speech. What evidence did Hill present to substantiate his position?
2. Whom did Judge J. Segar Gravatt, the legal counsel for the county, refer to as the "good people" of Prince Edward, and how was this a reflection on race relations in the county? Whom did Oliver Hill describe as the "good people" of the county?

Prince Edward County Items

Harry Boyte
April 11, 1962

In August 1961, Harry Boyte replaced Helen Baker as head of the AFSC field office in Farmville. Boyte, a white Quaker who had previously worked for the American Red Cross, sought out local whites to privately discuss their views on the county's dilemma. Over the course of the nine months he spent in the county, Boyte regularly reported on the situation to AFSC officials.

Shortly after this report was written, Boyte was assaulted by four white men in Farmville because of his civil rights work. Wishing to protect the AFSC's work there, Boyte did not report the event to local police, and the attackers were never apprehended. The AFSC transferred Boyte from the county a few months later.[1]

The deep pain and loss of faith in the white people of this area by the Negro community is a very difficult condition to explain vividly. Apparently for many decades there has been a residual trust among the members of the Negro community in the good faith and sincere interest of the white people in the health and welfare of the total population of the County. The extremity of the statements made through the past several years by many of the leading citizens of the white community indicating their attitudes toward the general Negro citizen served to undermine this residual good will. The closing of the public school system in 1959 came as a surprise, not only by the large majority of the Negro population, but also to the majority of the white people of the County. Three years have now passed and in my judgment the majority of citizens of Prince Edward County, both Negro and white, have repeatedly expected the public schools to have been reopened; the Negro community because of its confidence that the white decision-makers would recognize their obligation to the Negro community and particularly the high school and elementary school students and the white community out of a recognition of the economic hardships placed upon it by the absence of a public school system. . . .

One can hear this point of view expressed repeatedly by various segments of the Negro community. . . . For example, Mrs. N. P. Miller, wife of the only Negro dentist in Prince Edward County, and a former school teacher here, has discussed with me several times the change which she now feels toward the members of the white community. She speaks wistfully of the time when she enjoyed so much teaching school nearby. She says that she never imagined that the white people of this county would do such a thing as they have done to the Negro children of Prince Edward County. . . . She elaborated by explaining that she felt considerable reluctance to even walk downtown because of what she considered the atmosphere prevailing among the white citizens toward Negroes. . . . Mrs. Miller said that she had noticed how eagerly the white merchants downtown sought her purchases. She pointed out that she had detected no discrimination on their behalf when they were seeking expenditures of funds from the Negro citizens. She, however, has not opened any new accounts with these merchants because in her opinion they have no interest actually in her welfare or the welfare and happiness of the Negro people. She feels a hurt that obviously goes quite deep and includes what she considers a rejection by the white community of the large Negro population of the County. She also feels a hostility prevalent among the white people toward the Negroes.

One hears many complaints these days in the Negro community of the reputed discrimination by the County Department of Public Welfare toward Negro clients. In attempting to investigate such complaints, I visited the office of Mrs. Frances G. Moon, superintendent of Public Welfare of Prince Edward County. I asked Mrs. Moon to give me the written statement of eligibility for the various classes of welfare recipients for whom her department was responsible. Mrs. Moon was considerably reluctant to do this although when I insisted and pointed out that this was a legal obligation she had to make this information available to any citizen she then supplied me with these documents. In reading through the pamphlet published by the State of Virginia on the Aid to Dependent Children Program, I noticed that it was Virginia law that any child who is under sixteen years of age or under eighteen years of age and regularly attending school could receive ADC assistance. This, of course, assumes that such individual meets the residence and other requirements of need. I immediately asked Mrs. Moon if this stipulation regarding children eighteen years of age or under had been changed in view of the fact that there was no public school system in this county. She angrily answered me that it certainly had not been changed. When I attempted to discuss with her the injustice involved here with Negro children who reached age sixteen and met all other requirements than of attending school, she answered me by stating that any Negro child who reached his sixteenth birthday was automatically cut off from any further ADC assistance. I asked her then if this was the practice with white children who reached age sixteen and she said, of course not because there were schools in this county which they were attending and thus they continued to be eligible for ADC assistance until they reached their eighteenth birthday. Thus it can be easily seen that the injustice of denial to the Negro child of any opportunity of attending a school system in this county spreads its ugly and vicious by-products into many other areas of the Negroes' community and economic life.

I certainly am no legal expert but it is not difficult to imagine that the above discrimination in the Welfare Program of Prince Edward County violates the law. This is one item among many others which in my opinion should be brought to the attention of the Federal authorities. . . .

Last week while riding in the country down a lonely country road, I came upon two Negro boys—approximate age—nine or ten. Across their backs they had large empty fertilizer sacks filled with water cress which grows wild and which they had picked near the river bed. I gave these two boys a ride in my car and we drove for almost four miles until we reached their house which was really appropriately termed a shanty. These boys informed me that each day one of their tasks was to go out and seek some type of food for their family. Water cress, I am informed, can be cooked as a sort of vegetable or can be used as a type of salad. It often is used as greens for the meal of the poorer rural family. These were very large and well-filled fertilizer sacks and certainly if these two boys had lugged these sacks the approximately four miles to their homes they would have been completely exhausted, although this was what they were undoubtedly doing. Both expressed to me a real desire to go back to public school. They were of particularly good initiative and I felt that any opportunity for them to receive an education would certainly prepare them well to assume some responsible place in our society.

Prince Edward County Records, 1962, American Friends Service Committee Archives, Philadelphia.

NOTE

1. Titus, *Brown's Battleground*, 102.

QUESTIONS

1. What were the most important effects of the school closings in Prince Edward County described by Harry Boyte?
2. How did Boyte describe race relations in the county?

Virginia's Black Belt

Martin Luther King Jr.

April 14, 1962

In 1954, Reverend Martin Luther King Jr. became pastor at Dexter Avenue Baptist Church in Montgomery, Alabama. He replaced noted preacher Reverend Vernon Johns, a native of Prince Edward County who was the uncle of school strike leader Barbara Johns (see p. 42).

On December 1, 1955, Rosa Parks refused to give up her seat to a white passenger on a city bus in Montgomery and was arrested for violating a local segregation ordinance. The NAACP filed a lawsuit against the ordinance, based in part on the desegregation ruling in *Brown v. Board of Education*. Montgomery's black community began a thirteen-month-long boycott of the bus system that concluded with a federal court ruling that bus segregation was unconstitutional.

Inspired by events in Montgomery, King formed the Southern Christian Leadership Conference (SCLC) in 1957 to promote nonviolent protest and encourage southern black churches to press for civil rights. In the spring of 1962, King visited Prince Edward County where he encouraged the community: "Things will get better. Do not despair, do not give up, but just stand firm for what you believe in, and people all over the United States will say there are black people in Prince Edward County who have injected new meaning into the veins of civilization."[1]

I did not realize until our "People to People" tour swung through the Black Belt of Virginia last week that the South gave to our nation nine of its first twelve Presidents. Seven of them were Virginians. How strange it is that this southern Commonwealth has failed so miserably in giving moral leadership to the South. The idea of "massive resistance" was spawned not in Georgia or Alabama—but in the heart of Southside Virginia, commonly known as the Black Belt.

This section of Virginia is the bulwark of Harry Byrd's political dynasty that holds Virginia's liberal bent in a strangle-hold. The anti-NAACP laws, the infamous trespass ordinances aimed at thwarting the Sit-Ins, the Pupil Placement laws—all children of "massive resistance," had their origin and loudest support from this same Negro majority section of Virginia that makes up most of the Fourth U.S. Congressional District.

What a pity that this state of such early historical distinction has missed an opportunity for real greatness in one of her nation's most critical hours!

It may well have been that the severe social change that is taking place in the South today might have been considerably accelerated had not Virginia, "the mother of Presidents" led the South backward into "massive resistance."

It is refreshing, however, to observe even from this brief vantage point of the struggle's history, that social crises at times produce their greatest need. The nonviolent thrust of the Negro community in the South and Virginia has met "massive resistance" with "massive insistence."

This is a part of the aim of the Southern Christian Leadership Conference "People to People" program. I am convinced, as I have said many times, that the salvation of the Negro is not in Washington, D. C.

The Supreme Court, the Justice Department, the President of the United States, and the Congress can aid immeasurably in the emancipation process of the Negro, but the major responsibility of securing our full freedom depends on the Negro himself.

Our constitutional guarantees will not be realized until Negroes rise up by the hundreds and the thousands, community by community, and demand their rights through nonviolence and creative protest.

As our SCLC task force traveled over the Black Belt of Virginia last week, I could see the potential of this. In just two days, we touched the lives of nearly 10,000 people. We could see the deep hope and yearning for freedom in the eyes of thousands of Negroes and the sincere commitment to human equality in many whites.

The Black Belt of Virginia has a potential of 100,000 voters in the Negro community but there are barely 17,000 registered at the present. The Fourth District is similar to many parts of Mississippi with many Negroes who are tied to the land as sharecroppers. Economic suppression is the rule rather than the exception and the poll tax requirement adds to the burden of general apathy in Negro voter registration. It is towards this enormous task in Virginia's Black Belt that our "People to People" tour was directed. . . .

We joined Fourth District leaders in Petersburg on the first day of our visit and spent the afternoon literally knocking on doors in the First Ward in a voter registration canvass.

We could discern from the response of the occupants of the more than eighty homes visited, that many of our people just need the information as to what they must know and exactly where they must go and what they must do.

In Lynchburg the same evening, up in the western half of the state, along with Ralph Abernathy and Wyatt Tee Walker, we recruited 118 volunteers to work in voter registration. I was overwhelmed by a nine-year-old white lad, Chuck Moran, who came forward and said he wanted to help in this struggle. The example of this tender spirit triggered the response of many of the others who joined the Freedom Corps that night.

Nine a. m. the next day, we saw first-hand the tragedy of Prince Edward County. This is the Virginia county that closed down its public schools rather than comply with the Supreme Court decision of 1954. This is the third year that there has been no public schools for any child white or black.

We could see the obvious lines of strain and weariness in the face of Prince Edward's peerless leader, the Rev. L. Francis Griffin.

He has refused the compromise of a half loaf of freedom and the parents and children have backed him unanimously in this position. Think of it! Closed schools in Virginia, the mother of Presidents.

Virginia State College afforded us another thrill. This was a homecoming for Mrs. Dorothy Cotton, Director of the Citizenship Schools, who accompanied us. The students jam-packed Virginia Hall auditorium (capacity 2,500) in a voluntary assembly that a college official said was the first such occasion in history.

It evidences a new breed and a new generation in our Negro community with this kind of enthusiasm and interest.

We rounded out our Virginia tour by attending the trials of 62 Sit-Inners in Hopewell, Virginia and visiting two rural communities in Dinwiddie County, just south of Petersburg.

More than 400 people talked with us informally and expressed their interest in the freedom struggle.

The last public meeting held at Petersburg's First Baptist Church was a standing room only affair where 158 joined our Freedom Corps to work in voter registration.

As we winged our way back to Atlanta, it came to me that the tremendous response we had found in Virginia held promise of changing the political climate in Virginia, and perhaps—perhaps, Virginia might once again produce a president.

New York Amsterdam News, April 14, 1962.

NOTE

1. "'Do Not Despair,' Negro Leader Urges at Rally," *Farmville Herald*, March 30, 1962.

QUESTIONS

1. According to Martin Luther King Jr., what was the unique role of Virginia in the nation's history? How was this reflected in the school integration struggle?
2. King visited Prince Edward County as part of his trip. What were his impressions of the county and its leadership? How do you think African Americans in Prince Edward County responded to King's visit?

The Shame and the Glory

Alfred P. Klausler

August 15, 1962

The *Christian Century* was founded in 1884 as an ecumenical progressive magazine. Notable contributors in the early decades included Progressive reformer Jane Addams and German theologian Reinhold Niebuhr. In 1963, the *Century* was the first major periodical to publish the full text of "Letter from Birmingham Jail," written by Martin Luther King Jr. when he was jailed there. Reverend Alfred P. Klausler, executive secretary for the Associated Church Press, visited Prince Edward County in 1962 and reflected on the spiritual struggles and the role of the clergy in the Prince Edward public school crisis.

Farmville, a pleasant country town of 6,000, is the center of Prince Edward County where, since 1959, there have been no public schools. The grade and high school buildings are locked, desks in the classrooms are covered by a layer of dust, and school buses, long unused, stand forlorn in parking lots. The county's 1,700 Negro children have lost all contact with formal education. A few weeks ago the county's board of supervisors unanimously refused to provide funds for public schools in 1962–63, as it had refused for the past three years. It remains to be seen what they will do now that the district court has unequivocally ordered them to reopen the schools.

Meanwhile Prince Edward County is a troubled area. The beautiful Virginia landscape may lull the senses of the visitor, but he soon becomes aware of a feeling of fear and tension among the residents. The whites and blacks seem to glance at each other warily. The visitor's discreet questions draw guarded responses.

The feeling of tension is reflected in the white clergy. One white minister, who asked specifically not to be mentioned by name or be directly quoted, carefully discussed the county's problem with your reporter. While declaring emphatically that there is no personal animosity between the races in his county, he admitted that Negro and white clergy do not meet in conferences. In answer to a question he said that the subject of school integration and segregation is never broached by clergy or laity in any type of formal or informal group in white churches. There is no sense in crusading, this minister declared, because that would only inflame the people, and any prophetic utterances from the pulpit would deepen antagonisms. This is not the time, he added, to undertake a definite program of education in racial relationships.

Yet, it became clear to your reporter as he talked to them, the white clergy feel that these are truly troubled times, that Prince Edward County suffers from a moral blight, and that the message of the gospel must somehow be brought home to a town and a county where hatred smolders beneath the surface. One white clergyman in particular conveyed to me the deep sense of helplessness that plagues him and his colleagues. Perhaps this man longed for the courage of some of the Negro ministers who unhesitatingly apply the healing Word to the local wounds.

The undercurrent of fear is also caught in the almost secretive answers given by the teachers at one of the remedial schools—or "activity training centers," as they are called—held at various places throughout the county for Negro children during the summer months. Here is High Rock Baptist, a dilapidated country church off busy Colonial Highway, not too far from the site of Lee and Grant's last pitched battle, Sayler's Creek. The paint is peeling from the shabby siding. The dusty yard becomes a sea of mud after a rain. There is one outdoor pump for drinking water. About 90 Negro children come here every day in summer for several hours of training, some from as far as six miles away.

In the church nave four grade groupings gather on either side of the aisle. The pews are low-backed and uncomfortable. The teachers, some white and some Negro, are college students or recent graduates from Yale, Oberlin, Wellesley, Amherst, Harvard, Columbia. Chief supervisor or principal is Ruth Turner, a Negro, an Oberlin alumna and holder of an advanced degree from the Harvard school of education. During the regular school season Miss Turner teaches in Cleveland, Ohio. The improvised classroom hums with activity. There is a complete absence of busy-work. The teachers attempt to give their pupils some knowledge of spelling, geography, history, reading. In other parts of the church, in the sacristy and the basement, primary students are taught some of the rudiments of the English language. . . .

A hundred yards from High Rock Baptist stands the district school. It is closed. On an outside wall adjoining the door is a tattered "No Trespassing" sign. Weeds grow in the playground. An almost eerie quiet hovers over the scene. White parents in the county have banded together and donated or lent money to establish a private school for their children. This school does not have all the frills of modern education, as a white minister explained, but it does manage to field athletic teams for various events. Meanwhile the Negro children receive no formal schooling. They are the pawns in the age-old battle between the federal government and proponents of states' rights.

All this is part of the shame of Prince Edward County. It is true that there are courageous whites who deplore this shame. C. G. Gordon Moss, dean of Virginia's oldest state teachers' college, Longwood, which is located in Farmville, was recently reported by the *Richmond Times-Dispatch* as one of a number of whites who urged the board of supervisors to show a positive leadership in opening the schools and raising the tax levy. "You have an opportunity to furnish leadership in Virginia with positive action, not negative, delaying action," Dr. Moss said.

Not until one visits the Rev. L. Francis Griffin, president of the Prince Edward County Christian Association, does the glory of Farmville and the surrounding area come to light. It is a glory compounded of persecution, determination, and the essentials of the gospel.

A husky former football player, college and seminary educated, Griffin, a 44-year-old Negro Baptist, conveys a sense of moral strength which must be unsettling to those who face him in the endless segregation disputes. Although he is constantly subjected to direct and indirect harassment from whites, Griffin faces the day's problems with grim, almost cynical humor. He asks no quarter and insists that no exceptions be made in his favor because of his role as leader. When his oldest son was offered a choice scholarship with all expenses paid at an outstanding eastern preparatory school, Griffin insisted that his children must suffer with the other Negro children of Prince Edward County and refuse to taste the sweets of a formal education. . . .

What are Griffin's reactions to the school board's dealing with the problem? His understandably ironic comments on the actions of his white fellow clergymen in Farmville and Prince Edward County carry both a sting and a feeling of compassion. "The clergy and their communicants are the most hardened of all about this situation," he says. "The majority of the ministers and their people fail to realize that there is any moral issue involved in this tragedy. They regard me and my fellow workers as troublemakers. I think it's because the gospel hasn't penetrated their hearts and they haven't communicated the gospel to their people. The prophetic voice is totally lacking among the white Protestant clergy. The Negro clergy may have also failed to communicate completely and properly, but let's remember what they have lived through and experienced these years.

"I believe the white ministers are dictated to by the pews. The pulpit in Farmville has relatively little to say to the pew. The [white ministers] will tell you that they preach the gospel and that they attempt to show their members how the gospel must be applied to their individual lives. But I have failed to see any results from that preaching in the last 12 years. I will not say it is all entirely their fault. But somewhere, somehow, my white brethren must be given courage to become prophets. And, believe me, it's hard being a prophet in Farmville and Prince Edward." . . .

As a stopgap measure, to give Negro children an idea of the group living and experience which schools provide, the Prince Edward County Christian Association organized a number of activity training centers, with the National Association for the Advancement of Colored People acting as supervisor. These centers are not to be confused with formal schools. They are merely a means to keep Negro youngsters in touch with some of the processes of education. The people in charge are called supervisors and assistant supervisors. To call them teachers would jeopardize the eventual integrated school system Negroes are demanding. The program is conducted in the summer months by the Virginia Teachers Association and the Student Christian Federation. The Virginia Education Association, the white teachers group, has so far remained aloof from the project.

This is the second summer the activity centers have been operating, often under the most primitive conditions. Some 600 Negro children attend. The supervisors are enthusiastic and dedicated people, motivated by a spirit of anonymous helpfulness. They are truly an unofficial Peace Corps. They are demonstrating that someone from the outside cares about Prince Edward's shame.

What is the prospect for the future? Griffin and other Negro leaders feel that it is only a matter of time before Negro and white children will be sitting side by side in classrooms. In Prince Edward County Negro and white families live in the same rural neighborhoods. It would be fantastically expensive to build two consolidated schools and operate two bus systems merely to perpetuate the myth of white superiority. . . .

Still, it must be remembered that, even though many school systems in Virginia have token integration—more perhaps than any other southern state—Virginia has a private school tradition far older than the public school idea. In a county like Prince Edward there is also the hidden establishment to be reckoned with. This establishment consists of families whose history goes back to colonial times. They cannot be touched by economic boycotts because their money is safely invested either in land or in banks in New York, Philadelphia and Boston. It is groups of this kind, small in numbers though they may be, that can and perhaps do incite the lower income groups to violent action against Negroes. The anonymous midnight telephone calls, the jovial threats of a necktie party, the taunts hurled at Griffin and his friends as they walk down Farmville's streets do not come from the establishment, but they are the result of its direct and indirect prompting of the white bully boys.

Along with all this it is painfully obvious, as Griffin points out, that in Prince Edward County the church has become a comfortable resting spot for the whites. It is no longer a transforming agency. The white ministers and their people have forgotten the realism of the gospel.

Yes, Prince Edward is a troubled county and Virginia is a troubled state. The Virginians themselves are gracious, cultured, kindly, the epitome of hospitality to the outsider. And yet one cannot escape the impression that they are embarrassed and even worried over this school problem.

Christian Century, August 15, 1962, 977–79. Copyright 1962 *Christian Century*, reprinted with permission.

QUESTIONS

1. What points did Alfred Klausler make to support his description of Prince Edward County as a "troubled area"?
2. Describe the public and private views offered by white clergy of Prince Edward County in this document. How did the author portray Reverend L. Francis Griffin?
3. What was Klausler's perspective on the education offered to black students in the training centers?

Address to the Charlottesville Chapter of the Virginia Council on Human Relations

C. G. Gordon Moss

October 25, 1962

Born in Lynchburg, Virginia, C. G. Gordon Moss moved to Prince Edward County in 1944 to accept a position as professor of history at Longwood College. In the 1950s, Moss was one of only a few white residents who advocated compliance with *Brown v. Board of Education*. Rebuffed by white segregationists, Moss was subjected to social ostracism, threats, economic intimidation, and efforts to terminate his position at the college.

In October 1962, Moss addressed a gathering of the Virginia Council on Human Relations (VCHR). Affiliated with the Southern Regional Council, the VCHR was created in 1955 to foster improved race relations and was the principal biracial organization seeking school integration in Virginia.

The first thing I want to say, is that I am not the only person, the only white person, in Prince Edward County who is violently opposed to what is going on there, has been going on there. There are really many others. I am simply the most garrulous of the oppositionists. . . .

Some people think that the present situation in Prince Edward County began in 1954, became rigid and confirmed in 1959, and so has been in development that brief number of years. I believe that is far from the actual truth of the matter. My first brief stay in Prince Edward County was back in the 1920's, as early as 1926. And though I left the county within two year's time, since I married one of its natives, I have had continuous contact with the county and return trips without any break. When I came back to the county in 1944, to resume residence . . . I saw from the beginning that it was a county where the paternalism, which the white people of Virginia have prided themselves upon in regard to our Negro fellow citizens, that that paternalism was probably more pronounced, more self-conscious, and the citizens thereof took more pride in it than in any other place that I have ever lived in the State of Virginia. I believe actually that that is the ultimate root of the present situation in the county. That the white people of Prince Edward County pride themselves upon their paternalism, which they do not admit is a condescending paternalism, but which certainly is such. They pride themselves upon it, and they would be very unhappy to be deprived of the solace to their own consciences which that paternalism gives them. Certainly, I am definitely sure that that is a basic explanation of Mr. J. Barrye Wall's attitudes and actions throughout recent developments.

But secondly, as I look back upon it now, and I'm certain that I was not too well aware of it earlier, the situation in Prince Edward County began to develop long before 1954 and 55. Because for all the years of the 30's and 40's, at least . . . it was absolutely obvious that the school facilities for the Negro part of the population were totally inadequate. The buildings were too few, too small in size, and too totally physically inadequate for any proper educational situation. And the white people of the county knew it. But they refused to do anything about it, or at least, they procrastinated in doing anything about it, and accordingly, it got worse and worse, more and more impossible, and certainly, more and more unbearable from the standpoint of both the Negro children and their parents who had to endure the inadequacies of it, and instead of admitting that it was an impossible situation, instead of after admission, doing something about it, I think the white population of the county made the basic mistake of . . . not doing, but promising that something would be done if and when they were financially able to do it. But promises for a new school, promises for the repair of a roof, promises for the transformation of a tarpaper shack into a real school building, such promises surely begin to lose any warmth when they are repeated year after year, year after year, decade after decade. And consequently, a Negro population that was the most, was and is, the most patient group of human beings that I have ever seen, that population with their hopes being postponed and denied year after year after year, eventually were no longer willing to wait any longer. . . .

For years I have been a member of a small discussion group of men in the town. It is not an organization in any way associated with the college whatsoever. It's a town discussion group, not a gown discussion group. And one evening, many years ago now, I heard a certain member of that discussion group say that he believed it would be a very fortunate and a very helpful thing if public schools, and he made no qualification there whatsoever, if public schools in the county were abolished completely for at least a period of time. That statement of opinion did come after the 1954 Supreme Court decision, yes, but it came some three or four years before any overt action in the county of a public nature. The man whom I heard express that belief was J. Barrye Wall, owner and publisher and editor of the *Farmville Herald*, and certainly the principal spokesman for the Prince Edward Foundation of recent years. Not upon that one assertion alone, but starting with that, I have believed ever since 1959 that our lack of schools in Prince Edward County actually was in no way, in no causative way, the result of the Supreme Court decision of '54, was in no way directly the result of the demand by the Negro population of the county for integration in the schools. Such matters have been merely the excuse used to accomplish, at least temporarily, a far deeper and a far more serious effort. We are a county with a very small economic upper class and the great majority of the population both white and colored of relatively low economic status. And I have contended, and I still believe my contention is true, that what has caused our situation there is that the small in number wealthy members of the county, for one thing, and this is the minor part of it, have desired to relieve themselves of the financial burden of being the principal supporters of a public school system and to substitute for that the financial burden of maintaining a private school for their own children. But that primary purpose is to destroy public education for both, yes, the Negro children of the county, but also the white children of the county in order that they might retain an unlimited cheap labor supply for the few, for the industries of the county. A cheap labor supply, a non-organized labor supply, and they don't have to bother about the fact that uneducated, it will be an unskilled labor supply. There are no industries in the county that need or require high skills. That, I believe, explains the fact, the depth and the length that people in the county have been willing to go to, to accomplish their purposes. In other communities in Virginia there has been opposition to integration of the schools, but . . . it has quickly collapsed. The adamant, the prolonged, the indefinite resistance to integrated public schools in our county, I believe, owes its existence and its length of existence to this, this belief on the part of the wealthier part of the population that they can get along better without public education. I grant you that it is one of the most cruel, heartless things I have ever seen in my lifetime for 1,700, 2,000 children regardless of the color of their skins to be denied education for one year, for two years, for three years, and now for the fourth year. But I ask you, despite our acute consciousness of such a thing, is it not an even more heartless, is it not an even more unbelievably cruel thing in the democracy of the United States of America dependent upon education for the continued existence of that democracy for the people in even one county to set out purposely, intentionally, not admittedly, but set out to destroy public education completely for the entire population of the county for as long as they are capable of maintaining such destruction? . . .

When in June of 1959, the Board of Supervisors refused to appropriate funds for public schools for the year '59–'60, one other white citizen of the county and myself, because somebody has to take the initiative, we began immediately to attempt to discover some way of preventing so calamitous a thing as the closing of schools. Of course, our remarks to the Board of Supervisors were nothing, accomplished nothing whatsoever. But by the end of August of that year of '59, we had found that the two men who could more nearly speak the mind of the Negro population of the county than any others did, of course, include the Reverend Mr. L. Francis Griffin, and a possibly less well known Negro citizen of the community, Roger Madison. This white friend of mine and myself sat down and discussed with those two Negro leaders several nights, days, I forget exactly how long, and we secured from them, what surely was, what I now realize was a far greater concession than I realized at the time, we secured Mr. Griffin and Mr. Madison's approval that they would advocate voluntary segregation in the schools for three years, if the public schools could be reopened. That was toward the end of August 1959, of course, before the schools had actually been closed in the sense of not reopening that fall semester. We took that promise, that agreement to J. Barrye Wall, and he refused to consider it one moment. He said he would not sit down and discuss the resumption of public schools with anybody. That the only thing he would do, and he would choose other Negroes rather than the two we were offering him, he would discuss with them private schools for the Negroes. I cannot be too specific in regard to the details of this, but we were able to tell Mr. Wall that though the Board of Supervisors had not appropriated for that, for such voluntary segregated public schools in '59–'60, we had been assured that the funds to run such schools could be found. And that was no mere pious wish. It was an absolutely assured fact. Then in the fall of '59, the Foundation people to protect themselves went through the motions of organizing a so-called corporation to run private schools of the county, and I would ask you to remember the circumstances of this rather carefully. It was in the fall of '59 that they created that corporation. By December of '59 they were finding it extremely difficult to operate their private white schools in the basement of various churches, in the Women's Club building, and such not. They were acutely aware of the fact that they needed better physical plants for their school system. So they promoted the idea of this offer of white assistance for private schools for the Negro children, and finally, shortly before Christmas of that year of '59, they told the Negroes of the county that they would give them until the first of the year to accept the offer or not. Of course, the Negroes did not accept the offer because of perfectly obvious reasons. Within two weeks time after the Negroes had not accepted the offer of white assistance in the organization of private schools, the reason for the whole thing became apparent. Because if the Negroes had accepted the offer, and had then asked for the use of the Negro schools for these private schools, the white children and white population could have done the same. So that within two weeks time after the Negroes had turned it down, the Prince Edward Foundation made its first formal bid or request to rent the white school buildings. Now ever since that time, they have protested and protested that the Negro children of Prince Edward County have gone without education because their Negro leaders wanted them to go without education. That they had been offered from the beginning white support for private education. The only offer that was given them was a mere token creation of a corporation and the mere statement that this corporation would help. The corporation never raised any funds, it never put on any campaign for the raising of funds. It has been a paper proposition entirely and nothing of reality whatsoever....

You may have seen in the newspapers in recent months some indication that the private school system, for the white children has begun, is beginning to run into difficulties. We learned down in Prince Edward County this past summer that white parents were receiving notices that if they didn't pay up the school would not be available to them....

They said that maybe a half dozen children, half dozen children of half a dozen families were denied. But we could not get any of the white families who had received those letters to say anything. I tried in every way I knew how to discover some of it and I couldn't get any of them to talk at all. Then, my friend, the Associate Editor of the *Lynchburg News*, decided to come into the county and see what he could do, and he secured, with some help by some of us, at least the names of a half dozen people that, for whose children it was known that they had been denied schooling this year. He went to see those half dozen people and found one of them only who was willing to talk.... That here were the children of a sergeant in the United States Army, who had not been able to meet the full cost of tuition last year and so his children were told they couldn't go to school this year and when he went to see Mr. Wall to insist upon some public statement, in regard to his children, being published in the paper, he was told that that could not be done....

One man protected by his Army status and not dependent upon employment in the county did speak up and force the Foundation to take his children back in the school. He is one, one person, whether he represents the half dozen families that the Foundation admits or the 180 families that public rumor has it or a larger number, I don't know, but we are definitely moving and this simply reconfirms me in my original interpretation; we're definitely moving in the direction of no public education for any children, colored, Negro or white, who cannot afford to pay the commercial cost of private education; we're definitely moving in that direction in the county....

Why could we not as Virginians who have had the opportunity in times gone by to be the leaders of the American Nation, why could we not simply say that the 19th Century is dead, the 20th Century is too far gone to deny it any longer and simply remove from our law books, simply remove all statutory and constitutional recognition of differences, distinctions, between people on account of their blood. And so negative an action as repeal seems to me, at least sufficient, to begin the thing; remove from our Constitution, remove from our statute books, all legislation that recognizes any distinction on account of the race or color of Virginia citizens.

Prince Edward County Records, 1962, American Friends Service Committee Archives, Philadelphia.

QUESTIONS

1. C. G. Gordon Moss had a unique perspective on the Prince Edward County situation. Why did Moss adopt this position, and how did this affect his place in the community?
2. What were the true reasons behind the closure of the public schools in Prince Edward County, as described by Moss?
3. How did he portray race relations in Virginia in the early 1960s? What steps did he recommend to move forward?

Three Apparent Effects of School Closing

Edward Harden Peeples Jr.

1963

Edward H. Peeples Jr., a white native of Richmond, was raised in a segregationist household, then experienced an intellectual and moral transformation while attending Richmond Professional Institute (now Virginia Commonwealth University) and began his work as a civil rights activist in 1955.

Peeples participated in sit-in protests in downtown Richmond department stores and public facilities in the early 1960s. In 1961, he heard Helen Baker of the AFSC (see p. 136) discuss the closed schools in Prince Edward County. Peeples then organized recreational and educational programs for the out-of-school children in the county and became closely associated with the ongoing work of the AFSC.

At the University of Pennsylvania, Peeples wrote his master's thesis on the public school crisis in Prince Edward. This was the first research paper written on the crisis and was later used as a briefing paper by the U.S. Department of Justice and the U.S. Office of Education in efforts by the Kennedy administration to reopen the public schools. This reading is a selection from his thesis.

Although there are suspected to be numerous uncovered effects accruing from the closure of public schools, we shall limit our discussion here to only three.

One outcome has been the increased awareness on the part of many Negroes of the importance of the ballot. The school issue has apparently become a catalyst for the heaviest registration of Negroes in recent history of the county.

Registration for voting in Prince Edward County, as all over Virginia, currently requires that a person must pay a poll tax of $1.50 six months in advance of an election and also that one shall have paid that tax for three years preceding the pending election. Registration is allowed by the state constitution and law to be largely at the discretion of the local registrar. However, there have been no known unmerited restraints on registration as far as this author can determine. The U.S. Department of Justice examined Prince Edward County registration procedures in 1961 and also found no faulty or unlawful practices.

PECCA has been working on increasing the number of Negro voting registrants. Some indication of their work is seen by the fact that nineteen Negroes registered between December 1, 1962, and February 5, 1963, while only four whites registered during that same period. There were, as of February, 1962, 5,559 registrants in the county including 4,433 whites and 1,126 Negroes. PECCA reported that there were only 900 Negroes registered in the county in 1961.

A second suspected effect of school closing has been what appears to be extensive and rapidly growing illiteracy. Most of the children of grammar school ages in Prince Edward have been without any competent instruction ever since school closing in June of 1959. Therefore, one would be led to believe that school closing has been directly responsible for unusual quantities of illiteracy. The question is—how widespread is illiteracy? To answer this query the author has ventured an extremely conservative estimate of "illiteracy" in Prince Edward County and the computing of this estimate follows.

The United States Office of Education defines an adult "illiterate" as an individual "eighteen and over with less than six years of schooling." The Office of Education also reports that 15.3 per cent of the state of Virginia's population falls into this category. We have for the purpose of estimation assumed that this 15.3 per cent is an excessively conservative estimate of the number of adult "illiterates" in Prince Edward County, the rationale being that it can easily be demonstrated with the 1960 census data that the county falls considerably below the state in "median school years completed" and significantly higher than the state in the percentage of those who have "completed less than five years of school." Thus, the estimate of adult "illiterates" is 2,161, rounded to the nearest whole number.

Using again the criterion of six years of school as the test for literacy, we find that an estimated 700 Negro children would, if schools had remained open, be "literate." This figure of 700 is a conservative estimate of the number of children who in 1958–59 were in the second, third, fourth and fifth grades and would have been expected (in the case of open schools) to proceed to the sixth grade and "literacy." This estimate of 700 includes a sizable deduction for those children among the second, third, fourth and fifth graders of 1958–59, who are surmised to have learned reading and writing skills to the satisfaction of our definition in their homes, in schools outside the county, and in various instructional programs conducted in the county. It also includes a deduction for dropouts, failures and those children whose families have moved out of the county.

There are, of course, an estimated 700 more children, ages two through six who in 1958–59 were pre-school or first graders and who would have achieved (had schools been open) by the conclusion of the 1962–63 session at least some of the language skills taught in the first through the fifth grades.

Neither of these estimates of 700 children, a total of 1,400, accounts for those children of other ages who have experienced the loss of reading and writing skills because of a failure to drill or to use these skills. Also, they preclude a figure for those whites who because of one reason or another have not reached the sixth grade or "literacy" in white private schools.

Thus, a total of 1,400 children, if they fail to receive any further language instruction, upon their eighteenth birthday will be "functional illiterates" by the definition of the U.S. Office of Education.

We now add the 2,161 adult "illiterates" to this projected estimate of 1,400 "will-be-illiterates." These total to 3,561 persons who have become or upon their eighteenth birthday are expected to become "illiterates." This means that, as of the spring of 1963, 25.29 per cent or about one in every four persons in Prince Edward County can be expected to become an "illiterate." In addition, the number of this estimate is expected to increase at least by 175 persons each year.

No matter what the weaknesses in this computation may be the figures still suggest unusual and alarming conditions relative to the learning of language skills.

A third effect of school closing revolves around physical and mental health. Public schools, especially in southern rural regions, play an important role in the health and hygiene of the families of public school pupils. Often the teacher or other school personnel are the only individuals in a given rural community who can recognize threats to the physical and mental health in the locality. Therefore, since school closing large numbers of the Negro youngsters, particularly in the rural areas of the county, have not come in contact (for years at a time in some instances) with any adult who can spot medical or social problems or who can offer assistance or advice in solving such problems. As a result, many serious maladies exist unnoticed or ignored by those who are uninformed.

All of the volunteer and professional projects in the county since 1959 report the discovery of severe problems associated with poverty, neglect and ignorance. Endless cases of malnutrition, decayed teeth, eye trouble, respiratory diseases and social and psychiatric disorders have been far too voluminous for the county's public health nurse to uncover and resolve.

There are, of course, many other educational, economic, psychological and social consequences directly attributable to school closing which have not yet been fully studied or explained. Some will not even be known until schools are opened and the problems of educating the human products of a school-less sub-culture are faced.

Edward Harden Peeples Jr., "A Perspective on the Prince Edward County School Issue" (M.A. thesis, University of Pennsylvania, 1963), 70–74.

QUESTIONS

1. What were the three effects of the Prince Edward County school closing discussed in this reading? Which of these three do you think was the most important, and why?
2. In what ways might the experience of the closed schools have had a continuing impact in the county even after the public schools reopened?

6

"The Free Schools"

On the centennial anniversary of the Emancipation Proclamation in March 1963, Robert F. Kennedy gave a speech in which he stated, "We may observe, with as much sadness as irony that outside of Africa, south of the Sahara where education is still a difficult challenge, the only places on earth known not to provide free public education are Communist China, North Vietnam, Sarawak, Singapore, British Honduras—and Prince Edward County, Virginia."[1] Racial tensions arising from the civil rights movement were high in the South in the spring of 1963, as nonviolent protests led by Martin Luther King Jr. were suppressed with fire hoses and police dogs at the order of Commissioner of Public Safety Eugene "Bull" Connor in Birmingham, Alabama. That summer in Danville, Virginia, ninety miles southwest of Farmville, peaceful black protests calling for desegregated public facilities, employment opportunities, and a voice in local government were met with equally repressive measures. In Prince Edward County, the African American community that had patiently waited years for legal recourse in the courts to reopen the closed public schools finally moved to direct action with a series of student protests in Farmville during July and August. The culmination of this period of black protest, the March on Washington for Jobs and Freedom, took place in the nation's capital on August 28, 1963, and included a group of black children from the county proudly marching with a banner proclaiming "Prince Edward County."

After four years of educational deprivation, the Prince Edward Free Schools Association was organized in the summer of 1963, under the auspices of the Kennedy administration, as an emergency remedial education program. William vanden Heuvel, special assistant to Attorney General Robert Kennedy, represented the administration in negotiating the establishment of the program with state and local officials and community leaders. Directed by Dr. Neil V. Sullivan, a public school superintendent from Long Island, New York, the association held classes and programs seven days a week for the eleven months of its existence in a concerted effort to reintroduce children to the experience of education.

The Prince Edward Free Schools were funded by philanthropic, corporate, and individual donations. Small monetary gifts came from schoolchildren across the country. Publishers donated books. The New York Philharmonic Orchestra contributed musical instruments. Washington Redskins football player Bobby Mitchell, who had desegregated the last all-white National Football League team only a year earlier, visited the Free Schools to encourage the students.[2]

The program began under challenging circumstances. After four years without public schools, Dr. Sullivan found "a student body that was mentally and emotionally whipped. The youngsters, living on isolated farms, had lost the few skills they had acquired while in school."[3] Sullivan and his staff had barely a month to hire teachers, prepare a curriculum, obtain books and supplies, and reopen the long shuttered school buildings to begin classes.

The arrival of the Free Schools program was not entirely welcomed in the county. School administrators, teachers, and students were subjected to threats of violence. On Sunday, September 15, 1963, the Sixteenth Street Baptist Church in Birmingham, Alabama, was bombed, killing four young black girls. The Prince Edward Free Schools opened for classes the next day.

Although this emergency educational program was now serving the African American children of Prince Edward County, the legal issues surrounding the closed public schools remained unresolved. The U.S. Court of Appeals had ordered Prince Edward County to desegregate its public schools in May 1959, five years after the original school desegregation ruling in *Brown*. County officials responded by defunding and closing the public school system. The NAACP immediately pursued new litigation focused on saving public education in Prince Edward County. For the next five years, the future of public education in the county remained mired in legal battles in state and federal courts. As noted by William vanden Heuvel, "The great irony is that the children who won the right to attend desegregated public schools ten years ago are still waiting to exercise that right" (see p. 183).

Yet in the face of these challenges, the African American students joyfully experienced the opening of the Free Schools. One young girl was asked about being back in school. Although lacking in grammar, she wrote with pride, "Virginia has rejoin the Union. I bet Thomas Jefferson is happy."[4]

NOTES

1. Robert F. Kennedy, Address at Kentucky's Centennial of the Emancipation Proclamation, Freedom Hall, Louisville, March 18, 1963, U.S. Department of Justice, http://www.justice.gov/ag/rfk-speeches.html.

2. Sullivan, Maynard, and Yellin, *Bound for Freedom*, 183.

3. Foster, *Status of Blacks*, 6.

4. Sullivan, Maynard, and Yellin, *Bound for Freedom*, 129.

A Program for the Education of Children of Prince Edward County

Albertis Harrison, William vanden Heuvel, and J. Segar Gravatt

July 30, 1963

By the summer of 1963, Prince Edward County's public schools had been closed for four years. While most of the county's white schoolchildren had attended the private Prince Edward Academy during that time, the majority of black youths had gone uneducated or received minimal education in "training centers" or summer remedial programs supported by the NAACP, the Virginia Teachers Association, and volunteer summer teachers.

Officials in the Kennedy administration had long expressed frustration with the closed public schools and sought a resolution to the educational crisis. In a special message on civil rights sent to Congress, Kennedy commented on "the case of Prince Edward County, Virginia, the only county in the nation where there are no public schools."[1] In the summer of 1963, William vanden Heuvel, special assistant to Attorney General Robert F. Kennedy, facilitated the creation of the Prince Edward Free Schools. Overseen by a biracial board of trustees composed of Virginia educational and political leaders, the program was funded by foundation grants and private donations as a temporary emergency program. The Free Schools brought an end to the educational drought for African Americans in Prince Edward County.

Memorandum of tentative agreement reached on July 30, 1963, between the Honorable Albertis S. Harrison Jr. Governor of Virginia, William J. vanden Heuvel, special assistant to the Attorney General of the United States, and J. Segar Gravatt, attorney for the Board of Supervisors of Prince Edward County, with respect to the development of a program for the education of children of Prince Edward County, in view of the fact that the public schools are not in operation.

It is understood that the School Board of Prince Edward County, which owns and controls the buildings, equipment and transportation facilities, are not a party, or have not been a party, to this conference, and that the tentative understanding hereinafter set forth is subject to the approval of Counsel for the School Board and to final approval of the School Board in its official capacity.

It is contemplated that a non-profit corporate association will be chartered under the laws of the Commonwealth of Virginia for the purpose of providing an educational program for children in Prince Edward County.

The proposed corporation is to have six trustees or directors who will be in charge of the program to be offered. Funds for the financing of the program are to be sought from private sources, and it is expressly understood that the trustees will have no obligation, nor will they be expected, to engage in the solicitation of such funds.

The trustees will select and employ the chief administrative officer of the educational program contemplated, and will employ teachers and other needed personnel incident to the program. It is contemplated that the School Board of Prince Edward County will make available the following buildings:

The R. R. Moton School Building, at Farmville
The Mary E. Branch Elementary School Building at Farmville
and Worsham Elementary School and High School Building located at
    Worsham,

together with such laboratory, shop and other equipment as may be needed and agreed to by the School Board, and that such transportation facilities as the School Board has and as may be needed will also be supplied, all subject to the final approval and agreement of Counsel for the School Board and of the School Board in its official capacity.

The lease of the above described facilities, or any other facilities which may be finally ascertained, will be for a period of one year, or for a lesser period, if the said buildings and facilities are required by the School Board, or any other agency of the State of Virginia, for the operation of public schools.

It is to be understood that neither the School Board, nor any agency of the Commonwealth of Virginia, assumes any responsibility whatever for any contractual obligations of the corporate association, nor any act or thing which said association may, at any time, do with respect to the conduct of the contemplated program of education. It is further contemplated that teachers formerly employed in the public schools of Prince Edward County will be given priority in preference for employment by the corporate organization conducting the said program. . . .

Based upon the foregoing understanding, the Governor will use his good offices to procure the services of the following persons, to fill three positions as trustees of the corporate association, in the following order of priority:

1. Colgate W. Darden Jr.
2. Dr. Fred B. Cole, President of Washington and Lee University
3. Dean F. D. G. Ribble, retired, of the Department of Law of the University of Virginia
4. Dr. Davis Y. Paschall, President of the College of William and Mary
5. Dr. George M. Modlin, President of the University of Richmond
6. Dr. H. Sherman Oberly, formerly President of Roanoke College
7. Dr. J. M. G. Finley, Director of George Mason College of the University of Virginia

It is further understood that three of the trustees of the said corporation will be selected from the following:

1. Dr. Thomas H. Henderson, President of Virginia Union University
2. Dr. Robert P. Daniel, President of the Virginia State College
3. Dr. Earl H. McClenny, President of St. Paul's College
4. Dr. Wendell Russell, Dean of Virginia Union University
5. Dr. James Howard Brewer, Professor of History, of Virginia State College

In the event the trustees of the private corporate organization determine that additional buildings are required for the conduct of an adequate educational program, and if the School Board of Prince Edward County shall concur in such determination that such additional buildings are needed by the private corporate organization, J. Segar Gravatt will use such influence as he may have with the leadership of the community in support of action by the School Board necessary to make such additional buildings available.

It is understood that the following will be provided to J. Segar Gravatt and to Counsel of the School Board, as well as to the Governor, a copy of the charter and by-laws of the proposed corporate organization, a copy of any conditions upon which private contributions are made to the private corporate organization, if any, and a statement of the general policy of the Board of Trustees in the conduct of the proposed educational program.

It is further understood that the facilities herein mentioned to be leased to the private corporate organization are to be used for educational purposes only, subject to such modification as the School Board, in its judgment, may wish to make with respect to the use thereof.

It is further here recorded that this Memorandum is the result of negotiations which were initiated in May of 1963 and have been in progress until the present.

It is further understood that, in view of the pending litigation in which the School Board is involved, a statement of the action here contemplated will be filed with the Judge of the United States District Court for the Eastern District of Virginia, and with the United States Court of Appeals for the Fourth Judicial Circuit, in which courts the litigation is presently pending.

Mr. vanden Heuvel is present in the capacity of offering the good offices of the Justice Department of the United States in bringing about the means by which children of Prince Edward County can be offered educational opportunity while the public schools of the County are unavailable to them.

Papers of the Prince Edward County Free School, Collection no. 1963–38, box 1, folder 10, Virginia State University Special Collections and Archives, Petersburg.

NOTE

1. "Excerpts from President's Civil Rights Message," *New York Times*, March 1, 1963.

QUESTIONS

1. By 1963, state officials supported the creation of a temporary, free, desegregated school system in Prince Edward County. This represented a dramatic change from the policies of state officials in the 1950s. Why do you think this change had occurred?

2. The governor was directed to choose six trustees for the nonprofit corporation that would oversee the Free Schools. Why do you think he was presented, in this document, with two lists to choose from? What did this signal about the Free Schools?

A Recess from Responsibility

Virginian-Pilot
December 5, 1963

The *Virginian-Pilot* was one of the few moderate white newspapers in Virginia during the civil rights era, and its editorial board supported compliance with *Brown v. Board of Education*. Published in Norfolk, the paper had also opposed the closure of the public schools in Norfolk by Governor J. Lindsay Almond in 1958, and the closing of the public schools in Prince Edward County in 1959. This editorial called for the opening of the schools and promoted public education, even if desegregated, throughout Virginia.

Governor Harrison, doing his soft-shoe best to ease a hard situation, suggested yesterday that Prince Edward County officials would move to open public schools within 48 hours if the United States Supreme Court upholds their right to close them.

By way of background, the story from the Governor's press conference noted that there have been numerous unofficial reports in the past that County officials would reopen the public schools "if a face-saving procedure could be found." An ultimate court decision upholding their right to close their schools "would provide the face-saving," said the Associated Press dispatch.

There has been, straight through, entirely too much concern about saving face for the Prince Edward authorities and too little thought about saving the lost school years of the County's children.

At nearly every turn in the case, local officials could have, without any loss of face, reopened the schools. Such a move would have been hailed as sensible, even statesmanlike.

There is no reason why, long ago, the classes could not have been resumed while the case continued in the courts. There is no reason why, now, with a favorable 6 to 1 ruling from the State Supreme Court, the officials could not remove all doubt about the future of public education by formulating and announcing plans to reopen schools in the Fall.

Instead, the County leaders will continue marking time until the United States Supreme Court forces them to do what could have been done in good grace long ago.

The highest court has an unhappy choice. On the one hand, it can present the woeful picture of the judiciary reaching over into the legislative sphere to order the Prince Edward County Board of Supervisors to appropriate school funds.

On the other, in a move reminiscent of massive resistance, it could enjoin Virginia from providing State school funds anywhere as long as Prince Edward schools are closed.

Either of these sad alternatives could set off a chorus of denunciation about Federal usurpation. We hope that the chorus will be short, and, once past, the County will get back in the business of public education.

Public education is no frill to be supplied or abandoned at will. Certain basic public education is as much a responsibility of government as tax-supported fire or police protection. The support of public education consumes at least half of the State of Virginia's general-fund budget.

The important thing has not been face, won or lost for one side or the other. It matters not what image Virginia presents in New Jersey or New Guinea. What matters is that Virginia permitted the withholding of a vital governmental function—public education—from a large portion of her population. Now, hopefully, the four-year recess is almost over.

QUESTIONS

1. How does this piece portray Prince Edward County's white officials? How does it portray Virginia's state officials?
2. How did the author portray public education? What threats faced public education in Virginia in 1963?
3. What events would bring an end to the conflict over the closed public schools in Prince Edward County, as described in this editorial?

The Tragedy of Public Schools: Prince Edward County, Virginia

J. Kenneth Morland
January 16, 1964

Dr. J. Kenneth Morland, a professor of anthropology and sociology at Randolph-Macon Women's College (now Randolph College), was commissioned by the U.S. Commission on Civil Rights to report on the Prince Edward County school situation. Morland enlisted the assistance of Edward H. Peeples, who had continued his extensive research in the county (see p. 166). The report was never officially released, according to Morland and Peeples, because of political pressure on the commission from southern members of Congress.[1]

Prince Edward County, Virginia closed its public schools at the end of the Spring term of 1959 in order to avoid a court order to desegregate them. At the time of this writing over four years later, there is still no public education for the white and Negro children of the County, a situation unique in the United States. While white children have had private schools during this period, Negro children had no regular schools open to them until the establishment this fall of a free school, supported by foundation and other gifts. For four years then, more than one half of the children of Prince Edward County did not have an opportunity for formal education in the county. They have been denied what many consider to be one of the most fundamental rights of American children—the right to a tax-supported education. This tragedy has taken place in a nation which constantly affirms its belief that education is essential to the development and maintenance of a democracy. It has occurred in a society founded on the belief in the worth of every individual and in the necessity of an education for the full realization of that worth. It has happened at a time when schooling is becoming more and more essential as improved technology demands more highly educated and skilled workers and eliminates jobs for the uneducated and the unskilled. It has taken place in a county that openly seeks new industry while denying most of its own children the chance for the schooling essential to the development of skills needed by any new industry that might come. It has happened in spite of the fact that white leaders who ordered the school closing have insisted that they want Negro children in the county to have an education. Yet, it has happened. The "unthinkable," has happened, here in Virginia and in America. . . .

The school-closing action brought warm commendation from white segregationists in the state and nation. The county was pictured as a small, brave group of whites pitting themselves against the power of the federal government and the NAACP. Contributions came from many sources, and segregationists visited the county to learn how the private schools were organized and operated. The president of the Prince Edward School Foundation declared in October of 1961 that he believed "more and more people are beginning to realize that Prince Edward is a test case for Southside Virginia and the entire South for that matter." With Prince Edward as a "cause célèbre" for segregationists all over the nation, any modification of their stand became difficult for the white leaders, as it would involve loss of face. This does not imply that there has been clear-cut evidence that the leadership wanted to retreat from its stand, but it does point out how a consideration of any modification was made difficult under the circumstances.

Negro leadership in the county has been resolute in seeking the goal of opening public schools to all children of the county without regard to race. Since the Negro high school children protested against unequal facilities in 1951, Negro leaders, aided especially by state and national NAACP legal counsel, have not wavered in the struggle to establish non-racial public schools. In spite of the fact that they and their children would be the ones to suffer most while segregation was being challenged, most Negroes have stood behind their leaders, as shown in their refusal to accept the offer by whites of private, segregated schools. . . . The court issues have been of great significance to the NAACP, whose lawyers have been the legal counsel for Negroes. And, as we have seen, different groups from the state and nation have tried to help Negro children in the county obtain some schooling. The stand of the leadership, then has been supported outside as well as within the county. If Negro leaders had been less determined, the challenge to racial segregation might have been too weak either to precipitate the actions against unequal facilities in the first place or to continue the long struggle for non-racial public schools after the schools had been closed.

There is little question, then, that leadership on both sides has been vitally important in the Prince Edward story. . . . However, there is no question about which leadership had the power to close or to open the schools. This power was, and still is, vested in the all-white board of supervisors. What in reality was said in blaming Negroes was that if Negroes had been willing to keep their segregated "place," the schools would not have closed. But this is equivalent to telling Americans that they must accept an inferior status, and this is something that Americans have never done willingly. . . .

The stated issues of the white leadership, according to our interpretation, rest ultimately on the conviction that racial segregation should be maintained in the schools. In this search for the causes of school closing, we come finally, then, to the question of why so many whites in Prince Edward County, and, indeed throughout the South and much of the rest of the nation, feel that it is so vitally important to keep Americans segregated by race. The answer is that such a feeling is an expression of what may be called "racism," a set of beliefs and attitudes that a person's race is very important, if not the single most important, thing about him. According to racism, a person is first of all a member of a race, and only after his racial designation has been made clear can be treated as an individual different from other individuals. Race even overrides the notion of the brotherhood of man, cherished by Prince Edward whites in their churches, for such "brotherhood" must be nourished in racially exclusive churches. As one white was previously quoted in defending the policy of racial segregation: "It is not a matter of religion, but of two different races."

In racist beliefs and attitudes, races are not only considered to be fundamentally different but also some are thought to be superior to others—and it is always one's own race that is the superior one. While the belief in the innate inferiority of Negroes is not flaunted by whites in Prince Edward, it clearly underlies their belief that Negroes must be kept separate. Belief in Negro inferiority is nourished by the system of forced racial segregation which assures unequal opportunities for Negroes and which educates everyone that racial differentiation is of paramount importance. The belief is also bolstered by treatises on the inferiority of Negroes, for such treatises were found to be very much in evidence in the conversations and on the bookshelves of dominant whites.

Belief in racial superiority of whites is convenient both for explaining and justifying the lower social and economic position of Negroes in the county. Negroes, so goes the explanation of the racist, have poorer jobs and less money, not because of racial segregation and discrimination, but because of lower innate ability. In other words, it is not the social system which is unjust, but the "natural" outcome of different racial abilities that produces the present result of unequal status. Exclusion of Negroes from white schools is not undemocratic for the racist, since the less able race will "pull down" the more able race if integration occurs. Such reasoning, then, can be used to support not only the desirability, but even the necessity of closing schools to avoid integration.

The basis on which racism rests, however, are refuted by the over-whelming majority of scientists who have devoted their lives to the study of race and race differences. A summary of the research and opinions of these scientists is beyond the scope of this report. Suffice it to say here that almost all geneticists, anthropologists, psychologists, and sociologists agree that there is no conclusive evidence to suggest that intelligence, or character or cultural development have anything to do with race directly. While members of the same race share genes which determine such physical features as color of the hair and skin and shape of the nose and head, there is no evidence for "racial" genes that determine the capacity to learn or to be creative or to develop sound character. While genetic factors clearly play a part in how much a person can learn and in his ability to create, these genetic factors are not racially based in any demonstrable way. Such views of scientists do not mean that they believe that all races are "equal" in innate ability, as is sometimes charged. This would imply that race somehow determines the "equality." The views indicate, rather, that race per se is not relevant to innate capacities of the individual to develop intelligence and other abilities. Of course, when race is seized upon as a basis for discriminatory treatment, as is true of forced racial segregation, then race can be an indirect factor in restricting the development of many kinds of skills. But this becomes a social, not a genetic, factor. . . .

In their studies of hundreds of different cultures in all parts of the world, cultural anthropologists have shown that the unity of a people lies not in similarities of their skin color or hair form but rather in the ideals and values they share. Thus the notion of the racist that basic unity lies in racial member-ship, as seen in such terms as "racial pride" and "racial integrity," conflict with anthropological findings. . . . The unity of Americans lies in their devotion to a democratic way of life, not in the particular physical features with which they are born. . . .

Most of America and many people throughout the world have been shocked that citizens of a democracy would deliberately close public schools in order to avoid desegregation. The dominant whites of the county claim that most persons outside the county "misunderstand" them, as indicated in the following *Farmville Herald* editorial of December 6, 1963:

"Prince Edward County, Virginia, has been misunderstood, maligned, and abused publicly by more people than probably any other county in the nation. It is understood, encouraged and admired privately by more people than any other county in the nation."

Criticism of Prince Edward comes not from misunderstanding but from disagreement with the goal of the majority, however sincerely and resolutely the majority may be devoted to it—the goal of maintaining forced racial segrega-tion even at the price of abandoning public education. And the encouragement and admiration for the county have not been so private, for we have seen that extreme segregationists have openly praised the county for fighting to maintain segregation. They have had no difficulty in understanding the issue.

It is difficult at this point to see what the county has gained by its long fight against the desegregation of public schools. Its reputation has been damaged, as the writer of the above editorial implies. Some of its own businessmen, as well as the Governor of the state, agree that the county has lost economically. Certainly the intellectual development of its Negro children has been seriously harmed. And from their responses to questions on their reactions to school closing and the placing of blame, most Negroes in the county hold deep resent-ment against the action of the dominant whites. Thus the sense of unity in the county has been hurt.

Perhaps we can find in these results the true lesson of Prince Edward County, namely that whenever some Americans try to keep other Americans in an inferior position, tragedy results. This nation is built upon the principle that every individual is of worth and deserves the opportunity to develop his abilities fully and to move freely in such development. To try to prevent some Americans from being treated as individuals brings disaster, both to those who set themselves up as superior and to those who are arbitrarily limited in their opportunities. All Americans need each other—in Prince Edward County, in the rest of Virginia, and throughout the nation. To the extent that we can assure equality of opportunity and recognition of individual worth and dignity for every American, without placing artificial restrictions on him because of race or creed or anything else—to that extent can we promote unity, utilize the talents of all, and thereby strengthen America to meet the challenge of today and the future.

Edward H. Peeples Jr. Papers, M342, box 14, folder 29A, Virginia Commonwealth University, Richmond.

NOTE

1. Edward H. Peeples, *Scalawag: A White Southerner's Journey through Segregation to Civil Rights Activism* (Charlottesville: University of Virginia Press, 2014), 102–3.

QUESTIONS

1. What led to the closing of the schools in Prince Edward County in 1959, as represented in this report?
2. How did Dr. J. Kenneth Morland explain the importance of race and racism in mid-twentieth-century Virginia?
3. What was the "tragedy" of public education in Prince Edward County, as described by Morland?

The Prince Edward County Situation

William vanden Heuvel
March 1964

The Prince Edward Free Schools were opened for classes on September 16, 1963, providing a long-delayed return to school for the county's black children. In March 1964,
as the protracted legal struggle for public education came to its conclusion before
the U.S. Supreme Court, William vanden Heuvel wrote a commentary on the Prince
Edward Free Schools program for the journal of the National Education Association.
One of the key figures behind the establishment of the Free Schools, vanden Heuvel
reflected on public education as the very foundation of American society and on the
damage that had been inflicted on the black children of Prince Edward County.

The problem of Prince Edward County, Virginia, is not a problem of civil rights
alone. It is also a problem that involves the fundamental integrity of free public
education in the United States.

If the doctrine that the state has no responsibility for free public education should spread to other parts of our nation, then what would become of
the American society, the very foundation stone of which has been free public
education? Free public education means that no child is born a prisoner of
any class, that the chains of poverty do not hang forever upon him, and that
the opportunities of a free and open society are ours and our children's and
our grandchildren's. That is what was taken away from the children of Prince
Edward County.

When the public schools in Prince Edward County were closed, a system of
private schools was established for the white children. These private schools,
which are still in existence, were supported, at first, by state tuition grants to
parents and by voluntary contributions. The supervisors encouraged many
contributions by granting tax relief to those who gave donations to the private
school foundation. The use of tuition grants and tax credits is presently enjoined by the courts.

In the meantime, many Negro children were sent to live with relatives outside the County so that they could attend school. Others—usually the brightest—were taken out of the County by groups such as the American Friends
Service Committee and sent to live with families in the North. The children
who left the County, however, represented at best no more than a sixth of the
Negro children of Prince Edward County.

The Virginia Teachers Association, which represents the state's 8,500 Negro teachers, did its best to help the majority of Negro children in the County by means of summer "crash" programs. Classes were set up in churches, lodge halls, and other available buildings. About 500 children attended VTA classes which, because of time and financial limitations, were confined to such basic subjects as reading and arithmetic.

Since 1959, the Prince Edward County case has gone back and forth through the courts. In 1961, a federal district judge ordered the schools reopened, but this judgment was vacated eight months later by an appellate court, which remanded the case to the state courts. The Virginia Supreme Court, with the chief justice dissenting, ruled in December that the state had no constitutional obligation to reopen the schools and that the supervisors could not be compelled to assess taxes and appropriate funds for support of Prince Edward's schools.

The Prince Edward case now stands, once again, before the U.S. Supreme Court, which will hear arguments on it March 30, 1964. The great irony is that the children who won the right to attend desegregated public schools ten years ago are still waiting to exercise that right. Even more ironic—in a County that is full of irony—is the fact that since September 1959 they have been denied the right to attend any public schools, much less desegregated ones.

The question that is now before the Supreme Court is whether the closing of public schools through the exercise of local option to avoid desegregation is a violation of the Fourteenth Amendment guaranteeing all citizens equal protection of the laws. The implications for public education throughout the South are obvious.

Since last fall, Negro children and some white children have been attending the Prince Edward County Free Schools. These schools, made possible in part through the voluntary contributions of NEA members and staff, reflect the personal concern of John F. Kennedy. As President, he could just as well have left it for the courts to resolve the Prince Edward problem. Instead, he commissioned the Department of Justice to see to it that the children of Prince Edward County had schools to attend this school year.

We hope that a great deal of lost ground will have been made up by the time these free schools close next August. At that time, the citizens of Virginia once again will have to decide whether or not public schools shall be open to all of the children in the state.

The leaders of Virginia with whom I have talked permit the optimism that some means will be found to reopen the public schools in Prince Edward County. Undoubtedly, those means are inextricably involved in the forthcoming Court decision. I, for one, hope that decision will come soon, that its terms and effect will leave no ambiguity so that the children of Prince Edward County can have public schools—and, perhaps more significant—that public education can be saved from further onslaughts that would debilitate its strength.

NEA Journal: The Journal of the National Education Association 53, no. 3 (March 1964): 13–15. Copyright 1964 National Education Association, reprinted with permission.

QUESTIONS

1. How did the Prince Edward County public school situation challenge the fundamental integrity of free public education in the United States?
2. What question is described as pending before the Supreme Court, and what implications would this hold for public education?

A Fresh Wind in Farmville

Peggy Bebie Thomson

April 1964

The *Progressive* magazine was founded in 1909 by U.S. senator Robert M. La Follette Sr. as *La Follette's Weekly*, "a magazine of progress, social, intellectual, institutional." In 1929, the magazine was renamed the *Progressive*, and it has continued to this day as a voice for social and economic justice, civil rights, and civil liberties. In December 1962, the *Progressive* published "A Century of Struggle," a special issue that won widespread acclaim for its exploration of the fight for civil rights during the one hundred years since the Emancipation Proclamation. In April 1964, the *Progressive* published this report on the Prince Edward County Free Schools.

In Virginia's rural Prince Edward County, on the south bank of the Appomattox, J. Barrye Wall, editor of *The Farmville Herald*, calls the news as he sees it and laces his opinions with the spine-stiffening admonition, "Prince Edward stand steady!"

Recently he wrote: "Prince Edward County has been misunderstood, maligned, and abused publicly by more people than probably any other county in the nation. It is understood, encouraged, and admired privately by more people than any other county in the nation. . . . Prince Edward stand steady!"

Whether or not it is as widely admired as he thinks, Prince Edward certainly is being watched. And a South balking at a commitment to integrated public education hopes a ruling on Prince Edward's case, presented to the Supreme Court on March 30, will vindicate this bitter-end segregationist county's contention that public schools are its whim, not its obligation.

So far as public education goes, Prince Edward could scarcely stand steadier without ossifying. It is right where it was in 1959. Practically everyone remembers how Prince Edward closed its schools rather than integrate—and became the only county in the country to abandon the concept of public education. Yet today many people can scarcely believe that the schools have never reopened. In decision after decision the Virginia courts have in effect upheld what the white community calls "the right to educate our children with the people we want."

While the white children have in the meantime been enrolled in the private Prince Edward Academy (its money raised by $250–$275 tuition fees plus contributions extracted from taxpayers "in lieu of taxes"), the Negro children have been on a four-year-long unhappy holiday. It was not until last fall that the Free School Association, set up on the initiative of the late President Kennedy and the Justice Department, the National Education Association, and a board of concerned Virginians, rented four of the old public school buildings and rang the school bells for these children again. Though the schools are private, they are desegregated, and they are re-engaging 1,700 Negro children, along with eight whites, in the business of education. "I'm going to lean on this bell and lean on it hard," one of the janitors said on that first school day, September 19, 1963. "It's been too long not ringing." . . .

When the hastily assembled staff of the Free Schools met for the first time last September, they were moved—some of them to tears—by the weight of the Negro community's hopes that rested on them and by the pitiful deprivation of children, many of whom had lost the ability to communicate. "I thought it would be a good thing to mark the opening day of school if we said allegiance to the flag together, the children and I," Superintendent Neil V. Sullivan remembers, "but the only ones who knew it were Bill vanden Heuvel of the Justice Department, the newsmen, and myself." In this same elementary school group only one youngster recognized the national anthem when it was played—and then only as "the baseball song."

What has happened in the Free Schools since then is so exciting, and of such a proportion, that a fresh wind is blowing through the county. It can no longer be said that the Negro community has suffered more than the white in the isolation of one from the other. The Free Schools have also blown in the notion that there may be a better way to live than "standing steady." . . .

Superintendent Sullivan, a tall, rangy figure with blue eyes that are quick to show admiration and a brow that rumples in concern as he listens and talks, speaks of the "greatest good fortune" that brought him from his top-notch Long Island school system to this demanding task. "I consider this the most important spot in American education today." His wife, who is deeply involved with the language arts program for one of the elementary schools, feels the same way. Colgate W. Darden Jr. a former Congressman, governor, and University of Virginia president, says he considers his post as the Free Schools' board chairman the most important service he has rendered his state. The assistant principal of the high school, T. L. Maynard, has "never had a more exciting job." Teachers spoke of the children's "remarkable dignity," "beautiful manners," "maturity," and "their quiet intensity." "It just seems," said the assistant librarian, "as if their minds are on what they're doing."

The politeness and deference were almost too much to take. The children walked along with proud carriage, greeted their teachers, rushed up to a principal with a new book. They smiled.

A little girl gave Mrs. Sullivan a quick hug as she passed.

All this, we learned from the teachers, was in contrast to the first weeks of school. "In the fall," one teacher told us, "the children would slink down the halls with their faces to the walls. They wouldn't look at us when we spoke to them. They wouldn't, or they couldn't, tell us their names." Another said, "We noticed for a while that even when the children greeted us openly here, they would pretend not to see us in town. Now they wave right on Main Street and say hello." . . .

Early September was a most unlikely time to find teachers. Some Peace Corps returnees and newly retired teachers, highly qualified, volunteered as soon as they heard of the need. Some currently teaching asked to be released from their jobs for the year; several Virginia teachers, whose boards refused to release them, came anyway. The hope was that most of the teachers would be from Virginia, and Negro; about seventy per cent are Negro. And teachers drawn from Maine to California are at Farmville. . . .

Actually, lack of money—except at the precarious start—has not stood in the Free Schools' way. Most of the schools' $1 million budget—filling the five-year gap—has been made up by foundations—Ford, Field, Danforth, Babcock. Virginia industries have anonymously given $125,000; individuals from all over the country, particularly school teachers, $75,000. An outpouring of contributions has included 40,000 free textbooks, out-of-town newspapers, thirty television sets, modern teaching machines, art supplies. Children can apply for clothing for themselves or their families, so that now they have proper shoes. The girl who missed school because she shared a winter coat with her mother now has a coat of her own. The high school's library, already sizeable, has been promised 25,000 new books. And Scott-Foresman publishers have given each child a dictionary as the start of a home library.

How much can be done in the one year allotted before the Court settles the issue—to make up for the lost years—the Free School teachers can't tell. Certainly nine and ten-year-olds who begin reading for the first time are progressing faster than six-year-olds. Testing at the start of the year was virtually impossible. Twelve-year-olds had to be shown how to hold a pencil. Many couldn't sign their names or recognize them in print. Some looked at the papers and burst into tears. "We just had to jump right in with teaching," one teacher recalled. Even the IQ tests given by a University of Michigan team did not seem to be accurate. The children had been so isolated and were so non-verbal that the first scores didn't reflect their intelligence; only a few weeks later they tested higher. "In fact," Sullivan tossed out, "we have three children who are over 150. The national average would be two."

Visible proof of how far these Negro children have to go are the cards tacked up everywhere in the lower schools. Each window carries a card on it lettered "window," each door, "door," "plant," "desk," "cupboard," and, in the cafeteria, "spoon" and "cup." "We're teaching every minute of the day," we were told. Nothing is allowed to interfere with the reading or language skills periods. According to Phyllis Mielke, a young Wisconsinite teaching eight and nine-year-olds, grammar is hard to teach because the children don't know what sounds right. "Looks, looking, looked—at home it's all the same to them."

Even more striking, however, is how far the children have come. Boys and girls in the art class, most of whom had never even held a crayon before this year, were doing sophisticated three-color silkscreen prints the day we visited. The teacher had even arranged for them to show their work in the window of a bank on Main Street. (The white-only Academy has no art teacher.) . . .

The children we saw were applying themselves to books like puppies to bones. Now that they are learning, they want to talk. The same children who last fall put their hands to their sides and refused to touch the library books ("I can't read") are crowding around the library tables, swapping opinions. High schoolers are using up to 6,000 volumes a month.

The teachers are living and working at a pitch probably no group could sustain over a long haul, but knowing they have just this one year colors everything they do. The year started with staff meetings every night—to spell out goals, discuss methods, acquaint everyone with the ways of "ungraded classrooms" (by which flexibly grouped students can progress at their own rate) and "team teaching" (by which a master teacher and several inexperienced teachers handle one group of children together).

One thing working in the Free Schools' favor is that the teachers, being new, have no other commitments in town. Living and working as an integrated staff, they are not welcome socially in restaurants and movies. "We have had to make our own society." They have a choir, evening movies at school, dinner meetings with homemade entertainment, and a topnotch basketball team. The Free Schools' faculty team is the only such integrated team in the South, and Superintendent Sullivan (who is ten feet tall) plays in every game.

The night we watched one of the faculty games, a teacher looking down the rows of students and faculty seated on the bleachers said, over the shouting and laughter, "I just wish the people in town could see what a wonderful people these are." . . .

The Free Schools comprise a rural school system unique in all the South, run on lines that are advanced even for many progressive white schools. Superintendent Sullivan, the architect of the ungraded system, has been asked to speak in Richmond, in Roanoke, and in cities from the East to the West Coast. So far he has never been asked to speak before any Farmville group, including Longwood College where, as one teacher laughingly pointed out, "The motto is, 'we teach to teach, education for all!'"

As the person who is the most linked to the destiny of the Prince Edward Negro people, Sullivan unashamedly uses every gimmick—entertainment, refreshments—to bring out parents wholly unused to turning up for PTAs. When he gets them together, sometimes 600-strong, he urges them to involve themselves.

"The tragedy of the Southern Negroes," he said, "is that they have abdicated their rights so far as schools are concerned. I tell them, 'Don't accept classes of fifty. Insist on good libraries. Above all, keep your children coming to school. You're going to get equal rights. That's coming. But this is where you fall down.' It is criminal that Virginia has no compulsory attendance law. The whites stay in school perhaps eleven years. Negroes, only six or seven. It's where you have good schools in the South that you have an aggressive Negro community with doctors and lawyers. It's where you get children wanting to stay, too."

The worry, of course, is what next year may bring. The white community is heavily committed financially and in loyalties to the Academy. If compelled by the Supreme Court to open the public schools, will it give only the worst it can get by with and send only the children of its most financially distressed families? This question, which sits uneasily on every mind, came up in our talks with the two men who have stood up tall through Prince Edward's schoolless years—Dean C. G. G. Moss of Longwood College and the Reverend L.

Francis Griffin, who is NAACP state president and minister of the Negro First Baptist Church.

Dean Moss, who reaches retirement age this year, is a Southern gentleman who has been "the conscience of the white community"—the one man to have spoken out for the Negroes in all the years that schools were closed. He is obviously pleased that his seventeen-year-old son elected to spend his senior year in the Free Schools. When we talked to him he was deeply troubled, though, by what he considered a hardening attitude on the part of the white community, at least regarding himself—a kind of personal hatred which he had never been made to feel in even the most vehement disagreements before last summer. "I guess it's some right wild dreaming of mine to get the local community to accept the Negroes as citizens."

The Reverend Griffin was more hopeful. Through all the years since 1951, when the Negro high school students in Prince Edward successfully struck for a "more equal" separate but equal high school, he has been the leader of the Negro movement. He finds some amusement in how perplexed the whites have been by the Negroes' refusal of their offer of separate private schools. He himself was pleasantly surprised by the solidarity. "I knew they would never accept. But even I was amazed that only one Negro family answered 'yes' to the whites' questionnaire five years ago."

If Superintendent Sullivan is worried about what is to come after the Free Schools end their one-year term, he shows it by putting an extra spurt of elbow grease into making this year shine. He is enormously encouraged that a number of his teachers intend to stay on in Farmville for at least a few more years. And he believes that in just the last few weeks the white community has been showing the first signs of concern. Members of the old county school board have come on a tour of the Free Schools; there has been a rumor that the Superintendent may be asked to speak in town.

Meanwhile, a relative newcomer in Prince Edward, the Reverend Arthur Field, a young white Presbyterian minister and faculty member at Hampden-Sydney College, has managed to bring together a group of twenty-one white citizens. "We don't dare to call it a committee, really. Certainly not a human relations committee," Sullivan explained. "It is just twenty-one people who are willing to talk and listen. They have invited a bi-racial group from the school to speak to them. And the Reverend Griffin. It's unprecedented for here."

In the first issue of the Moton high school paper, *The Eagle*, which made its appearance last month, the student editor's query was: "What about schools in '64–65?" Even if public schools are open and desegregated, "how good will they be?"

Those questions are a touching evidence of progress; students so long concerned with getting any schooling at all are now concerned with how good the schooling will be. The answer rests largely with the white community, on whether it too has progressed in its attitude—from unfailing courtesy to an appreciation of the rights of all American children to public education.

Collins Denny Jr. the Prince Edward lawyer who begged his doctors to keep him alive long enough to plead the whites' case before the Supreme Court on March 30 (an extension they were unable to grant), requested that "instead of flowers" donations in his memory be sent to the Free Schools as well as to his beloved Prince Edward Academy—a hint, perhaps, of a new spirit in Farmville.

The Progressive, April 1964, 23. Reprinted with permission.

QUESTIONS

1. What was the "fresh wind" blowing through Prince Edward County?
2. What opinion did the author express with regard to Prince Edward County's closed schools? How does this essay portray the county's white residents?
3. In what ways did the Prince Edward County Free Schools offer more than a typical education to the children of the county during the 1963–64 school year? How did the author portray the Free Schools?

Introduction to *Bound for Freedom*

Robert F. Kennedy
1965

In 1965, Dr. Neil Sullivan published a memoir of his year as the superintendent of the Prince Edward County Free Schools. Robert F. Kennedy, now serving as U.S. senator from New York, wrote the introduction to the book. Kennedy offered a reflection on the importance of the Free Schools, Dr. Sullivan's role, and the struggle for education in Prince Edward County.

The longest, most intensive litigation in the history of the civil rights struggle involved Prince Edward County, Virginia. It began in 1951. In some aspects it is still continuing. The case was part of the landmark decision of *Brown v. Board of Education* which on May 17, 1954, established the constitutional right of American children to attend public schools which were not segregated because of color. Five years later, under federal court order to desegregate, the Board of Supervisors of Prince Edward County refused to assess taxes to support the public school system, and the schools were closed. For the next four years the Negro children of Prince Edward County were the only children in the United States—in fact, in the entire Western world—who did not have an opportunity to have free basic public education.

This brief outline of the conflict does not begin to measure its anguish and bitter tragedy. The litigation languished in the state and federal courts as difficult constitutional issues developed—and the schools remained closed. In 1963, President Kennedy refused to permit further injury to the children and ordered the Justice Department to find some way to reopen the schools. His personal concern inspired an extraordinary project known as the Prince Edward Free School Association.

The Free Schools did not make up for the years of educational opportunity that had been lost, but they did stop the human erosion, and in the process served as a pilot project for the nation in showing what remarkable progress could be made with disadvantaged children if excellent teachers, modern techniques, and adequate funds were available. In an important sense, the Free Schools provided the experience that justified the war against poverty as enacted in the Economic Opportunity program. The concept of a National Teacher Corps as advocated by President Johnson was also part of the lesson taught by the Free Schools.

The project owed its success to the heroic efforts of many individuals, including those of Neil Sullivan. The trustees of the Free School Association are among them. They were six unusual men—three white, three Negro, all Virginians and all in the highest ranks of their state's academic circles. They had the basic responsibility for the operation of the schools, and in good measure their courage and wisdom assured the project's success. They chose Dr. Sullivan, the author of this book, to be the superintendent of the system.

There are many others whose efforts should be acknowledged—the teachers who were recruited in a month's time from all over the nation and who served without concern for personal cost or inconvenience; United States Commissioner of Education Francis Keppel and his dedicated staff who did so much in helping the teacher recruitment and planning the curriculum; the foundations, corporations and thousands of individual contributors who gave the funds that permitted the Free Schools to operate for a full year; the National Education Association which also helped recruit teachers and supported the project with contributions from many of its chapters; the administrative staff, headed by Neil Sullivan, which sustained both the quality and the spirit of the Free Schools throughout their existence; the citizens of Prince Edward County, both Negro and white, who encouraged the project and held it safe from violence; and the children of Prince Edward County who attended the Free Schools—their conduct and performance set an example that made the nation proud.

The name of Robert E. Lee is a heroic legend in southside Virginia, but too often it is his military genius and not his qualities of character and compassion that are remembered. He bid fellow Virginians to end the Civil War and return to the task for which they had already done so much—building a great nation dedicated to freedom and justice for all of its citizens. He saw education as the hope for his people and dedicated his last years to that cause. Appomattox and Prince Edward County are side by side. As one marked the end of a cruel war, how significant it would be if the other symbolized the end of the struggle that has oppressed the Negro and left him less than a full citizen of his own country. At least one generation of children in Prince Edward County will always carry the scars of the conflict that closed their schools. But perhaps even they will disregard the cost if their children are permitted to share the American dream.

Neil V. Sullivan, *Bound for Freedom: An Educator's Adventures in Prince Edward County, Virginia* (Boston: Little, Brown, 1965), ix–xi. Copyright 1965, reprinted with permission of Little, Brown and Company.

QUESTIONS

1. What were some of the most important lessons to be learned from the struggle for public education in Prince Edward County, according to Robert Kennedy?
2. What parallels did Kennedy draw between the life of Robert E. Lee and public education in Prince Edward County?

7

"Too Much Deliberation and Not Enough Speed"

On May 25, 1964, ten years and eight days after the original school desegregation ruling in *Brown v. Board of Education*, the U.S. Supreme Court ruled in *Griffin v. County School Board of Prince Edward County* that the public schools must be reopened. The Court held that the public schools were closed for one reason only, to ensure that white and black children would not attend the same school, a violation of the equal protection clause of the Fourteenth Amendment. The Court further noted that all other counties in Virginia operated public schools, thus the children of Prince Edward County were denied equal protection. Justice Hugo Black stated in the opinion of the Court, "There has been entirely too much deliberation and not enough speed in enforcing the constitutional rights which we held in *Brown v. Board of Education*, had been denied Prince Edward County Negro children" (see p. 196).

The first words of the *Griffin* decision stated, "This litigation began in 1951," a clear indication of the long legal battle for integrated public education set in motion by the student strike at Robert R. Moton High School on April 23, 1951, thirteen years earlier. The initial lawsuit, filed in May 1951, was *Davis v. County School Board of Prince Edward County*. In 1957, the lawsuit was refiled as *Allen v. County School Board of Prince Edward County*, seeking compliance with the *Brown* decision. And in 1962, the case was refiled again, with Reverend L. Francis Griffin and his children as named plaintiffs, when the NAACP sought legal remedy to reopen the closed public schools.[1] In 1964, the Supreme Court rebuked the county's refusal to comply with *Brown v. Broad of Education*, ordered the Prince Edward public schools reopened, and ordered the county to levy taxes to fund public education. NAACP general counsel Robert L. Carter declared that the Court ruling on "Prince Edward County's experiment in ignorance" had "brought to an end one of the most shameful chapters in the history of the school desegregation crisis" (see p. 206).

For many African American children, however, the schools' reopening came too late. A year-long study on the effects of the school closings, funded by the U.S. Office of Education, conducted by Dr. Robert L. Green of Michigan State University, documented the breadth of the damage. Many children were grades behind in their studies. Too long out of school, many teenagers simply never returned rather than restart their education in the elementary grades. One student, now eighteen years old, was drafted into the army and upon appeal was told by the county draft board that he was too old to be in high school—with no acknowledgment of the county actions that had delayed his education. The educational damage was extensive, and the challenges to public education would be ongoing.

In an expression of continued opposition to the courts, the county Board of Supervisors appropriated $189,000 to reopen the public schools while also authorizing $375,000 in tuition grants for white students at the private academy despite ongoing legal actions regarding the legality of those grants. The county school board refused to provide any additional funding for special education or remedial reading teachers in the public schools, claiming the county had no need for such programs. And in spite of overcrowding at several of the reopened schools, the board refused to ever reopen the previously white Farmville High School building. No African American child would ever cross that educational threshold. In a letter to William vanden Heuvel in 1964, Reverend L. Francis Griffin wrote, "After thirteen years of litigation we have only succeeded in reopening a type of public school system vastly inferior to the one in existence in 1959" (see p. 207).

Following five years of work in support of educational rights of black children, the American Friends Service Committee turned its efforts to supporting the reopened public schools. A survey by AFSC fieldworkers indicated that as many as two hundred or more white children had left school by 1965. With the loss of state tuition grants and local tax credits, which the courts had declared illegal, many poor whites could no longer afford the private academy but were reluctant to return to the now primarily black public schools. The grievous, ongoing effects of the public school crisis also fell on poor white residents of Prince Edward County.

Court battles over financial aid to the private school and funding for the public schools continued through the 1960s. In 1972, one public elementary school had a student enrollment of 450 students in a school built for 180, the same, overcrowded conditions that had precipitated the Robert R. Moton High School strike twenty years earlier. The county Board of Supervisors was compelled that year to increase the public education budget by 48 percent in order to meet the new minimum state funding standards set by the Virginia General Assembly.[2]

The public schools of Prince Edward County were closed for five years in a defiant, last-ditch expression of massive resistance. The schools were now reopened, but the damage that had been inflicted on the county and its children would last for years to come.

NOTES

1. *Allen v. County School Board of Prince Edward County, Virginia*, 249 F. 2d 462 (1957); *Griffin et al. v. County School Board of Prince Edward County et al.*, 377 U.S. 218 (1964).

2. Dr. James M. Anderson Jr., interview with Brian Grogan, Farmville, Virginia, May 18, 2004.

Griffin v. County School Board of Prince Edward County

U.S. Supreme Court
May 25, 1964

Ten years after the original court ruling in *Brown*, the black children of Prince Edward County had yet to benefit from the decision. In 1964, the Prince Edward school struggle returned to the U.S. Supreme Court in *Griffin v. County School Board of Prince Edward County*. In a historic decision with national implications for the future of public education, the Court ruled that the black students had been denied the equal protection of the laws guaranteed by the Fourteenth Amendment and ordered the immediate reopening of the public schools.

This litigation began in 1951 when a group of Negro school children living in Prince Edward County, Virginia, filed a complaint in the United States District Court for the Eastern District of Virginia alleging that they had been denied admission to public schools attended by white children and charging that Virginia laws requiring such school segregation denied complainants the equal protection of the laws in violation of the Fourteenth Amendment. On

May 17, 1954, ten years ago, we held that the Virginia segregation laws did deny equal protection. On May 31, 1955, after reargument on the nature of relief, we remanded this case, along with others heard with it, to the District Courts to enter such orders as "necessary and proper to admit (complainants) to public schools on a racially nondiscriminatory basis with all deliberate speed. . . ."

Efforts to desegregate Prince Edward County's schools met with resistance. In 1956 Section 141 of the Virginia Constitution was amended to authorize the General Assembly and local governing bodies to appropriate funds to assist students to go to public or to nonsectarian private schools, in addition to those owned by the State or by the locality. The General Assembly met in special session and enacted legislation to close any public schools where white and colored children were enrolled together, to cut off state funds to such schools, to pay tuition grants to children in non-sectarian private schools, and to extend state retirement benefits to teachers in newly created private schools. The legislation closing mixed schools and cutting off state funds was later invalidated by the Supreme Court of Appeals of Virginia, which held that these laws violated the Virginia Constitution. In April 1959 the General Assembly abandoned "massive resistance" to desegregation and turned instead to what was called a "freedom of choice" program. The Assembly repealed the rest of the 1956 legislation, as well as a tuition grant law of January 1959, and enacted a new tuition grant program. At the same time the Assembly repealed Virginia's compulsory attendance laws and instead made school attendance a matter of local option.

In June 1959, the United States Court of Appeals for the Fourth Circuit directed the Federal District Court (1) to enjoin discriminatory practices in Prince Edward County schools, (2) to require the County School Board to take "immediate steps" toward admitting students without regard to race to the white high school "in the school term beginning September 1959," and (3) to require the Board to make plans for admissions to elementary schools without regard to race. Having as early as 1956 resolved that they would not operate public schools "wherein white and colored children are taught together," the Supervisors of Prince Edward County refused to levy any school taxes for the 1959–1960 school year, explaining that they were "confronted with a court decree which requires the admission of white and colored children to all the schools of the county without regard to race or color." As a result, the county's public schools did not reopen in the fall of 1959 and have remained closed ever since, although the public schools of every other county in Virginia have continued to operate under laws governing the State's public school system and to draw funds provided by the State for that purpose. A private group, the Prince Edward School Foundation, was formed to operate private schools for white children in Prince Edward County and, having built its own school plant, has been in operation ever since the closing of the public schools. An offer to set up private schools for colored children in the county was rejected, the Negroes of Prince Edward preferring to continue the legal battle for desegregated public schools, and colored children were without formal education from 1959 to 1963, when federal, state, and county authorities cooperated to have classes conducted for Negroes and whites in school buildings owned by the county. During the 1959–1960 school year the Foundation's schools for white children were supported entirely by private contributions, but in 1960 the General Assembly adopted a new tuition grant program making every child, regardless of race, eligible for tuition grants of $125, or $150 to attend a nonsectarian private school or a public school outside his locality, and also authorizing localities to provide their own grants. The Prince Edward Board of Supervisors then passed an ordinance providing tuition grants of $100, so that each child attending the Prince Edward School Foundation's schools received a total of $225 if in elementary school or $250 if in high school. In the 1960–1961 session the major source of financial support for the Foundation was in the indirect form of these state and county tuition grants, paid to children attending Foundation schools. At the same time, the County Board of Supervisors passed an ordinance allowing property tax credits up to 25% for contributions to any "nonprofit, nonsectarian private school" in the county.

In 1961 petitioners here filed a supplemental complaint, adding new parties and seeking to enjoin the respondents from refusing to operate an efficient system of public free schools in Prince Edward County and to enjoin payment of public funds to help support private schools which excluded students on account of race. The District Court, finding that "the end result of every action taken by that body (Board of Supervisors) was designed to preserve separation of the races in the schools of Prince Edward County," enjoined the county from paying tuition grants or giving tax credits so long as public schools remained closed. At this time the District Court did not pass on whether the public schools of the county could be closed but abstained pending determination by the Virginia courts of whether the constitution and laws of Virginia required the public schools to be kept open. Later, however, without waiting for the Virginia courts to decide the question, the District Court held that "the public schools of Prince Edward County may not be closed to avoid the effect of the law of the land as interpreted by the Supreme Court, while the Commonwealth of Virginia permits other public schools to remain open at the expense of the taxpayers." Soon thereafter, a declaratory judgment suit was brought by the County Board of Supervisors and the County School Board in a Virginia Circuit Court. Having done this, these parties asked the Federal District Court to abstain from further proceedings until the suit in the state courts had run its course, but the District Court declined; it repeated its order that Prince Edward's public schools might not be closed to avoid desegregation while the other public schools in Virginia remained open. The Court of Appeals reversed, Judge Bell dissenting, holding that the District Court should have abstained to await state court determination of the validity of the tuition grants and the tax credits, as well as the validity of the closing of the public schools. We granted certiorari, stating:

"In view of the long delay in the case since our decision in the *Brown* case and the importance of the questions presented, we grant certiorari and put the case down for argument March 30, 1964, on the merits, as we have done in other comparable situations without waiting for final action by the Court of Appeals."

For reasons to be stated, we agree with the District Court that, under the circumstances here, closing the Prince Edward County schools while public schools in all the other counties of Virginia were being maintained denied the petitioners and the class of Negro students they represent the equal protection of the laws guaranteed by the Fourteenth Amendment. . . .

The case has been delayed since 1951 by resistance at the state and county level, by legislation, and by lawsuits. The original plaintiffs have doubtless all passed high school age. There has been entirely too much deliberation and not enough speed in enforcing the constitutional rights which we held in *Brown v. Board of Education*, supra, had been denied Prince Edward County Negro children. We accordingly reverse the Court of Appeals' judgment remanding the case to the District Court for abstention, and we proceed to the merits.

In *County School Board of Prince Edward County v. Griffin* (1963), the Supreme Court of Appeals of Virginia upheld as valid under state law the closing of the Prince Edward County public schools, the state and county tuition grants for children who attend private schools, and the county's tax concessions for those who make contributions to private schools. The same opinion also held that each county had "an option to operate or not to operate public schools." We accept this case as a definitive and authoritative holding of Virginia law, binding on us, but we cannot accept the Virginia court's further holding, based largely on the Court of Appeals' opinion in this case, that closing the county's public schools under the circumstances of the case did not deny the colored school children of Prince Edward County equal protection of the laws guaranteed by the Federal Constitution.

Since 1959, all Virginia counties have had the benefits of public schools but one: Prince Edward. However, there is no rule that counties, as counties, must be treated alike; the Equal Protection Clause relates to equal protection of the laws "between persons as such rather than between areas." . . .

Virginia law, as here applied, unquestionably treats the school children of Prince Edward differently from the way it treats the school children of all other Virginia counties. Prince Edward children must go to a private school or none at all; all other Virginia children can go to public schools. Closing Prince Edward's schools bears more heavily on Negro children in Prince Edward County since white children there have accredited private schools which they can attend, while colored children until very recently have had no available private schools, and even the school they now attend is a temporary expedient. Apart from this expedient, the result is that Prince Edward County school children, if they go to school in their own county, must go to racially segregated schools which, although designated as private, are beneficiaries of county and state support.

A State, of course, has a wide discretion in deciding whether laws shall operate statewide or shall operate only in certain counties, the legislature "having in mind the needs and desires of each." A State may wish to suggest . . . that there are reasons why one county ought not to be treated like another. But the record in the present case could not be clearer that Prince Edward's public schools were closed and private schools operated in their place with state and county assistance, for one reason, and one reason only: to ensure, through measures taken by the county and the State, that white and colored children in Prince Edward County would not, under any circumstances, go to the same school. Whatever nonracial grounds might support a State's allowing a county to abandon public schools, the object must be a constitutional one, and grounds of race and opposition to desegregation do not qualify as constitutional. . . .

We come now to the question of the kind of decree necessary and appropriate to put an end to the racial discrimination practiced against these petitioners under authority of the Virginia laws. That relief needs to be quick and effective. The parties defendant are the Board of Supervisors, School Board, Treasurer, and Division Superintendent of Schools of Prince Edward County, and the State Board of Education and the State Superintendent of Education. All of these have duties which relate directly or indirectly to the financing, supervision, or operation of the schools in Prince Edward County. The Board of Supervisors has the special responsibility to levy local taxes to operate public schools or to aid children attending the private schools now functioning there for white children. The District Court enjoined the county officials from paying county tuition grants or giving tax exemptions and from processing applications for state tuition grants so long as the county's public schools remained closed. We have no doubt of the power of the court to give this relief to enforce the discontinuance of the county's racially discriminatory practices. It has long been established that actions against a county can be maintained in United States courts in order to vindicate federally guaranteed rights. The injunction against paying tuition grants and giving tax credits while public schools remain closed is appropriate and necessary since those grants and tax credits have been essential parts of the county's program, successful thus far, to deprive petitioners of the same advantages of a public school education enjoyed by children in every other part of Virginia. For the same reasons the District Court may, if necessary to prevent further racial discrimination, require the Supervisors to exercise the power that is theirs to levy taxes to raise funds adequate to reopen, operate, and maintain without racial discrimination a public school system in Prince Edward County like that operated in other counties in Virginia. . . .

An order of this kind is within the court's power if required to assure these petitioners that their constitutional rights will no longer be denied them. The time for mere "deliberate speed" has run out, and that phrase can no longer justify denying these Prince Edward County school children their constitutional rights to an education equal to that afforded by the public schools in the other parts of Virginia.

The judgment of the Court of Appeals is reversed, the judgment of the District Court is affirmed, and the cause is remanded to the District Court with directions to enter a decree which will guarantee that these petitioners will get the kind of education that is given in the State's public schools. And, if it becomes necessary to add new parties to accomplish this end, the District Court is free to do so. It is so ordered.

377 U.S. 218 (1964).

QUESTIONS

1. What did the Supreme Court order in *Griffin v. County School Board of Prince Edward County*? What was the legal basis for its decision? What was the impact of this ruling in Prince Edward County?
2. In the conclusion, the justices discussed how county officials might comply with this pronouncement. What were the Court's recommendations?

The Door Unlocked

Washington Post
May 26, 1964

The *Washington Post* lauded the *Griffin* ruling and recognized the courage of the African American community of Prince Edward County. While criticizing the failure of political leadership in Virginia, the paper also called for a state and federal role in meeting the vital educational needs of the children of Prince Edward County.

"The time for more 'deliberate speed' has run out," the Supreme Court held yesterday, nine years after it introduced that celebrated phrase into the Prince Edward case, and now the County must at last reopen its schools. The gross delays in the recent litigation are owed, not to any great complexity of the issues, but rather to the earnest desire of the Federal judges to let Virginians work out their own solution among themselves. But Governor Harrison, to his State's great misfortune, was never able to summon up the courage to lead Prince Edward County toward the rule of reason that prevails throughout most of Virginia. And the State's Supreme Court, over the trenchant objections of its own chief, insisted upon a reading of the Fourteenth Amendment that ignored all of the great decisions of the last two decades. The Federal courts must end this affront to the Constitution because the men elected to lead Virginia have repeatedly refused to do so.

The 1,700 Negro children of Prince Edward County have a right to the same education afforded by the public schools everywhere else in Virginia, the Supreme Court said, and if necessary the lower court will force the County Supervisors to levy school taxes and unlock the classrooms. No doubt the blind stubbornness that has brought the county to its present circumstances will not be dissipated over night, but surely the Supervisors can perceive the benefits of voluntary compliance. The children of both races will be best served by local operation of the schools under the conditions of equality set by this long line of decisions.

The Court's decision does not reach the interesting question of a state's authority to close all of its public schools to preserve total segregation. Virginia, happily, no longer stands in peril of that monumental folly. The era of massive resistance has ended. Some 3,700 Negro school children, in 55 of Virginia's 130 school districts, attend desegregated classes. Those desegregated districts contain two thirds of the State's population, and as a matter of political reality the State's schools will stay open.

When public education is recommenced in Prince Edward next September, the children who were four years without schools will need more help than other children in the adjacent counties. The Court can only set a rough standard of equality; to compensate for time lost will require, for a time, a higher expenditure than is customary in that part of Virginia. Prince Edward is not a rich county, and it will need special assistance. It is time for the State and Federal authorities to consider their responsibilities to these children who have carried forward one of American history's great tests of right, and have suffered for it.

QUESTIONS

1. How does the editorial portray Virginia's leaders and the state's court system? On whom did the editorial call to promote equal rights in Prince Edward County?
2. What special considerations would be needed when the county's public schools were reopened in September?

That Horrendous Decision

Richmond News Leader
May 26, 1964

The *Richmond News Leader* and its editor, James J. Kilpatrick (see p. 107), had been prominent in the fight to maintain segregation in Virginia since the 1954 ruling in *Brown v. Board of Education*. Following the *Griffin* decision, the newspaper attacked the Supreme Court on its editorial page, just as it had attacked the *Brown* decision ten years earlier. This editorial refers to funding public education in the county as a "discretionary act contrary to the expressed wishes of their people," reflecting the paper's dismissive view of the expressed wishes of the African American community in Prince Edward County.

The Supreme Court of the United States, speaking through Mr. Justice Black, yesterday erected another of its milestone decisions—a milestone, that is, to the decay of the Constitution and to the arrogance of judges.

This latest chapter in the Prince Edward County case put squarely before the Court one of the most profound questions of constitutional law ever brought before our highest tribunal. In its simplest terms, the question was whether the Federal courts have power to compel a local legislative body to levy taxes in order to perform a discretionary act. This was a question that demanded full and serious exposition, for the question was founded on bedrock principles of American government—the principle, among others, that taxation without representation is tyranny.

The Court did not grapple with these principles at all. Mr. Justice Black's opinion amounts to no more than a bland assertion that of course the Federal courts are possessed of such power. "The district court may, if necessary to prevent further racial discrimination, require the supervisors to exercise the power that is theirs to levy taxes to raise funds adequate to reopen, operate, and maintain without racial discrimination a public school system in Prince Edward County like that operated in other counties in Virginia."

That is the heart of the opinion, wrapped up in a single sentence. The Court's seven-man majority did not spell out precisely how the district court is to accomplish this unprecedented step. "An order of this kind is within the Court's power." That was all the Court had to say.

The mind spins off in a dozen directions. The gist of the Court's opinion is that "the colored schoolchildren" of Prince Edward since 1959 have been denied the equal protection of the laws. This is because "Prince Edward children must go to a private school or none at all," while "all other Virginia children can go to a public school." But our own Virginia Supreme Court of Appeals has ruled that under the laws and constitution of Virginia, the State's system of public schools depends entirely upon local decisions. Within limits fixed by the State constitution, a county is free to operate no schools, some schools, or very elaborate schools. This is what our highest State court held in *Prince Edward County v. Griffin*, that in Virginia, the operation of local schools is a local responsibility. The U.S. Supreme Court, to the layman's bewilderment, said yesterday that "We accept this case as a definitive and authoritative holding of Virginia law, binding on us."

But the Prince Edward case is "unique." It has been characterized by "entirely too much deliberation and not enough speed." Despite the fact that the "colored children" of Prince Edward have not been denied one single benefit, opportunity, or advantage made available by the county to white children, in some fashion perceived only by the Supreme Court the colored children have been denied "equal protection." This is because they do not have public schools while all other counties do. But Prince Edward has no control over what all other counties do. That was the authoritative, definitive, and binding decision of the Virginia Supreme Court. One travels around in circles.

So District Judge Oren Lewis, who failed wretchedly in drafting an order in the first place, must now try again. He may "require the supervisors to exercise the power that is theirs to levy taxes." How much taxes? On what property or transaction? At what rate? If the supervisors refuse to levy taxes on their constituents against their will, are the supervisors to be imprisoned for contempt? If the supervisors resign, are new supervisors to be similarly jailed? Or suppose the supervisors, thus intimidated, levy appropriate taxes, and the resentful people of Prince Edward refuse to pay? To jail with them too?

Other questions come to mind. The supervisors, under this judgment, may be compelled to levy taxes sufficient to maintain a public school system "like that operated in other counties in Virginia." What other counties? Arlington? Fairfax? Henrico? Or at the other end of the economic scale, Tazewell, Scott, Buchanan? Total per pupil costs range from $170 or $180 in some parts of the State to $400 or $500 in others. In one recent year, Arlington appropriated in local funds alone $383 per child. Nansemond County appropriated $37 per pupil only.

The amount of taxes to be levied is a function not only of the quality of the school to be maintained, but also of the number of pupils to be educated, the ratio of teachers to pupils, the salaries to be paid, the frills to be provided.

It would seem to us inescapable that Judge Lewis, explicitly or implicitly, must pass upon all of these things, thereby assuming the role not merely of Federal judge, but also of county supervisor, school board, and school superintendent. Who elected him to these offices?

With this decision, the American Republic glimpses what Jefferson feared— a dictatorship imposed by judicial oligarchy. If the Supreme Court may order a tax imposed for one purpose, it may order a tax imposed for any purpose. The principles of the Court's 1954 decision, limited at the outset to public schools, swiftly were extended to parks, playgrounds, swimming pools, libraries, bus terminals, and hospitals. Many Southern communities are hanging back from public housing projects, lest they wind up with integrated housing projects. Are we to understand that in such communities, Negro plaintiffs may now compel the levying of taxes to construct public housing facilities like those of Boston or New York? . . .

Here the supervisors are ordered to levy an unspecified tax, for the indefinite future, to operate schools of undefined cost; under threat of imprisonment, they are ordered to perform a discretionary act contrary to the expressed wishes of their people. This was the milestone reached yesterday by the Court. It is a milestone that stands far down a darkening road.

QUESTIONS

1. The editorial argues that the black schoolchildren of Prince Edward had not been denied any opportunity offered by the county to white children. What justification was offered for this argument?
2. What fears are expressed about the implementation of the *Griffin* decision? What is your assessment of those claims?

NAACP Hails High Court Ruling on Virginia Schools

National Association for the Advancement of Colored People

May 29, 1964

While segregationists opposed the *Griffin* decision, the NAACP celebrated its hard-fought victory. Despite the length of time it took to get the case through the judicial system, the verdict signified important changes. Robert L. Carter, the head of the national NAACP legal staff, praised the Supreme Court's ruling and its ramifications, both in Prince Edward County and throughout the South.

The National Association for the Advancement of Colored People hailed the U.S. Supreme Court's ruling this week requiring "quick and effective" action to reopen the public schools in Prince Edward County, Va., on an integrated basis.

NAACP General Counsel Robert L. Carter, who argued the case before the High Court in March, stated that the decision was a portent of "general implementation of the historic 1954 anti-segregation ruling throughout the South."

The latest Supreme Court ruling on Prince Edward County was handed down on Monday, May 25. The Virginia case was one of five on which the Court based its edict of May 17, 1954, that segregated public education is unconstitutional. The case was argued before the Court in 1952, 1953 and 1955, as well as in 1964. . . .

Mr. Carter stated that this most recent ruling by the Supreme Court outlawing "Prince Edward County's experiment in ignorance" had "brought to an end one of the most shameful chapters in the history of the school desegregation crisis. . . . The decision has broken the back of the South's unlamented 'massive resistance' to school desegregation and should mark the end of open defiance of the Supreme Court's decree," he said.

"And finally," he added, "10 years after the ruling, school children in the county will begin reaping the benefits of the 1954 decision which ruled segregation in public education unconstitutional." . . .

Associated with Mr. Carter in the numerous and repeated appearances before state and federal courts in the 11-year-old case were NAACP Attorneys Spottswood W. Robinson, III, Oliver Hill, Henry Marsh, III, all of Richmond; S. W. Tucker, Emporia, Va.; Frank Reeves, Washington; and Miss Barbara Morris, New York City.

Papers of the NAACP, part 3, box A107, Library of Congress, Washington, D.C.

QUESTIONS

1. How did NAACP attorney Robert L. Carter describe the *Griffin* opinion and its importance?
2. Carter stated that the influence of the decision would reach beyond Prince Edward County. What impact did he ascribe to the decision?

Letter to William vanden Heuvel

L. Francis Griffin
November 25, 1964

In the fall of 1964, shortly after the public schools in Prince Edward County reopened, Reverend L. Francis Griffin wrote to William vanden Heuvel (see p. 183). In his letter, Griffin expressed his concerns about the newly reopened public schools and the failure of county leaders to comply with the law. Following decades of educational challenges and thirteen years of legal battles, Griffin voiced his frustrations and those of black citizens of the county.

Mr. William vanden Heuvel, President
International Rescue Committee
New York, New York

Dear Bill:

I have never formally thanked you for your efforts in securing a system of education in our county which benefited all of the community in general, and the Negro children in particular. I am fully aware that were it not for your efforts the Free School would not have come into being.

The Free School, under Neil Sullivan, accomplished much in the way of helping Negro children to close the gap created by four years of educational malnutrition. Neil's skill as an administrator was evident in the almost miraculous pulling together of persons and equipment in so short a period of time. We are certain that the present schools could not be in existence had it not been for the fact that Neil had organized a school here prior to the opening of the public schools.

What these schools did for the morale of the Negro community can not be measured. The vast majority of Negro people are fully aware that were it not for your deep concern for children, your interest in this community and your great skill in dealing with people the Free School would not have been a reality.

But the days of the Free School were numbered from the beginning, and I must share with you now some observations about the current community and school situation. For quite some while, I have been concerned that articles published in the national press do not, in my opinion, convey the real truth about the Negro plight in this little southside community.

The sufferings of the Negro people here are too public to be denied, too severe and long-lasting to need detailed reiteration. For generations, our people here had been denied the few rights and pleasures that could make life in this county even minimally bearable. For five years our community was without any public schools, and because of this a generation of our children are permanently crippled and disabled educationally.

For years, we have suffered the ways of peace and sought from the law the justice we have been denied so long. We suffered our children to be destroyed in order that the law might speak.

The law has spoken. We have yet to see it obeyed. For thirteen years we have been in the courts, and for thirteen years we have received—with one exception—empty promises and have been the dupes of false hopes.

For longer years than I care to remember, I have been the leader of the Negro people of this county and I have counselled the ways of peace. The Negro people have shown amazing patience and faith toward a county that has treated them so roughly and unfairly. We are a people of great patience; and our patience is not of infinite duration.

Having gone so far and achieved so little, the Negro people here are still willing to listen to my counsel. I am now in a stage of trying to decide what my advice to them will be for our future salvation.

In making this decision, I am afraid, in the light of recent press coverage of Prince Edward County, that a great many people throughout the nation are getting the idea that the Free School was a panacea for all the ills existing here.

As good as they were, one would have to be awfully naive to expect that any one agency could solve in a year's time problems which have been existing in this county for generations.

The total Free School project was such a noble gesture that I have been reluctant to hurl any sort of criticism against it. Yet, after talking to Gillian Walker, it occurred to me that I had discussed with her some aspects of the total situation in the county which are critical, and which I had not talked over with you; I wish to appraise you of them.

For one thing, any number of Negro citizens have manifested total disgust at the actions of the Board of Directors of the Free School. We have every reason to believe that they used their good office to meddle in community affairs which were not directly related to education. They made certain concessions to the authorities in Prince Edward County without consulting Negro citizens to discover their desires. Those hasty judgments have served to influence the present school authorities in opening and operating the only public schools since 1959 through creating the erroneous concept that the vast majority of Negro citizens would be happy and content just because public schools had been restored to the county. What a good many of us feared inwardly is now an actuality. After thirteen years of litigation, we have only succeeded in reopening a type of public school system vastly inferior to the one in existence in 1959.

These schools have not created an atmosphere where culturally deprived children can be respected, accepted and developed. They are under-staffed (and that with people whose qualifications are questionable), overcrowded, and grotesquely demoralizing. While they are not under-equipped, they are not organized to use the equipment that they had prior to the Free School and the equipment left by the Free School. I am afraid we are in the position which James Baldwin describes so well—the authorities aren't concerned with inspiring these children to excellence, but "in making peace with mediocrity."

It is possible that this system is equal or better than some of those in surrounding counties, but the fallacy in this is that none of these counties can boast of having had their schools closed for five years. Here, the children have to overcome both a natural handicap and one forced upon them by the local authorities, e. g.: their cultural background limitations and their residence in a community which did not offer formal education. The School Board takes the attitude that education for Negro children in Prince Edward County is a privilege, not a right. Cultural pluralism still exists and will exist so long as education in the county is run by a little oligarchy.

The weakness and lack of preparation of many of the teachers is so obvious that the children themselves are able to accurately point out the inadequacies.

As a result, many are trying to find ways and means to leave the county to complete their high school education.

There was an increased effort on the part of Negro citizens to point out the probability of poor schools before the opening of these schools, and strong attempts on their part to point out the weaknesses which are evident in the system since its actual operation. Committees have gone directly to the Superintendent of Schools and tried unsuccessfully to get him and the School Board to contribute something significant toward a just solution of the problem, but to no avail. These authorities go so far as to even refuse to admit that a problem exists. A great deal of this attitude can be traced back to the implications that the Free School had cleared up all the problems. We submit that the Free School did an excellent job for the one year, and we submit that this was the extent of their responsibility, but we are afraid that the impression has been given to the public that as a result of this one year the school population has reached its normal educational level.

This situation has served to further disillusion and bewilder the minds of the Negro citizenry to the extent that we are now in the process of organizing to hurl a challenge to the community authorities in the form of an all-out economic boycott and demonstrations by demand of the Negro citizens themselves. I have never noticed such enthusiasm on the part of the people for such action. Continued procrastination on the part of local authorities is going to bring the Negro press—if not the national press—back to the scene to reveal to the nation and the world the inconsistencies of this nasty situation.

I am sure that you share my deep concern about the plight that racial discrimination and segregation places upon our community and that you are eager to take whatever steps are within your power to help. Unfortunately, because we can not find help on a local level, we have to turn to others for aid. It seems that the local white authorities have decided that they can do anything to us they want to, and do it with impunity. It is for us to disavow them of this folly.

Something is going to be done; just what, we do not know. Personally, I think that if we all come together and honestly appraise the situation, we could certainly arrive at a better solution.

Old methods will not work. For example, money is needed to pay for such things as remedial reading instructors, special education, etc. However, the unsympathetic attitude of the School Board makes it unadvisable to direct outside financial aid through this channel. It seems to me that, both from the point of view of community support and interest, and for the welfare of the school, financial assistance must be channeled through sympathetic citizens' groups of white and Negro citizens.

In this same vein, we can not use the same approach in our attempt to find a solution as was used in bringing about the agreement to operate the Free School. First, the Negro leadership in the community and in the state had come to the realization that nothing should stand in the way of getting children back in school. Second, the opening and operation of the schools were to be entirely out of the hands of local people. Now, these two conditions do not exist. Such an approach would only be practical in a similar situation. I can not imagine Negro leaders being willing to make concessions to the extent they were made in our negotiations in any other situation.

I suggest that we get together with a fresh approach in order to identify the problem and honestly go to work on it.

I would appreciate hearing from you concerning these matters.

My fondest regards to you and Jean, and I do hope you are both enjoying good health.

Sincerely yours,
L. Francis Griffin

Prince Edward County Records, 1964, American Friends Service Committee Archives, Philadelphia.

QUESTIONS

1. Reverend L. Francis Griffin expressed frustration with the status of the reopened public schools in Prince Edward County. What were Griffin's principal complaints, and what did they suggest about the struggle for a successful, integrated public school system in the county?

2. What did Griffin mean when he said, "We suffered our children to be destroyed in order that the law might speak"? What does this tell us about the black community of Prince Edward County in 1964?

Speech at Annual Meeting of the
American Friends Service Committee

Nancy Adams
October 30, 1965

The American Friends Service Committee maintained a presence in Prince Edward County from 1960 through 1965 to provide assistance during the educational crisis. Helen Baker (see p. 136) and Harry Boyte (see p. 150) both served as AFSC field representatives. Throughout the school crisis, AFSC director of southern programs, Jean Fairfax was a passionate advocate, calling on federal government agencies and departments to reopen the public schools. The ongoing work of the AFSC in Prince Edward County reflected the commitment of the Quaker faith to peace and social justice and to its tenet, "Speak truth to power."

In 1963, Nancy Adams, an assistant dean of students at the University of North Carolina, accepted an assignment with the AFSC and moved to the county. Two years later, Adams gave a speech to the 1965 AFSC annual meeting. Her remarks offer an important perspective on the continuing struggle for public education in Prince Edward County.

I have just completed a two-year assignment in Prince Edward County and I hurry to tell you that you mustn't be deceived by this. The assignment is certainly not completed nor in any sense finished. There is a long history of racial disturbance in this County; there are a great many complexities which have developed because of the situation and the length of time the situation has been fermenting. I think it will be many years before AFSC or any of us who are concerned about the dignity of man will be able to forget Prince Edward County, Virginia.

Briefly may I remind you that this is the county which closed its public school system in order to avoid the threat of desegregating schools. This happened in 1959, very simply, just by the Board of Supervisors, which is an elected six-man board, refusing to appropriate any public monies for the operation of a public school system. When this happened all of the schools in the County were padlocked and they remained padlocked for five years—there was no public education. During this time, the September following this action, there was opened in Prince Edward County a "private Academy for whites" and this school is in operation today. Most of the white children who are able to afford the private Academy are in school there now. . . .

Now, the situation today in Prince Edward County. This is six years after the schools were closed. Today four schools in the County are open, seven are still padlocked. In the four schools are 1,500 Negro children and about twelve white children. The schools are terribly over-crowded, so much so that the County has recently bought four portable buildings to house the overflow of children in the elementary grades. This was at some little expense to the County and will take the County about ten years to pay for, and yet we do still have seven buildings which are padlocked, and of course, the maintenance on these is a problem.

In these schools there is absolutely no remedial work going on at the moment although there are plans to try and get some remedial help to these students. Many of the Negro students are 10, 11 and 12 years old struggling with first grade work. I should pause to tell you that the study done by Dr. Green indicated that there was not just a lack of four years, it was not just a matter of missing work but the lack of any formalized education in the lives of these students at certain crucial years has caused a definite mental retardation to take place. Dr. Green warned two years ago that unless there was immediate remedial help there was a question as to whether certain skills would ever be regained. There was an I. Q. depression which took place in some students of from one to fifteen points.

The white children in the County are by and large still in the Academy buildings attending school there. There are no tuition grants—tax paid tuition grants—any longer. They have been ruled out by the courts this past year. The economic press on the County, because they are enjoining tuition grants during the court struggle, has been very severe. This is a rural county, many of the white farmers are far from affluent people. The tuition is $320 per child and this is from first grade on up. This is a severe drain on the average family. We know that there are white children out of school altogether. We don't know how many—it is impossible to know how many—the number may run as high as 600.

My assignment when I first went to Prince Edward two years ago was to work primarily in the white community, to try and develop a spirit of compliance among the white residents of the County for a peaceful desegregation of the public school system. This is what I would like to speak with you about today. . . . I begin with the Supreme Court decision concerning the Prince Edward case which was given in May 1964. The court found that Prince Edward would have to open its schools; it found that closing the schools was a violation of the 1954 *Brown* decision, and Prince Edward children were among the original claimants in the *Brown* decision. . . .

On June 23 just two months before the schools were to be reopened the Supervisors met. This was a very dramatic, a very tearful session. The Supervisors had no choice but to open the schools but they were not at all willing to do so. One Supervisor stood and with tears in his eyes and his voice, read the following statement. This is an excerpt from his statement: "I love the nigger children of Prince Edward County but I will never vote 'Yeah' to something which destroys the American democratic way of life. I am proud that five years ago I voted to close the schools of this county rather than allow them to be taken over. I am fighting to preserve democracy. I will not back down." So, after a very lengthy discussion, the Supervisors voted four to two to comply with the United States Supreme Court. After this order they then appropriated $189,000 local monies to run the school system. At the same time they appropriated $320,000 to be paid out in the form of tuition grants for the white children of the County. There was some doubt as to whether they could use this $320,000, however, because during the past four years they had been stopped by injunctions.

However, on August 4 word was quietly passed in the white community; there was a committee which called itself the vigilantes and they rode door-to-door from midnight until three in the morning alerting white residents of the county who either did not have telephones or where there was fear that there might be a Negro on the party line. They summoned these people immediately and all night long until about nine o'clock in the morning checks were dispensed at the county armory. By ten o'clock in the morning there were five lines at the bank and they were two blocks long. The police were out with walkie talkies directing traffic and there was a spirit of victory in the air. I went to the bank and I shall never forget standing in this tragic circumstance and watching the orderly excitement which prevailed. From time to time the crowd would break into choruses of "Dixie," and members of the vigilantes coming back from their all night experience were congratulated as they approached. There was this feeling of community spirit in the air. So, if there was any doubt in anyone's mind that the four years of very tragic pathos which surrounded the Negro children or the presence of the very elaborate Free School with instructors from all over the country had in any way enlightened the Prince Edwardian citizens, I think by this time we were convinced that this was not so.

However, we were able to form an interracial group in which to begin our work. It was touch and go at first but there were a number of college professors from the two schools who were agreeable to trying to work in the situation. We had about 50 people actively involved in the group. There were in the group mostly college professors and their wives; there were two townspeople, one college chaplain. The Negro membership of this committee that did become very active were mostly farmers or laborers and their wives as well as a few Negro professional people, a Negro doctor and a dentist. The group became known as the Citizens for Public Education and they began by devoting their interest to quality of the schools and their immediate needs. The first project was a reading project. The reading needs, as you may well imagine, were extremely severe and they prepared a documented report to present to the school board. . . .

The Board meeting was a real lesson in democracy, Prince Edward style. We went armed with our report—about thirty members of Citizens for Public Education—white and Negro. We had an appointment but were about an hour and a half waiting in the hall while the Board discussed whether or not it had to honor the appointment and had to admit us, once they had seen the nature of the group. When we were admitted we were shown into a very small room ordinarily housing the desk of the superintendent, not a meeting room. It was quite cramped and uncomfortable. No one could sit down except the members of the School Board who sort of lolled back in their chairs and yawned as we stood around the room in our very crowded and uncomfortable circumstances—on one foot and then the other. . . . We began to present the report, and the School Board Chairman was very rude. He took a look at the report and said, "This is entirely too complicated and would waste our time, you'll have to leave." We asked if we could only present the request at the end of the report at which he turned to one of the Negro ladies in the group and, hoping, I am sure, to embarrass her, said, "you have one and a half minutes to give a succinct synopsis." She took a deep breath, folded her report and gave one of the most amazing succinct synopses I have ever heard.

We realized after this meeting that, if the group were to make any progress, it would have to attempt to reach the general public, the average citizen. . . . The first attempt was to put an ad in the newspaper. We thought it was very logical. This was the ad which appeared in the *Farmville Herald* which is the bi-weekly paper in Prince Edward County. It says at the top that public education is the only answer, it asks a series of questions dealing very calmly and rationally with the economics of the County, the needs of children, etc. Down at the bottom it has a coupon which was to be clipped out and returned to us. It simply says: "Please mail me information on public education—name and address." It was asking for no commitment and was not in any way a radical response.

At the same time, in addition to the newspaper approach, we began a series of teas in the homes of the white members of the Citizens for Public Education. At this point you see our emphasis had switched to attempting to reach the white parents to bring their children back to public education, recognizing that this was the only way to get a larger public base with which to work, to put pressure upon the officials to do something about the schools. We had a series of teas. We had a series of conferences with businessmen in town. This, we might say, was the second phase of this committee's work.

The response to the ad, to the teas, to the conferences was absolutely nothing. We weren't overwhelmed with coupons; as a matter of fact, not one citizen returned a coupon from the ad in the paper. The teas, we had a number of them, and we reached a number of very nice citizens, and they all would say, "Yes, we understand, we're glad we heard your message, you go right ahead and I will, of course, keep my child in the Academy where all the white children are and where their friends are." The businessmen were very enlightened and very sympathetic. The economics of the town were suffering, they felt the economic straits of the community and some even went so far as to give us under the table donations, but they would not take a public stand for public education, and they would not work with us in any way.

At this point we had one other report that was necessary. We had felt early in the year that it would be necessary for private citizens to become experts in the area of public school financing and county financing if we were ever to convince the general public and the school board that it was possible to run decent schools to meet the needs of the children of this County. The Committee worked and prepared quite an extensive financial report and this was again presented to the school board. This was the last meeting before the school board—the representatives were asked never to return to the Board and not to waste their time with these reports as they were unduly time consuming. The reports were never answered and there was never any comment or reply from our public officials.

At this point the white citizens who had taken quite some risk, not endangering themselves but yet threatening their social lives and their community acceptance, were beginning to get quite discouraged about the work in the County. At the same time, we knew that there was a public to be reached. We had only to go to the back roads of the County, to ride on the dirt roads of the County where the poorer farms were to find white children out of school and to see that there was a tremendous need. Every day we heard rumors of families where one child was able to go to school, the rest were kept home. We knew that there was a need but the problem was how to get to these people. We have failed completely in every effort.

This time we decided to try mailing a brochure. . . . We mailed 7,000 of these to every white citizen whose name and address could be found. It is entitled "A Time To Speak and Act." It makes a very simple and moderate plea to white parents to save their own children from the plight that they are in and put them into one of the padlocked schools which would be an integrated school.

In each of these brochures was enclosed a card but this time, because of the lack of response from the newspaper ad, the card asked for no name or no address. It was to be sent back to us anonymously if there was any interest at all on the part of white citizens in public education for white children. . . .

But, at long last, response began to come and cards began to be mailed back in. These were some of the first ones that came in (cards with no written in big letters); there were very few of these. By the end of the month 150 people had responded with cards. We then had the problem of finding these people. We had 150 anonymous cards but we did not know where they were. At this point AFSC offered to finance a volunteer project to help to find these people. We used about 50 volunteers, mostly from Virginia, from various Friends Meetings in the state, from the Presbyterian Church, the Catholic women's organization, the League of Women Voters, and people poured into Prince Edward all summer long. By the end of three months 5,000 people had been visited, every road in the County had been covered, and we have uncovered 130 parents, representing 235 children, over 170 children in the elementary grades and 60-some children in the high school grades.

We were then ready to work with these parents to try and sign them up for public schools. The meetings we held in August with these parents toward the close of our program were one of the most enlightening and one of the most disheartening experiences I have ever had. The people were very low-economic situated white people. They were absolutely terrified. For example, at one meeting they refused to get out of their cars. They hid in their cars, occasionally peering with their eyes at the window level, because they had heard that there might be a trap at this meeting. Once in the meeting they were violently anti-Negro. These people are not in any way sympathetic, but they were desperate. They were willing to put their children in integrated schools simply because they had no schools to go to. They were bitter. They were frightened and they were hostile. They wanted the Superintendent to meet with them and assure them of the type of school that would be reopened and that they would not place their children in the currently operating schools with 1,500 Negroes where their children might be one of twelve white children. This was the only solution they would accept.

The Superintendent refused to meet these parents. His position was that if the parents came in and registered there will be a school. The parents' position was that they would not register without knowing in advance the type of school their children would go to.

By the end of the month of August, 30 white children had signed registration forms. Since this was not enough to open a school our last meeting consisted of a very solemn ceremony with the 30 parents tearing up the children's registration forms. This meant that these children would not return to any school in the fall. After they tore up the forms they begged us not to tell anyone that they had ever signed them. The project came awfully close but it failed and yet I think it was significant because for the first time, after struggling for two years, these particular white people were reached and we learned a great deal from it. In my opinion this is really a group of lost people in the South.

There is hope, there is leadership, and there is forward progress, however so painfully slow on behalf of the Negro people; but there is so little being done with this particular type of white Southerner who is terribly afraid, who is ignorant, who is a racist and who is caught in a change which he does not understand. We hear a lot about loving our enemies and understanding the people we work with, but I think for the first time I began to understand the type of Southerner who causes a lot of trouble in the South but who is himself a real victim of his own prejudice. I don't know the answer to this situation, but I know that it is worth pursuing because I know that these people are terribly in need. Thank you.

Prince Edward County Records, 1965, American Friends Service Committee Archives, Philadelphia.

QUESTIONS

1. How did Nancy Adams describe the county's political leadership and its actions?
2. What were the challenges described by Adams to developing white support for the reopened public schools, even among poor whites who could not afford tuition at the private academy?

The Lost Years

Joseph P. Blank
November 29, 1966

Look was a large-format general interest magazine published twice weekly during the mid-twentieth century. It had one of the highest circulations of that type of periodical in the United States. The magazine reported on Prince Edward County in the fall of 1966, two years after the public schools had reopened. Based on interviews with a variety of county residents, author Joseph P. Blank described the public schools and the continuing effects of five years of educational deprivation.

In the spring of 1959, rural Prince Edward County, Virginia, achieved uniqueness in American history by abolishing school taxes and closing its public schools. The move—an answer to the Supreme Court decision that classrooms must be desegregated—had scant immediate effect on the county's white children. A private foundation was set up to provide a combined elementary and high school, the Prince Edward Academy, for them. For most of Prince Edward's 1,700 Negro children, the move meant four years ripped out of their lives before a court order forced a reopening of public schools. This is a case history of the human toll wreaked by a spasm reaction of racism.

Less than one-third of the Negro children found ways to attend school in adjoining counties, more distant parts of Virginia and other states. The great majority that remained in the county received occasional schooling in summer courses taught by out-of-county volunteers and sporadic classes conducted by mothers, older teenagers and elderly schoolteachers in homes, church basements and tar-paper shacks. The teaching effort generally was aimed at keeping the children aware of the existence of the three R's.

But the experience of 14-year-old Charles Carter is probably most typical of the way Negro children whiled away their precious youth. "I just began to learn to read and write when school closed," he says. "I don't remember what I did for those four years. Mostly walked around. Sometimes caddied and cut lawns. I forgot how to read and write and spell and do arithmetic." Now a desperately struggling student in the reopened public schools, Charles is thinking of dropping out, like so many of his schoolmates.

All Negro families with school-age children suffered. Reginald White, a slim, serious Farmville man who had his five children in school in 1959, says: "Some whites still don't understand what they did. They don't care. Others have told me they didn't like what was going on, but couldn't do anything about it. To think: They closed the school doors in my children's faces because we asked that they have the same educational opportunities as other children! This fact is going to stay with me the rest of my days."

White and his wife Harriet were determined that their children would not miss a day of school. "We thought of moving out of the county," Mrs. White says, "but my husband is a partner in a dry-cleaning business, and we couldn't afford to give that up. So we sent the children off to relatives in Baltimore. It was a terrible thing to have to break up our family so our children could have an ordinary public school education." After two years, the Whites brought their children home and sent them to schools 20 miles away in adjoining Cumberland County by renting a house and establishing a second residence in Cumberland, a severe financial burden.

Yet the Whites were more fortunate than most Negro families. In 1964, Dr. Robert L. Green of Michigan State University and four associates tested several hundred Prince Edward Negro children. The team found that many children in the 6-to-12 age group could not follow simple instructions, like "turn the page." Some had never learned to hold a pencil. A large number of 14-to-18 year olds were able to read only on a fourth-grade level. Interrupted schooling had depressed their intelligence scores 15 to 30 points and had also depressed their ambitions, self-esteem and hope for the future.

The children who went away to school were quick to notice the changes in the stay-at-home youngsters. Rodman Lee, a bright, intelligent boy of 14, says: "When I got back here, I felt that closed schools closed people up. Kids forgot how to work, learn and get along with others. In my class, most are between 16 and 19. A lot don't care. They're mixed up and withdrawn. They feel no push. They can't put into words the things that are going on inside them."

Most of the teenagers are either resigned or determined about completing high school. Eunice Dove, a spirited, immaculately groomed girl of 17, says, "I could see what was happening to myself and others in those four years. I sat around a lot and got tired. I felt lost. Now and then, mother tried to keep up with lessons, but she had eight children to look after. Some kids never went back to school, but I'm going to finish—and then I'm going to leave this county."

In 1963, Negro children were at last able to attend the ungraded Free School, backed by private funds raised at President Kennedy's instigation, before legal action finally reopened the public schools. The first year, 1964—65, was understandably chaotic and more or less a shakedown cruise to fit the pupils to the proper grades. Actually, many older children did not return: In 1959, the Negro high school graduated 55; in 1965, the number was 25. Before the school year ended, it was obvious that the primary problem was reading. According to the Rev. L. Francis Griffin, a round-faced, middle-aged Negro leader whose sense of humor and wisdom saved him from bitterness: "Some 400 to 500 youngsters between 14 and 18 years old couldn't read well enough to get any information from a school book. This deficiency made school meaningless."

The first thrust at the problem was taken by the Prince Edward Community Action Group, Inc., an organization financed by the Federal Government's antipoverty program. It was headed by Robert E. Taylor, a segregationist but fair-minded businessman, who brought in Mr. Griffin as co-director. They contracted with an organization called Institute of Educational Research, Inc., to employ a special "Reading in High Gear" technique that calls for programmed learning and is specifically designed to let children catch up at their own speed.

Results have been promising, and the Government has granted $186,000 for the continuance of "High Gear."

Fitting children of wildly varying ages into proper classes was a more painful problem. In the fourth grade, children ranged in age from 9 to 14, with 25 percent 12 or older; the eighth-grade range is 12 to 19; the eleventh-grade, 16 to 21. Many still cannot adjust to the proper grade, and maladjustment means trouble. Emotional and mental obstacles that hamper the children are formidable.

"They are not aware of their loss because they can't compare themselves to others," says one of the few whites among the 70 teachers laboriously recruited to restaff the county's public schools. "Their attention span is short. Words mean little to them, and they have trouble grasping ideas and making generalizations. School has become a place where they are embarrassed by their ignorance."

In contrast to the teenagers, the younger children are eager, ambitious, spontaneous. George Hatcher, a bright-eyed, interested boy of ten, says, "I don't miss a day of school, even when I'm not feeling well. I study. I like that new reading program because it makes me feel I'm learning." George enrolled for 1966 summer school because "It's important to learn, and I'm not doing too well in arithmetic." Three out of four elementary-school pupils attended the summer school, a record that delighted Superintendent Bryant Harper because it indicated the purposeful attitude of both the young pupils and their parents. But Mr. Griffin wonders, "Can they stay that way, or will they, too, become beaten down as they get older?"

While the Negroes have taken the crippling brunt of Prince Edward's action to keep the races separated, the whites also have suffered. In this low-income-level, tobacco-and-pulpwood area, some 65 miles from Richmond, many white families find it a hardship, even though for years they paid no school taxes, to send their children to the Academy, where tuition fees average about $300 a year per child. To meet the expense, families have had to second-mortgage their farms and other property. Dr. C. G. G. Moss, a reflective, white-haired professor of history at Longwood College, one of the county's two institutions of higher learning, believes some families have found a tragic solution to the problem. "There's no question that we have white children who are not in school," he says. "You see them around farms during school hours. The families won't admit they're not in school, out of shame and a reluctance to be heard complaining."

Robert Taylor, a policymaker at the Academy, insists, "There is no reason why any white child cannot attend the Academy. If it's a question of money, we have scholarship funds to deal with that problem. Incidentally, we do have integrated public schools." Only 12 white children are enrolled in the public schools, but many white families would now like to find a painless way to integration. A survey has shown that 130 of them want their 247 children in the public schools, providing they would not be tremendously outnumbered by the Negroes. Most whites, however, are satisfied—some placidly, some uneasily—with school conditions and race relations as they are.

"I think things are improving at a fine rate," Taylor says. But hear Mrs. Etta Lee try to explain her feelings: "The grown-ups, like the children, are frustrated and bewildered," she says, staring at her folded hands. "We can't sit down with the whites and talk about problems. Everything is so elusive. We make a request for a school improvement, like hiring a psychologist or introducing an art course, and the answer is 'We'll let you know.' Eventually comes a letter of refusal. After a while, you give up."

Dr. Moss, a Southerner with unimpeachable Confederate credentials, who changed his point of view after he was 60 years old and argued against closing the schools, is well-acquainted with this feeling of frustration. "We can't make contact to work out solutions," he says. "The people here are as indifferent as ever to the feelings of Negroes. The Negroes have gained nothing in terms of education. And the whites have hardened their view toward moderates like me. I've been criticized by members of my church, derided behind my back, ignored. I encounter a blind stare and silence when I try to talk about human problems. The whites want me to leave this community. But I've come to terms with my conscience. I'm staying . . . and I will keep expressing my conscience."

A senior at Longwood—a native Virginian—sees Prince Edward as a never-never land. "Here we're being trained as teachers in the public-education system," she says heatedly, "and we don't acknowledge the crisis right at the steps of the college. No one dares discuss it in or out of the classroom. It's medieval."

Thanks to peaceful but determined pressure, Negroes have here and there broken through the wall between the races. Some non-menial jobs have opened up for them in the county, and "a few officials are a little more courteous." But the oppressive school situation has driven young faculty members at both Longwood and Hampden-Sydney College out of Prince Edward County. "I'm leaving," says one, "not because I want to, but because I have to. I feel conscience-stricken about pulling out of the fight, but I have an obligation to my three sons to see that they are properly educated. All the children in this county are getting below-standard education. I've always felt a strong obligation to my family and my community. In other places, you can fulfill both responsibilities. But not here."

"As far as I can see, everybody—Negroes, whites and the community as a whole—has lost in this struggle."

Look, November 29, 1966, 73–75.

QUESTIONS

1. What were the experiences of black children in Prince Edward during the years of the closed schools as described by Joseph Blank?
2. What special challenges confronted the reopened public schools, and what steps were taken to meet them?
3. How did Blank describe the impact of the school closings on the white community?

Epilogue

"A PRETTY GOOD PLACE TO LIVE"

Prince Edward County never experienced the overt violence witnessed in the Deep South during the civil rights movement, priding itself on its Virginia gentility. In Prince Edward County the bleeding was internal. "To rob young people of education at such a critical point in their human growth and development was, in effect, dooming them and their offspring to a life of illiteracy, poverty, and dependency," wrote Prince Edward native and scholar Gerald Foster.[1]

In *The Strange Career of Jim Crow*, the classic history of the segregation era in the South, historian C. Vann Woodward described a culture of a "permission-to-hate" that permeated American society at the beginning of the twentieth century. Political leaders, the courts, academia, and the press advocated intellectual and social justifications for racism. The conditions were set for the creation of a segregated society that marginalized and suppressed its black citizens for more than half a century.[2]

The 1951 student strike at Robert R. Moton High School was one of innumerable expressions of the quest by African Americans for their full and equal constitutional rights as citizens in the decades-long battle to dismantle the onerous restrictions of Jim Crow society. From the school strike to the courts, to the decision in *Brown v. Board of Education*, to the fight to save public education in the county—all were steps on a long road to freedom.

As the struggle in Prince Edward County moved forward, so too did political changes on the national level. The Civil Rights Act of 1964, signed into law by President Lyndon Johnson on July 2, outlawed discrimination in public facilities and accommodations in the United States, and provided legal means to hasten the process of southern school integration. The Voting Rights Act of 1965 forbade discriminatory practices in voting and restored the ballot to black voters in the South, who had been largely disenfranchised since the turn of the century. With federal support and protection, a growing number of African Americans in the South registered to vote, cast ballots, and slowly began to influence the political direction of their communities.

Political change would be slow to come to Prince Edward County. Still, one notable change to education occurred when Dr. James M. Anderson Jr. was appointed the superintendent of the Prince Edward public schools in 1972. Anderson later described his first meeting with the Board of Supervisors where one member confronted him, "Let me tell you one thing. You can come in here and ask for any and everything you want to. But I will never vote for one single thing for the public schools."[3] In spite of that outspoken opposition, his twenty-year tenure would eventually revitalize public education and gradually bring the majority of the students in the county, black and white, back into the public school system.

The Prince Edward Academy and other segregationist private schools in Virginia remained segregated through the 1970s. The Internal Revenue Service revoked the tax-free status of nonprofit discriminatory private schools, including Prince Edward Academy in 1978, which forced many of them to abandon segregationist policies. The academy finally opened its doors to all students in 1986. In 1993, Prince Edward Academy became the Fuqua School, named for J. B. Fuqua, a wealthy businessman and native of the county whose major financial contributions helped save the school from insolvency. Founded to preserve segregation, the academy now moved to identify itself as a model private school for children of all races and ethnic backgrounds.

In 1993, the African American community that had once fought for public education now rallied to save from demolition the school building where the struggle had begun almost half a century earlier. The campaign was first led by Vera J. Allen, president of the Martha E. Forrester Council of Women, the local African American women's group, which had been a leading advocate for the construction of the school in 1939, and James Ghee, a local African American attorney. The community that had once fought to save public education now worked to save the history of that struggle. The county would eventually sell the building to the Council of Women to become a museum to the struggle for public education.

The *Farmville Herald* newspaper, the longtime segregationist voice of the county that had written passionately against public school desegregation, now argued with equal force to preserve the school building that was the birthplace of the movement. "Should blacks and whites join hands to create a museum out of the Moton school, it would be a healing act of affirmation in Prince Edward County," wrote editor Ken Woodley.[4] In a series of editorials he supported the effort to save the site of the 1951 school strike from demolition and to honor its place in American civil rights history as part of an effort for reconciliation in the county (see p. 240).

Journalist R. C. Smith (see p. 35) returned to Prince Edward in the mid-1990s for the first time in thirty years and observed, "I have come to believe that this county can make out of its regrets for the past and out of its pride for what has happened since those dark days a ringing statement for the past and for the future. I think that the very fact of this darker history will make that important for the healing process within the county. If so, the county will end up teaching many who otherwise would have scorned its name."[5]

The Moton school was designated a National Historic Landmark by the U.S. secretary of the interior on August 31, 1998, the highest level of recognition offered by the federal government to a site deemed of exceptional importance in the history of the nation. On April 23, 2001, the fiftieth anniversary of the school strike, the Robert Russa Moton Museum was formally established in the historic building.

The long overdue recognition of the historical importance of the public school crisis in Prince Edward County came in several forms in the following years. In February 2003, the Virginia General Assembly passed a resolution expressing "profound regret" over the 1959–64 closing of the public schools in Prince Edward County.[6] In June 2003 and June 2004, Prince Edward County High School held honorary commencement ceremonies and presented diplomas to students who had been denied an opportunity to graduate from Moton High School when the schools were closed.

In recognition of the fiftieth anniversary of *Brown v. Board of Education*, the Virginia General Assembly established the *Brown v. Board of Education* Scholarship Program Fund in 2005 "for the purpose of assisting students who were enrolled in the public schools of Virginia between 1954 and 1964, in jurisdictions in which the public schools were closed to avoid desegregation," who wished to complete or further their education.

In 2006, the Faith and Politics Institute in Washington, D.C., sponsored a congressional pilgrimage to Farmville, led by famed civil rights leader Congressman John Lewis of Georgia, and including several members of Congress, to pay homage to the role of Prince Edward County in the civil rights movement. A notable participant in this event was Reverend Peter Storey of South Africa, who in 1995 was appointed by South African president Nelson Mandela to help select members of that nation's Truth and Reconciliation Commission. Storey noted in his speech, "Here in Prince Edward County I have been struck by sad echoes of what happened in South Africa under apartheid. . . .

The destruction to black education is one of the acts of apartheid that today's South Africans find hardest to forgive." Storey went on to note the motto of the Truth and Reconciliation Commission of South Africa, which said, " 'Without forgiveness, no future.' Forgiveness cannot be forced or organized or legislated. We can only make space for it, and then wait. If and when it comes, it comes as a sacred gift. I pray that this sacred gift may grow here in Prince Edward County, setting free both the victims of this place's sad past and their oppressors of old, for a new future."[7]

The history, and a new future for Prince Edward County, received long overdue recognition on July 21, 2008, when the Virginia Civil Rights Memorial was dedicated on the lawn of the state capitol in Richmond, honoring Barbara Johns and her fellow students; Reverend L. Francis Griffin; NAACP lawyers Oliver Hill and Spottswood Robinson; and the long struggle for public education in Prince Edward County. Engraved in the granite monument are Barbara Johns' visionary words, "It seemed like reaching for the moon."

The historic effort by the African American community of Prince Edward County for educational opportunity, the defiant closing of the public schools, and the later successful resurrection of public education in the county comprise one of the notable, unheralded stories of the civil rights era and of the history of public education in the United States.

In the words of Reverend Griffin, "If you're looking at it on a national scale, I'd say we won a victory. I believe you could say the black people of Prince Edward County saved the public schools of the South, particularly in Virginia. Had we given in, I think perhaps massive resistance might have become the order of the day throughout the South. So in that sense we won a tremendous victory."[8]

NOTES

1. Foster, *Status of Blacks*, 10.

2. C. Vann Woodward, *The Strange Career of Jim Crow* (New York: Oxford University Press, 1955).

3. Dr. James M. Anderson Jr., interview with Brian Grogan, Farmville, Virginia, May 18, 2004.

4. Ken Woodley, "Prince Edward Can Make History By Preserving the Moton-Branch School," *Farmville Herald*, December 9, 1993.

5. R. C. Smith, "Prince Edward County: Revisited and Revitalized," *Virginia Quarterly Review* 73, no. 1 (Winter 1997): 27.

6. House Joint Resolution no. 613, "Expressing the General Assembly's Profound Regret over the 1959–1964 Closing of the Public Schools in Prince Edward County, Virginia," Virginia General Assembly, 2003 session, http://www.doe.virginia.gov/administrators/superintendents_memos/2003/inf105a.pdf.

7. Reverend Peter Storey, "Healings from the Wounds of South Africa," address at the Faith and Politics Institute Congressional Pilgrimage, Longwood University, Farmville, Virginia, May 29, 2006, copy in possession of the editors.

8. Smith, *They Closed Their Schools*, 265.

Prince Edward County, Virginia, 30 Years After: "A Pretty Good Place to Live"

Wilbur B. Brookover, Arthur Dudley, and Robert L. Green

November 2, 1993

In 1963, Dr. Robert L. Green of Michigan State University conducted research in Prince Edward County for the U.S. Office of Education on the educational impact of the closed public schools. In the years and decades following, Green completed several additional studies on the effects of educational deprivation in the county. Nearly thirty years after Prince Edward County's public schools reopened, Green revisited the county with colleagues to study how residents now viewed the crisis and how race relations had changed during that time. Their report was published in the *Journal of Negro Education*.

Recollections and Assessments of the 1959–1964 Period

We interviewed all the surviving supervisors and school board members from the 1959–1964 period. The three surviving supervisors concurred that they did "the right thing" by forcing the school closings and stated that they would not have done anything differently. One supervisor indicated that his vote to close the schools was the result of his perception that it was "what the people wanted"—the people, of course, being the voting White population. The surviving school board members, who all voted to keep the schools open, also indicated their belief that they too did the right thing, despite strong pressure from the supervisors and the White population to fight the desegregation rulings. The school board members' decision to at least respect the desegregation order was perhaps an exception to the predominant opinion of Whites in Prince Edward County. Certainly, many of the other surviving White leaders of the period remain confirmed segregationists. Most, however, realized that school desegregation was bound to occur, and they generally expressed the opinion that it would have been much better if they could have done it in their own way. Many of these older Whites condemned the involvement of the National

Association for the Advancement of Colored People (NAACP), which entered into the Prince Edward County situation and promoted the court action. They contended that desegregation might have been accomplished sooner and with less tension if the residents of the county had been left to work out their own methods and timetables. This, however, is doubtful because no evidence exists that the board of supervisors would have appropriated money for desegregated public schools during the early 1960s. On the contrary, it is quite evident they would not have. It is convenient, of course, to blame the school closing on "outsiders" such as the NAACP legal staff.

It is interesting to note that many of these older White leaders believe that serious conflict and violence might have occurred in Prince Edward County had it not been for the leadership of the Reverend L. Francis Griffin. Griffin was an Afro-American Baptist minister who was then the president of the local NAACP. He participated in the court action and supported the national NAACP action, but at the same time was able to maintain communication with the local White population. Consequently, he played a part in preventing what probably would have been a violent situation. The authors' experiences in the county and our acquaintance with the situation at that time confirm this assessment, which was made by many White as well as Afro-American residents active during the period.

When asked the question—"Looking back, are there any things that you think should have been handled differently?"—most respondents were of the opinion that the school closings should not have happened. Both Afro-American and White respondents expressed a strong assessment that the situation should have been handled differently. A few White respondents approved of the action taken in closing the schools, but no Afro-American respondents thought the situation was handled properly. Many Afro-Americans who lived through the school closings period recalled that they felt helpless to act during the conflict years. Although the surviving White supervisors defended their defiance of the desegregation order, little support was found among contemporary Prince Edward County citizens for what happened in the county from 1959 to 1964.

After 30 years, many White residents of Prince Edward County would rather not talk about this episode in the county's history. A few Afro-American residents also preferred not to talk about it. A few White residents actually blamed the desegregation conflict on the Afro-American population, indicating that they would have preferred to maintain segregation. Other Whites felt sad about the situation, but recognized that they were in the minority when they expressed feelings in favor of integration. Those Afro-American respondents who lost years of schooling from 1959–1963 expressed considerable anger and resentment over what had happened and how they had been treated. There were even a few, but not many, White respondents who felt that what happened was wrong and that Afro-American as well as White children should have remained in school. There were also many White respondents, particularly those who had been in leadership positions during the school closings era, who resented being forced by outside interests to change their system. However, some Afro-American residents, particularly the older ones, felt satisfied that they had fought a battle and won over the forces of segregation.

The Prince Edward County public schools are officially desegregated, with about 60% Afro-American and 40% White students. . . . Some classes, particularly in the secondary schools, are nearly all-White, while others are nearly all-Afro-American; but there is no evidence that any systematic organization of classes on the basis on race accounts for this. The teaching staffs are also racially mixed, and three of the eight school board members are Afro-American. Thus, it is safe to conclude that desegregation has occurred in the public schools.

Nonetheless, an element of segregation persists in the existence of the Prince Edward Academy, whose enrollment remains almost all-White. About 20% of the White student population in Prince Edward County attends the Academy, which draws its students from 10 other counties as well.

It is hard to discuss current desegregation and integration efforts in Prince Edward County's public schools without, at least briefly, acknowledging the difference between desegregation or integration and discrimination as these two phenomena affect the individuals involved. For the purposes of this article, the authors feel compelled to acknowledge that desegregation and integration has occurred in the county's public schools. However, this acknowledgment must stop short of claiming that discrimination no longer exists. Much differentiation of educational programs and classroom placement has been noted in the county's public schools. Prince Edward County, and other counties like it, will not truly end discrimination in their school systems until they are prepared to address, and take affirmative action toward eliminating, the effects of past discrimination over and beyond mere integration. . . .

The three publicly elected bodies in the county—the board of supervisors, the school board, and the Farmville City Council—are all multiracial. Of the seven supervisors, who are elected by districts, three are Afro-Americans. The eight school board members, who are appointed by the board of supervisors, also include three Afro-Americans. There are two Afro-American city councilmen. The county sheriff's staff and the Farmville police force were also integrated.

It is generally believed that White county officials exert more power than do Afro-American officials, but there is evidence that, among both the board of supervisors and the school board, few decisions are made that are not acceptable to the Afro-American minority. This is not the case with regard to the Farmville city council. One Afro-American member of the council claims that he feels powerless on that body. . . .

The perceptions of race relations in the county vary greatly. About half the respondents reported that race relations are "good," "better," or "fine." Such perceptions were almost equally reported by Afro-Americans and Whites. However, a number of White respondents had reservations about whether race relations are any better than in the past, and some were particularly opposed to affirmative action programs to improve these relations. Generally, older White residents are more likely to be concerned about the changes that have occurred over the last 30 years. Newer White residents and those with a higher social status have more congenial relations with Afro-Americans than do their older or less well-educated counterparts. Many Afro-Americans are still angry with Whites for closing the schools and feel that the closings are the cause of the current problems experienced by Afro-American county residents.

Most Afro-American respondents claimed that their situation has improved and they are in a much better position today than they were 30 years ago. Indeed, the position of Afro-Americans in the Prince Edward County community has changed noticeably over the past 30 years. One result of this is that some White residents have great difficulty in accepting Afro-Americans on any kind of equitable basis. One professional White man who was an active, committed segregationist 30 years ago, now claims that he has been converted from his segregationist views, but Afro-Americans and some Whites who know him have a somewhat different perception of him. They noted that he interacts much more freely with some Afro-Americans than he did formerly, but he only relates to those Afro-Americans he views as nonthreatening or those he perceives as "knowing their place." Afro-Americans who challenge the traditional racial relationships and who do not accept a subservient role in that relationship are highly condemned by this "former" rabid segregationist. Another older White man, who is perceived as much more liberal in his attitude toward Afro-Americans, reported that he still has some difficulty accepting them in new relationships. For example, he reported that he finds it difficult to accept the fact that an Afro-American man who has worked for him for several years now comes to the front rather than the back door of the house to discuss his work from day to day. By contrast, he reported that when a young

Afro-American woman who rents a house from him came to the front door to pay the rent, he and his wife invited her in for ice cream and cake together. Clearly, for Whites in general, particularly older ones, acceptance of new race relations, on an equal basis, with Afro-Americans is difficult. . . .

Although the patterns of segregation that characterized Prince Edward County 30 years ago have changed drastically, the attitudes and patterns of race relations are not completely comparable. Many Whites, particularly older ones, are uncomfortable and disturbed by desegregation. They find it difficult to accept the new patterns of interaction between the races. Most of the Afro-American residents feel that race relations in Prince Edward County are decidedly better and that they can "do what they want to." Other Afro-Americans feel that racial relationships have not changed much.

We have sought in this brief account to examine the county's unique situation and the changes that have occurred since its public schools were closed for four years in 1959. Some Prince Edward County residents persist in saying that no changes have occurred, but many changes have occurred. Afro-American and White children now go to school together, with occasional bouts of tension, but no serious incidents of conflict have been reported. Afro-Americans and Whites work side-by-side in many roles that were restricted to one race or another 30 years ago. Although still a minority, Afro-Americans presently are elected and appointed to county governing bodies in significant numbers and have significant influence on public policy and practice. Afro-Americans move freely in public facilities and eat with White citizens in all restaurants. There may be a few places where Afro-American citizens do not feel free to go but these places are not numerous.

With all these changes, it would be inaccurate to say that there is complete equality and no discrimination in Prince Edward County. Many White citizens have accepted the changes very reluctantly; older citizens particularly persist in their belief that Afro-Americans are inferior and should maintain subordinate roles in society. On the surface, some Whites seem to accept the changes, but feel some resentment, particularly against the courts that forced the restructuring of their society. Such reluctance is frequently reflected in discriminatory behavior that these Whites may overtly deny, yet their reluctance is readily apparent to the Afro-Americans who are being discriminated against. Other Whites rather completely accept the new structure of racial relationships; however, these Whites noted that on occasion they still feel somewhat uncomfortable when the Afro-American worker comes to the front door. Other Whites seem to completely accept and support the changes, but they feel some resentment that such changes were forced upon them. They feel that desegregation would have been handled better if they had been permitted to make the necessary changes themselves.

By and large, the Afro-American population of Prince Edward County has welcomed and embraced the very significant transformation from a rigidly segregated society to one approaching equality and nondiscrimination. Many White residents of the county join them in welcoming the new Prince Edward County. Remnants of discrimination and unequal treatment remain, but for the most part it is a new society. This is symbolically expressed by the responses of two prominent citizens interviewed for this study. These two respondents occupied opposite positions in the continuum from equality to segregation. When asked if there were anything else he would like to tell the senior researcher about Prince Edward County, the first, a recognized activist leader of the Afro-American community, replied, after some thought: "This is a pretty good place to live." Similarly, at the end of his interview, a White county resident who had been an active, militant segregationist 30 years ago and certainly still resents the position of the Afro-American interviewee noted above, had the following to say in response to the same question: "As you know, I am retiring this week. My wife and I have decided to stay here. This is a pretty good place to live."

Journal of Negro Education 62, no. 93 (1993): 162–70.

QUESTIONS

1. The authors noted that "after 30 years, many White residents of Prince Edward County would rather not talk about this episode in the county's history." Why do you think this was the case?

2. Residents expressed a variety of opinions on the school closings. What were some of the most commonly held beliefs? How did blacks and whites view these events differently?

A Model for the Nation

Timothy M. Phelps

May 17, 1994

Thurgood Marshall was the lead attorney for the NAACP legal team in *Brown v. Board of Education* and later was the first African American appointed as a justice of the Supreme Court. Following Marshall's death in 1993, journalist Timothy M. Phelps was inspired to visit and report on the five communities that were part of the *Brown* case. In his article on Prince Edward County, Phelps examined the changes that had occurred since the public schools were reopened in 1964. Based on his observations and comparisons to the other case locales, Phelps portrayed the Prince Edward County public schools as "A Model for the Nation." The article was published in *Newsday*, a New York daily newspaper, on May 17, 1994, the fortieth anniversary of the *Brown* decision.

The Appomattox River slides gently through the tobacco and dairy country of southern Virginia, its name a reminder that the Civil War ended nearby with the surrender of Robert E. Lee at Appomattox Courthouse.

But the white people of Farmville and surrounding Prince Edward County fought on in their way, and when the Supreme Court 40 years ago today ordered them to send their children to school with blacks, they simply closed the public schools.

The white children went to a private academy organized for the purpose, but most of the black children went nowhere for five years, until the Supreme Court got around to ordering the schools reopened. The result is a "lost generation" of semi-literate African-Americans, ill-equipped to educate their own children in turn.

Yet despite those bitter events, Prince Edward County is the success story of the five cases that were decided with the *Brown vs. Board of Education* decisions in 1954. The same community that treated its black children like so much trash is now a model for the nation.

Today the schools of Prince Edward County are both integrated and of high quality, spawning National Merit Scholars like minnows. The debating society has become the state's best and boasts of the proud moment when it vanquished Prince Edward Academy, until recently for whites only. Test scores match the national average, despite the rural poverty of many of the students.

Integration has been achieved without further court intervention, without manipulating school boundary lines, without forced busing.

"Prince Edward's schools are head and shoulders above other school systems in this area," says James Ghee, 48, a local black lawyer who is a national board member of the NAACP. Ghee, who found a sponsor to send him out of state to school, is one of the few in his generation in the county to have done well.

The point at which this remarkable story turned from hatred to hope was 1972, when the district was looking for a new superintendent.

The schools had been reopened for seven years. But they were 94 percent black and terribly underfunded, because white voters were unwilling to pay taxes for schools they didn't patronize. At the same time, they were struggling to educate children who had been out of school for five years. Most white children went either to the academy or to a private school that Longwood College, a publicly funded teachers' college, set up for the children of its faculty.

When Prince Edward was reborn as a mostly black school system, it was treated as a pariah by neighboring schools, which refused to send football or other athletic teams to compete.

But in 1970, Dr. James M. Anderson Jr. the white principal of Buckingham High School in an adjoining county, organized a breach in the boycott, sending his baseball teams to play Prince Edward and persuading several other schools to do the same.

So it was natural that the black community in Prince Edward would reach out to their open-minded neighbor, especially because the appointed school board was still controlled by whites with connections to the private academy.

Ghee said the Farmville area has had strong black leadership since the first days after the Civil War, strong enough to make compromises with the white community that had treated its children so badly.

When a prominent white businessman from Farmville, whom Anderson will not identify to this day, called him to say that the whites, too, wanted him as superintendent, he agreed.

That businessman had ties to the private school. "But his point was, 'It's our tax money. We know you. We know your family,'" Anderson said. "They were interested in their tax money being spent wisely."

"I don't think they knew what they were getting," Ghee said. In fact, one school board member said that Anderson's success in rejuvenating the public schools has caused consternation among "the private school people," as that segment of the community is known. Only several years ago, this member said, sales clerks who knew she sent her children to the public schools refused to wait on her.

Anderson, whose family had lived for eight generations in tiny Andersonville
—a town 20 miles north of here named after the family—was local enough to
win the support of the white community, progressive enough to rally the black
community, and also enough of an outsider to have been neither a pawn nor a
knight in the terrible controversies of the previous decades.

"It was a unique situation," Anderson said, "being local and being able to
work with people of different races. We had always shopped in town [Farm-
ville], done our business in town." The fact that he went to a rural one-room
school with no indoor plumbing—an experience shared by many blacks his
age—also helped, Anderson said.

There is no hint of anything particularly progressive, much less radical, in
this 61-year-old, unusually soft-spoken man who is fighting a losing battle with
his hair line. On his desk are some dried flowers, behind it the American flag
and pictures of his children on the wall. He looks like a small-town insurance
agent who would slip out to a Kiwanis or Lions Club meeting at lunchtime.

But through this demeanor, a sense of passion, courage and determination
seeps through—not from his manner but his words. An incident from his first
weeks on the job made that clear to those working for him.

"At my first home football game in 1972, I was the only white person there,"
Anderson recalled. "After a while I noticed there was a deputy sheriff standing
next to me, and after the game he escorted me to my car. My staff had done
this to protect me, but I told them this is not going to happen again. I've never
felt threatened here, and I have always insisted that no one will feel unsafe in
my schools."

Though Anderson insists it was his students and faculty who turned
things around, community leaders believe that no one else could have done
what Anderson has done in the 22 years he has been superintendent of Prince
Edward Schools.

"It was Dr. Anderson," said Nancy Shelton, who works in the alumni office
at Longwood College and chairs the school board. "He started out with a
vision, and he has slowly been able to make that vision a reality."

But there are other factors that have contributed to Prince Edward County
schools' becoming about 60 percent black and 40 percent white. (Although
the U.S. Census Bureau reports that the population of the county is roughly
the reverse, local officials point out that the census includes the predominantly
white and out-of-town students at two local colleges.)

Just as Anderson was moving to his new job at Prince Edward, the Virginia
legislature changed the state constitution to require a minimum level of local

funding and to set minimum standards of quality. Though the levels were low, they boosted the funds available by 45 percent.

By Anderson's third year on the job, white enrollment had jumped to 16 percent. So when Longwood College decided to close its private school in the mid-'70s, its faculty members felt they had a choice, and many sent their children to the public schools rather than to the academy.

Anderson says that he never recruited students, white or black. He believes that it was his emphasis on academic excellence, as well as programs that he set up to appeal to one race or the other, that worked.

When he arrived, younger students were not allowed to check out books from the schools' libraries and were taught reading on speed reading machines without even opening a book.

"I want books in the hands of children," he said, ordering a freer lending policy. "I want children to love books."

The high school taught only beginning French and Spanish in 1972. Now it offers four or five years of those, plus Latin, German and a course in Japanese.

Algebra used to be the highest math offered; now students can take trigonometry as well as calculus. The brightest students can take courses at the two local colleges.

At the same time, he established an ambitious vocational-technical program for students not headed to college, set up comprehensive special education and offered an athletic program that included sports with special appeal to white students, such as soccer, tennis and golf.

Another advantage was the presence of the colleges. Faculty turnover at Longwood, with 166 teachers, and Hampden-Sydney, a small, private liberal arts college for men, with 63, provided an influx of families not burdened by the events of the 1950s and 1960s. It also provided a natural constituency for public education.

The size and design of the school district, which has 2,600 students and is about 25 miles across, is also a help. The three schools—elementary, middle and high—are in one central complex just outside Farmville, a substantial, prosperous and pleasant college town where, despite its isolation, you can buy an alfalfa-sprout sandwich. Every student in the same grade goes to the same school. Anderson says that this way, there is no chance of there being a "white school" or a "black school" based on residential patterns. And Anderson says that everyone in Prince Edward is bused, so that is not an issue, either.

"I don't know where busing has worked anywhere" as a means of achieving integration, Anderson says disdainfully. "It is an attempt to undo social evil, but it doesn't succeed. I think the way to succeed is to improve the fundamental basic educational system, to have the best system for each individual child based on what that child needs."

There have been deep changes in the institutions and people of Prince Edward County that have contributed to the success of the schools as well.

The owners of *The Farmville Herald*, a thrice-weekly newspaper here, were among the staunchest supporters of the school closing and the establishment of the academy, both with their newspaper and their pockets. Today another generation of the same family has hired a young white editor who writes impassioned editorials supporting integration and the public schools and proudly volunteers the fact that he is a member of the Prince Edward branch of the NAACP.

The private academy itself is changing, too. It started admitting blacks about eight years ago. Last year it changed its name from the Prince Edward Academy —a name that had become a national symbol of resistance to integration—to the Fuqua Academy after an Atlanta businessman and Prince Edward native, J. B. Fuqua, donated $10 million. With the name change has been a symbolic change in the school colors and, J. B. Fuqua insists, a real change in attitude. Trustees of the school are actively soliciting funds in the community for additional scholarships for blacks.

Even Farmville's mayor of 22 years, J. David Crute, admits to some change in his attitude. Crute, owner of Crute's Pharmacy, looks and talks like a relic of the past, with his suspenders and white, crew-cut hair. He is not bashful about having supported the school closing and segregation.

Asked if he still supports segregation, he said, "I did at the time. "Today it's different. It doesn't seem to make much difference."

Newsday, May 17, 1994. Reprinted with permission.

QUESTIONS

1. Why did Timothy Phelps believe that the Prince Edward County public schools could be a "model for the nation" in 1994? What is your assessment?
2. How had the county's schools changed since their reopening in 1964? What decisions made after the schools reopened did the author believe had been most important?

Shall We Tear Down America?

Ken Woodley
February 15, 1995

The *Farmville Herald* was the leading segregationist voice in Prince Edward County in the 1950s and 1960s. Publisher and editor J. Barrye Wall was a leader both in the closing of the public schools and the formation of Prince Edward Academy. By the 1990s, however, change had come to the county and the newspaper. Editor Ken Woodley reflected this change. Woodley's many editorials on Prince Edward's painful history and the need for healing and reconciliation were acknowledged by lawyer Oliver Hill, one of the lead NAACP attorneys on the first school desegregation lawsuit in the county in 1951. In a letter to Woodley, Hill wrote, "It was one of the tragedies of the times that during the fifties and succeeding years we did not have more people with your insight and sensitivity to help work out solutions to our racial problems in Prince Edward County, in Virginia, and in the rest of the United States."[1]

When county officials considered proposals to sell the building and property of the former Robert R. Moton High School, site of the 1951 school strike, it immediately stirred a vigorous community debate. On the same editorial page that had once argued for segregation, Woodley issued a stirring call for the preservation of the school as a historic landmark.

If we're going to tear down the former R. R. Moton High School—now Farmville Elementary School—let's go ahead and tear down Independence Hall, too, and dump the Liberty Bell in the river. Let's use the oldest extant copy of the Declaration of Independence to make a paper airplane and throw it off the Washington Monument, which will also be torn down and replaced with a fast-food restaurant.

America tends to trivialize virtually everything, from marriage to life itself, so that tearing down one of just five *Brown v. Board* school sites in the nation may be within our distorted sense of values.

Seem far-fetched? Well, in fact, we do have Prince Edward's board of supervisors deciding, not in open session but over the phone, to step in and delay consideration of this supremely historical school building for inclusion on the Virginia Landmarks Register and the National Register of Historic Places.

The process is now stopped dead in its tracks.

One county official has even pointed out that if the school is torn down the property's value would increase dramatically because the land could be used commercially. Prince Edward doesn't need the value of the property to increase.

The building is already priceless. History—and I can't believe I feel compelled to make this point—is more important than hamburgers.

County officials believe they are acting for the best because the building's prospective buyer, Longwood, would prefer the property not be listed on the state and national registers. Without that designation, Longwood could do what it wants with the building, including tear it down. Prince Edward, like anyone selling real estate, wants to make the land more attractive to its prospective buyer. Proceeds will help pay for important new school construction but I believe that, correctly seen, the former Moton High School adds to the value of property.

Some county officials may also mistakenly think that the recreation center across the street, not the elementary school, is the historic *Brown v. Board* property and so the delay, in their eyes, is inconsequential.

I believe that if county officials understood the true significance of the building they would participate in its preservation. There is still time for the county to ensure that nothing and nobody tears down an American monument to what is best about this country: the triumphant struggle toward freedom by human beings.

The building must not be destroyed.

It was in those walls, not the recreation center across the street, that students gathered to listen to Barbara Johns on April 23, 1951. It was from this building that students marched out on strike that day, precipitating Prince Edward's inclusion in the monumental *Brown v. Board* case that drove a stake through the heart of separate but equal.

Separate but equal? One R. R. Moton High School classroom was in a bus. Others were in glorified chicken coops dubbed "tar paper shacks" because of their appearance. Three classes were held simultaneously in the auditorium. Built for 180 students, enrollment at the school was 477 in 1950. It was in this building, and no other, that history was made. The building must not be torn down.

Would we destroy Independence Hall in Philadelphia? Never. Then we must preserve this school building. For millions of people in Prince Edward and Virginia and the United States of America, the words and deeds of April 23, 1951 precipitated a far more meaningful revolution than that spawned on July 4, 1776 by words that were only half true and deeds that left too many people untouched by liberty.

The Farmville school building is no less a monument to human courage in the belief that all human beings are created equal than Independence Hall. The building is a monument we should be proud of, both because of what happened there 44 years ago and because of the county's stature as the lone success story among *Brown v. Board* communities. We shouldn't sweep any of it under a rug. We should proclaim 1951 and 1995 from every rooftop. This is a monument we should protect. We should do nothing to help anyone tear it down. . . .

We're not talking about a pile of bricks. We're talking about the soul of America.

Farmville Herald, February 15, 1995.

NOTE

1. Oliver Hill to Ken Woodley, June 7, 1994, copy in possession of the editors.

QUESTIONS

1. What assertions did Ken Woodley make for the preservation of the Moton High School?
2. Why did members of the county Board of Supervisors support the sale or demolition of the old school? How did Woodley respond to their concerns?

Far Away from Home: One Woman's Passage through Segregation

Sara Fritz

Summer 2006

In 1955, James Bash, then the principal of the white Farmville High School, spoke against the closing of the public schools and the establishment of private schools in Prince Edward County. In 2003, he reached out across the ensuing decades to one of the black students who experienced the educational and emotional trauma of losing her opportunity to attend public school. Rita Moseley's story reflects both the healing and lingering hurt, as well as the efforts toward truth and reconciliation, in Prince Edward County. Sara Fritz was an award-winning political journalist and, later in her career, an executive for the Faith and Politics Institute of Washington, D.C., which sponsored the congressional pilgrimage to Prince Edward County in 2006.

Rita Moseley was in sixth grade in 1959 when her mother sent her away to live with strangers in Blacksburg, Virginia. She still remembers the day her mother took her there.

"It was one of the worst moments of my life," Ms. Moseley recalls. "My mother walked away; she never looked back. I don't know how she did it."

Ms. Moseley's mother was not abandoning her. Instead, she was making certain that Rita would get an education after the public schools closed down in their hometown of Farmville, Virginia.

Ms. Moseley was one of about 2,000 African American children in Farmville who were left in the lurch when the Prince Edward County school board voted to shut down the schools in 1959, rather than integrate them. A private, Christian academy was created for the white children, but blacks had no similar alternative. The Prince Edward schools remained closed until 1964.

It was not until many years later, according to Ms. Moseley, that she allowed herself to feel the pain of her long separation from her mother. In fact, it was not until June 2003, when she received a letter from a total stranger that she acknowledged how much she suffered during her years in Blacksburg. The letter came from Jim Bash, a retired University of Virginia professor who had been high school principal at the white Farmville schools in 1959. Mr. Bash recalled in the letter that he had opposed closing the schools.

"That was the first time I actually cried," Ms. Moseley said. "Until then, I didn't know anyone cared. I thought all the white people favored closing the schools."

The letter was the beginning of a wonderful friendship between Ms. Moseley and Mr. Bash—a relationship that exemplifies the dramatic impact of various efforts to bring about reconciliation between the races in Farmville.

Mr. Bash decided to write to Ms. Moseley after reading in the *Charlottesville Daily Progress* about plans to award honorary diplomas in June 2003, to the African-Americans who had been deprived of education. Rita Moseley, now an employee at Prince Edward County High School, was one of the organizers.

"The idea to hold a ceremony for the purpose of awarding honorary diplomas to those now-grown children is testimony to the truth that progress continues," Mr. Bash wrote. "Truly, all of you are touched with a special gift for healing to have been able to conceptualize and bring to fruition this important and poignant occasion."

Mr. Bash, in his letter, recalled how he had spoken out against the school closing at a meeting of townspeople on June 7, 1955. He said the plan would only create another form of enslavement for African-Americans. Then, after the meeting voted to proceed with the school closing, he said, he submitted his resignation as principal.

In a return letter to Jim Bash, Ms. Moseley said she had "always wondered if any of them (white citizens) had a conscience, and if so, how would they have done this to us—changed who we were or whom we were going to become, changed the course of our lives by turning it completely around and in a lot of cases destroyed so many lives, forcing us to be in circumstances, places and situations no child should have had to endure."

She also explained why she had failed to shed any tears about the school shutdown until she read Mr. Bash's letter.

"I am a person who rarely feels—rarely feels happiness, anger and seldom feels hurt," she wrote. "I often wonder if I conditioned myself as a child. I never felt the anger, bitterness, and hatred I saw all of my life in others. I never allowed myself to feel it as a child to protect myself and as an adult to protect my two children. I was determined they would not grow up with it either.

"Trust is also very hard for me because, if you couldn't trust a whole town of people to do the right thing, whom could you trust? But while reading your letter with tears in my eyes and running down my face, I can honestly say this is the first time I actually allowed myself to feel any emotion about what happened to me and other black children in Prince Edward County."

Now in her late 60s, Rita Moseley, thanks to her friendship with Jim Bash, is finally learning to trust.

Conscience and Courage 2 (Summer 2006): 5. Copyright 2006 Faith and Politics Institute, reprinted with permission.

QUESTIONS

1. Many black children of Prince Edward County were forced to leave home to continue their education when the public schools were closed. How did Rita Moseley describe the emotional impact of this experience?

2. Honorary diplomas were awarded to former Prince Edward students who had been denied the opportunity to graduate from their community high school. How do you perceive the purpose and effect of this effort?

A Resolution of the Board of Supervisors of the County of Prince Edward, Virginia

July 8, 2008

In the summer of 2008, the Prince Edward County Board of Supervisors adopted by a seven-to-one vote the following resolution. It celebrates the actions of Barbara Johns and her fellow Moton High School students, who launched the historic student strike

of 1951. Now composed of new members, the Board of Supervisors, which had condemned the strike in 1951 and closed the public schools in 1959, praised the students,
expressed regret for the closing of the public schools, and honored the children for
their role in promoting civil rights in Virginia and the nation.

Whereas, on April 23, 1951, students at Robert Russa Moton High School went
on strike in protest of separate and unequal schools for African American students in Prince Edward County; and

Whereas, these students and their families filed suit against the County to
end segregation in public schools; and

Whereas, that legal case, *Davis v. Prince Edward County*, was decided on
May 17, 1954, when the United States Supreme Court ruled against segregated
schools in the United States with the landmark *Brown v. Board of Education*
decision; and

Whereas, the United States Supreme Court *Brown II* decision on May 31,
1955, orders the pace of integration to occur with "all deliberate speed"; and

Whereas, the Commonwealth of Virginia implemented a strategy of "Massive Resistance" to public school integration between 1954 and 1959; and

Whereas, in June of 1959, the Prince Edward County Board of Supervisors
voted to close the Prince Edward County Public School System rather than
operate an integrated public school system by appropriating zero dollars for
public education; and

Whereas, following four years without public schools, the Prince Edward
County Free School system was created in 1963, funded through foundation,
corporate and private support, and leasing equipment and buildings from the
County; and

Whereas, on May 25, 1964, the United States Supreme Court ruling in *Griffin v. County School Board of Prince Edward County* ordered Prince Edward
County to reopen its public school system; and

Whereas, the Prince Edward County Public Schools were reopened in the
fall of 1964; and

Whereas, in 1995, the Robert Russa Moton school building was retired from
service by the Prince Edward County School Board and was sold by Prince
Edward County to the Martha E. Forester Council of Women to be used as a
museum dedicated to the study of civil rights in education; and

Whereas, in 2003, the Virginia General Assembly adopted a Resolution of
Profound Regret for the state's role in the closing of the Prince Edward County
Public Schools; and

Whereas, on July 21, 2008, the Virginia Civil Rights Memorial will be dedicated on the Capitol grounds in Richmond, honoring the struggle begun in Prince Edward County on April 23, 1951;

Now, Therefore Be It Resolved, that we, the undersigned members of the Prince Edward County Board of Supervisors, believe that the closing of public schools in our county from 1959 to 1964 was wrong, and we grieve for the way lives were forever changed, for the pain that was caused, and for how those locked doors shuttered opportunities and barricaded the dreams our children had for their own lifetimes; and for all wounds known and unknown, we regret those past actions; and

Be It Further Resolved, that on July 21, 2008, the Prince Edward County Board of Supervisors will illuminate The Light of Reconciliation in the courthouse bell tower in honor of Barbara Rose Johns and the students of Robert Russa Moton High School and all the children of our county, for their historic role in ending public school segregation in the United States, and with sorrow for closing schools; hoping that when we raise our eyes to see this light, may we also incline our hearts and minds to shine our own light of reconciliation toward all people.

Minutes of the Board of Supervisors, 2008, Office of the Clerk of the Court, Farmville, Virginia.

QUESTIONS

1. What did the Board of Supervisors say about the 1959–64 school closings in this statement?
2. What other actions in the 1990s and 2000s, mentioned in this document, reflected changes that had occurred in Virginia, and in Prince Edward County, since the 1960s?

Our Past

Richmond Times-Dispatch
July 16, 2009

During the 1950s, the leading newspapers in Virginia, the *Richmond Times-Dispatch* and the *Richmond News Leader*, supported segregation and massive resistance while attacking the NAACP and proponents of civil rights and integration. The newspapers provided intellectual leadership for the South in the fight against the Supreme Court ruling in *Brown v. Board of Education* and to preserve racial segregation. Fifty years later, the two papers having merged in 1992, the *Richmond Times-Dispatch* published the following editorial expressing regret for the positions the newspapers had taken.

Sometimes the era seems ancient; sometimes it resembles yesterday. Fifty years ago Virginia had a rendezvous with destiny and came up wanting. It scorned human rights and the promise of the Declaration of Independence and instead took a course known as Massive Resistance....

Throughout the episode, Richmond Newspapers played a central role— but not a centering one. The hour was ignoble. Editorials in *The News Leader* relentlessly championed Massive Resistance and the dubious constitutional arguments justifying its unworthy cause. Although not so intimately engaged, *The Times-Dispatch* was complicit. The record fills us with regret, which we have expressed before.

Massive Resistance inflicted pain then. Memories remain painful. Editorial enthusiasm for a dreadful doctrine still affects attitudes toward the newspaper. Many remember. We understand. Words have consequences. Artful paragraphs promoted ugly things. Stylish sentences salted wounds. Euphemism was profligate. As members of the Fourth Estate these pages did not keep a proper distance, either. The debate is over. It is done.

Virginia long has prided itself on its gentility. The state's political tradition has lacked firebrands such as Gene Talmadge, Orval Faubus, George Wallace, Bull Connor, Theodore Bilbo, and James K. Vardaman. Massive Resistance shattered pretensions. Although the commonwealth's campaign to evade *Brown v. Board of Education* did not produce the pyrotechnics seen in other states, it was directed towards the same dead end. Pride, humanity learns ever again, is not a virtue but a sin. Forgive us our trespasses, as we forgive those who trespass against us.

Hubris prevailed. Those who railed against oppressions visited upon sovereign states by an allegedly imperial Washington relied on government's coercive might to deny the full humanity of their fellow citizens. Massive Resistance was neither a departure nor an exception but the extension of Jim Crow and the attitudes informing it. Segregation and its associated indignities were in retreat. Massive Resistance formed a last stand.

"Empathy" has been politicized and in some circles invites derision. Yet, properly understood, empathy leads away from hatred and cruelty and opens hearts to the loving-kindness men and women are intended to magnify. "As I would not be a slave, so I would not be a master," Abraham Lincoln said. Many simply could not see the harm they did to so many others. Jefferson trembled for his country when he reflected that God is just.

Yesteryear's words cannot be revoked. They endure on newsprint yellow and brittle, on microfilm, and in the computer files into which they have been translated. They belong to history, and history lives. It is well and good that the words be remembered, as a warning perhaps best. We will not forget.

QUESTIONS

1. The *Richmond Times-Dispatch* expressed regret for the policies adopted in the 1950s and 1960s and strongly promoted by the newspaper against school integration. How does the newspaper reflect on those policies here?

2. In what ways does the newspaper seek forgiveness from those who may have been offended by its earlier support for massive resistance?

SELECTED BIBLIOGRAPHY

The following is a select bibliography of archives, articles, scholarly research, publications, and court decisions pertinent to the public schools history in Prince Edward County, Virginia.

Archives

Archives of the American Friends Service Committee, Philadelphia

Brown et al. v. Board of Education Case Files, National Archives, Washington, D.C.

Farmville 1963 Civil Rights Protests, VCU Libraries Digital Collections, Special Collections and Archives, Virginia Commonwealth University, Richmond

Brian Grogan Prince Edward County, Virginia, Public Schools Desegregation Research Collection, Special Collections and Archives, Virginia Commonwealth University, Richmond

Papers of the Prince Edward County Free Schools Association, Archives and Special Collections, Virginia State University, Petersburg

Edward H. Peeples Prince Edward County (Va.) Public Schools Collection, Special Collections and Archives, Virginia Commonwealth University, Richmond

Articles and Scholarly Research

Brookover, Wilbur B. "Education in Prince Edward County, Virginia, 1953–1993." *Journal of Negro Education* 62, no. 2 (1993): 146–62.

Brookover, Wilbur B., Arthur Dudley, and Robert Green. "Prince Edward County, Thirty Years After: 'A Pretty Good Place to Live.'" *Journal of Negro Education* 62, no. 2 (1993): 171–89.

Du Bois, W. E. B. "The Negroes of Farmville, Virginia." *Bulletin of the Department of Labor, No. 14, January 1898*. Washington, D.C.: Government Printing Office, 1898.

Egerton, John. "A Gentlemen's Fight in Prince Edward County, Virginia." *American Heritage*, August 1979, 56–65.

Green, Robert L., and Louis J. Hoffman. "A Case Study of the Effects of Educational Deprivation on Southern Rural Negro Children." *Journal of Negro Education* 34, no. 3 (1965): 327–41.

Green, Robert L., Louis J. Hoffman, and Robert F. Morgan. "Some Effects of Deprivation on Intelligence, Achievement, and Cognitive Growth." *Journal of Higher Education* 36 (1967): 5–14.

Green, Robert L., et al. "The Educational Status of Children during the First School Year Following Four Years of Little or No Schooling." *Cooperative Research*

Project No. 2498, United States Office of Education. Washington, D.C.: Department of Health, Education and Welfare, 1966.

Green, Robert L., et al. "The Educational Status of Children in a District without Public Schools." *Cooperative Research Project No. 2321, United States Office of Education.* Washington, D.C.: Department of Health Education and Welfare, 1964.

Green, Robert L., and Robert F. Morgan. "The Effects of Resumed Schooling on the Measured Intelligence of Prince Edward County's Black Children." *Journal of Negro Education* 38, no. 2 (1969): 147–55.

Hale-Smith, Margaret E. "The Effect of Early Educational Disruption on the Belief Systems and Educational Practices of Adults; Another Look at the Prince Edward County School Closings." *Journal of Negro Education* 62, no. 2 (1993): 171–89.

Heaton, Paul. "Childhood Educational Disruption and Later Life Outcomes Evidence from Prince Edward County." *Journal of Human Capital* 2, no. 2 (Summer 2008): 154–87.

Lee, Brian E., "A Matter of National Concern: The Kennedy Administration's Campaign to Restore Public Education to Prince Edward County, Virginia." Ph.D. diss., University of North Carolina at Greensboro, 2015.

Lee, Brian E., and Brian J. Daugherity. "Program of Action: The Rev. L. Francis Griffin and the Struggle for Racial Equality in Farmville, 1963." *Virginia Magazine of History and Biography* 121, no. 3 (2013): 251–87.

Madison, Sybil. "And Still They Rise: Factors Related to Resilience in African American Students Affected by the Prince Edward County School Closing." Ph.D. diss., University of California at Berkeley, 1998.

Morland, J. Kenneth. "The Tragedy of Public Schools: Prince Edward County, Virginia." Report for the Virginia Advisory Committee to the U.S. Commission on Civil Rights, January 16, 1964.

Peeples, Edward H. "A Perspective of the Prince Edward School Issue." M.A. thesis, University of Pennsylvania, 1963.

———. "Prince Edward County, the Story without an End." Unpublished manuscript prepared for the U.S. Commission on Civil Rights.

"Prince Edward County, Virginia: The Most Important Spot in American Education Today." *New York State Education* 51 (March 1964): 16.

Smith, Robert C. "Prince Edward County, 1979: Just Say That We Remember." *Southern Exposure* 7, no. 2 (1979): 64–71.

———. "Prince Edward County: Revisited and Revitalized." *Virginia Quarterly Review* 73, no. 1 (1997): 1–27.

Spreng, Jennifer E. "Scenes from the Southside: A Desegregation Drama in Five Acts." *University of Arkansas at Little Rock Law Journal* 19, no. 3 (1997): 327–412.

Steck, John C. "The Prince Edward County, Virginia Story." Farmville, Va.: Farmville Herald, March, 15, 1960. Copy in Southern States' Pamphlet Collection, box 25, no. 15, Albert and Shirley Small Special Collections Library, University of Virginia, Charlottesville.

Turner, Kara. "It Is Not at Present a Very Successful School: Prince Edward County and the Black Educational Struggle, 1865–1995." Ph.D. diss., Duke University, 2001.

U.S. Commission on Civil Rights. *Civil Rights U.S.A.: Public Schools/Southern States, 1962.* Washington, D.C.: Government Printing Office, 1962.

Waugh, Dwana. "'The Issue Is the Control of Public Schools': The Politics of Desegregation in Prince Edward County, Virginia." *Southern Cultures* 18, no. 3 (2012): 76–94.

Books

Bonastia, Christopher. *Southern Stalemate: Five Years without Public Education in Prince Edward County, Virginia.* Chicago: University of Chicago Press, 2012.

Branch, Taylor. *Parting the Waters: America in the King Years, 1954–63.* New York: Simon and Schuster, 1988.

Daugherity, Brian J. *Keep on Keeping On: The NAACP and the Implementation of Brown v. Board of Education in Virginia.* Charlottesville: University of Virginia Press, 2016.

Egerton, John. *Speak Now against the Day: The Generation before the Civil Rights Movement.* New York: Knopf, 1994.

Foster, Gerald A. *The Status of Blacks in the Commonwealth of Virginia: From Prince Edward County to the Election of 1985.* Hampton, Va.: Hampton University, 1986.

Foster, Vonita W., and Gerald A. Foster. *Silent Trumpets of Justice: Integration's Failure in Prince Edward County.* Hampton, Va.: U.B. and U.S. Books, 1993.

Green, Kristin. *Something Must Be Done about Prince Edward County: A Family, a Virginia Town, a Civil Rights Battle.* New York: Harper, 2015.

Heinemann, Ronald L. *Harry Byrd of Virginia.* Charlottesville: University Press of Virginia, 1996.

Holland, R. *The Story of Prince Edward Free Schools.* Charlottesville, Va.: Michie Company, 1964.

Irons, Peter. *Jim Crow's Children: The Broken Promise of the Brown Decision.* New York: Viking, 2002.

Kilpatrick, James J. *The Southern Case for School Segregation.* New York: Crowell-Collier, 1962.

Kluger, Richard. *Simple Justice: The History of Brown v. Board of Education and Black America's Struggle for Equality.* New York: Knopf, 1976.

Lassiter, Matthew D., and Andrew B. Lewis. *The Moderate's Dilemma: Massive Resistance to School Desegregation in Virginia.* Charlottesville: University Press of Virginia, 1998.

Moton, Robert R. *Finding a Way Out.* New York: Doubleday, Page, 1920.

Muse, Benjamin. *Virginia's Massive Resistance.* Bloomington: Indiana University Press, 1961.

Smith, Bob. *They Closed Their Schools: Prince Edward County, Virginia, 1951–1964.* Chapel Hill: University of North Carolina Press, 1965.

Stokes, John, with Lois Wolfe. *Students on Strike: Jim Crow, Civil Rights, Brown and Me.* Washington, D.C.: National Geographic Press, 2008.

Sullivan, Neil V., Thomas LaSalle Maynard, and Carol Lynn Yellin. *Bound for Freedom: An Educator's Adventures in Prince Edward County, Virginia.* Boston: Little, Brown, 1965.

Titus, Jill Ogline. *Brown's Battleground: Students, Segregationists, and the Struggle for Justice in Prince Edward County, Virginia*. Chapel Hill: University of North Carolina Press, 2011.

Williams, Juan. *Eyes on the Prize: America's Civil Rights Years*. New York: Viking Penguin, 1987.

Selected Court Decisions

Allen v. County School Board of Prince Edward County, Virginia, 249 F. 2d 462 (1957)

Brown et al. v. Board of Education of Topeka, Kansas, 347 U.S. 483 (1954)

Brown et al. v. Board of Education of Topeka, Kansas, 349 U.S. 294 (1955)

Davis et al. v. County School Board of Prince Edward County, 103 F. Supp. 337 (1952)

Griffin et al. v. County School Board of Prince Edward County et al., 337 U.S. 218 (1964)

Plessy v. Ferguson 163 U.S. 537 (1896)

INDEX

Recent Books in the Carter G. Woodson Institute Series

CPSIA information can be obtained
at www.ICGtesting.com
Printed in the USA
LVHW091251050920
665116LV00007B/191